CAMBRIDGE STUDIES IN
INTERNATIONAL AND COMPARATIVE LAW

General Editors:
H. C. GUTTERIDGE, H. LAUTERPACHT, SIR A. D. MCNAIR

I
COMPARATIVE LAW

COMPARATIVE LAW

An Introduction to the Comparative Method of Legal Study & Research

BY

H. C. GUTTERIDGE

*One of His Majesty's Counsel; Bencher of the Hon. Society of the
Middle Temple; Emeritus Professor of Comparative Law and
Fellow of Trinity Hall in the University of Cambridge;
LL.D. Cambridge and London; Doctor (Honoris
Causa) of the Universities of Paris,
Lyon and Grenoble; Associate of the
Institute of International Law*

CAMBRIDGE

AT THE UNIVERSITY PRESS

1946

CAMBRIDGE
UNIVERSITY PRESS

University Printing House, Cambridge CB2 8BS, United Kingdom

Cambridge University Press is part of the University of Cambridge.

It furthers the University's mission by disseminating knowledge in the pursuit of education, learning and research at the highest international levels of excellence.

www.cambridge.org
Information on this title: www.cambridge.org/9781107594722

First published 1946
First paperback edition 2015

A catalogue record for this publication is available from the British Library

ISBN 978-1-107-59472-2 Paperback

Contents

General Introduction

THIS series has been designed to fill certain gaps that are to be found in that part of English legal literature which is concerned with international relations. Three separate branches of the law are involved and we desire to say a few words about each of them.

In the field of Public International Law there is a growing need, at a time when the foundations of the new international order are being laid, for a fuller treatment of questions of International Law and Organisation than is possible within the limits of text-books devoted to the subject as a whole. It is hoped that the task of progressive codification of International Law, which suffered a temporary set-back in the decade preceding the second world war, may be assisted by research and studies such as are contemplated in this series. We are, further, of opinion that it may, perhaps, be possible to give a generous interpretation to the phrase 'International Law' so as to permit of the inclusion in the series of volumes dealing with certain aspects of diplomacy and international relations in general.

Private International Law, or the Conflict of Laws, is a subject which is of growing importance, both practically and academically, owing to the rapid development of means of transport and communication and to the increasing contact between the citizens and commercial organisations of different countries. Until recently it has, no doubt, been possible to deal adequately with this subject in a single volume, such as Dicey's magisterial treatise, in the same way as two hundred years ago it was feasible to write a book on the Law of England as a whole. But Private International Law has now reached a stage at which a certain measure of disintegration of its content has become necessary, because in no other way can proper provision be made for the needs of those, other than students, who are interested in the subject. Certain topics such as the law of contracts, marriage, jurisdiction and the like can, in our view, be dealt with more advantageously in a series of monographs than in a text-book covering the whole of the area of conflicts of law and jurisdiction.

Comparative Law is an unfortunate but generally accepted label for the comparative method of legal study and research which has come to be recognised as the best means of promoting a community of thought and interests between the lawyers of different nations and as an invaluable auxiliary to the development and reform of our own and other systems of law. In particular, a very important part is played by Comparative Law in the movement for the unification of private law—a movement which seems destined to gain strength as the nations are increasingly brought into contact with one another and the world tends more and more to become an entity in an economic as opposed to a social or political sense. At present the literature of Comparative Law is scattered, fragmentary and often difficult of access. It is our hope that this series may hereafter be of some service in helping to provide materials for those desiring to avail themselves of the comparative method of legal study or research.

H. C. G.
H. L.
A. D. McN.

CAMBRIDGE
April, 1946

Preface

THIS book is not intended to be a treatise on foreign law. It represents an attempt to meet the need for an English book which deals with Comparative Law in a systematic manner.

My task has been of a threefold character. I have tried, first of all, to explain the origin and meaning of the somewhat curious phrase 'Comparative Law'. In the second place, I have endeavoured to describe the various purposes for which the comparative method of legal study and research can be utilised and the manner in which it functions. Finally I have attempted to arrive at an estimate of the value of Comparative Law as an instrument for the growth and development of the law. Some explanation may, perhaps, be required of the fact that, when dealing with the functional aspects of Comparative Law, I have confined the discussion of this question, for the most part, to the problems which arise if comparison is made between the rules of the Common Law and those of the Civil Law. I may seem, therefore, to have ignored or belittled the importance of comparison between the laws of the different English-speaking nations, but the apparent omission is due to other reasons. I felt it necessary, in the case of a book such as this, written primarily for English readers, to stress the fundamental differences which divide the Common from the Civil Law rather than to call attention to the questions which may arise when the comparison is concerned with the kindred systems based on the principles of the Common Law. No special form of technique seems to be called for if the comparison is, for instance, between Australian and Canadian law or between English law and the law of the United States. It has been necessary to deal—though only in outline—with certain features of foreign law such as the authority of precedents and the interpretation of statutes in systems of law governed by codes. In so doing, I have been mindful of the grave risks incurred by anyone who writes about any law other than his own. But I have embarked on this somewhat perilous adventure because I feel that the nature of the obstacles to be surmounted by English lawyers who may wish to adopt the comparative method of legal study can best be described and explained to them by one of themselves. If I have fallen into error I hope for leniency, having regard to the difficulty of the task.

I am grateful to the many friends, here and abroad, who have encouraged and helped me in various ways. I am specially indebted to Professor Édouard Lambert, Sir Arnold McNair, K.C., Professor Lauterpacht,

Professor René David, and Dr K. Lipstein. Mr C. J. Staines of the Squire Law Library at Cambridge has rendered me much valued assistance. I also wish to thank the members of the staff of the Cambridge University Press for their unfailing courtesy and readiness to help in the difficult and distracting conditions of the present time.

I have, in all humility, ventured to dedicate this volume to the memory of a former Master of my College who has more profoundly influenced the development of comparative legal study than any other English lawyer.

The materials for certain chapters of this book have been taken from articles appearing in the *Tulane Law Review*, in the *Journal of Comparative Legislation*, in the *British Year Book of International Law* and in the *Transactions of the Grotius Society*. I am under a special obligation to the Editors of these publications for permission to make use of those materials.

H. C. G.

TRINITY HALL
CAMBRIDGE

Abbreviations

British Year Book of I.L. = British Year Book of International Law.

Cambridge L.J. = Cambridge Law Journal.

C.L.J. = Cape Law Journal Reports.

Chicago L.R. = Chicago Law Review.

Clunet = Journal de Droit International Privé.

Columbia L.R. = Columbia Law Review.

Fordham L.R. = Fordham Law Review.

Harvard L.R. = Harvard Law Review.

Illinois L.R. = Illinois Law Review.

Journal of C.L. = Journal of Comparative Legislation and International Law.

Journal of the S.P.T.L. = Journal of the Society of Public Teachers of Law.

L.Q.R. = Law Quarterly Review.

Recueil des Cours de l'Académie de D.I. = Recueil des Cours de l'Académie de Droit International.

Recueil Lambert = Introduction à l'Étude du Droit Comparé. (*Recueil d'Études en l'Honneur d'Édouard Lambert.*)

Tulane L.R. = Tulane Law Review.

Yale L.R. = Yale Law Review.

Table of Cases

Table of Statutes

Chapter I

THE PROVINCE OF COMPARATIVE LAW

A DISTINGUISHED comparative lawyer[1] has said that the phrase 'Comparative Law' is a strange one. How strange it is becomes manifest when attempts are made to define it or to ascertain its relation to other forms of learning. Much of the atmosphere of doubt and suspicion which envelops comparative legal study and has proved, in the past, to be so hostile to its development, would disappear if it were generally recognised that the phrase 'Comparative Law' denotes a method of study and research and not a distinct branch or department of the law. If by 'law' we mean a body of rules, it is obvious that there can be no such thing as 'comparative' law. The process of comparing rules of law taken from different systems does not result in the formulation of any independent rules for the regulation of human relationships or transactions. Not only are there no 'comparative' rules of law but there are no transactions or relationships which can be described as comparative. When we speak, for instance, of the comparative law of marriage this does not mean that comparative lawyers have devised a new set of rules to govern the relations between husband and wife; it merely indicates that the marriage laws of several countries have been subjected to a process of comparison in order to ascertain how far, and in what respects, they may differ one from another. There is no 'comparative' branch or department of the law in the sense in which a lawyer speaks of 'Family Law' or 'Maritime Law' or the other departments into which law is conventionally divided for the purpose of indicating the particular type of subject-matter with which each department deals.

The emptiness of the phrase has been realised by German-speaking lawyers who use the term *Rechtsvergleichung*, which connotes a process of comparison and is free from any implication of the existence of a body of rules forming a separate branch or department of the law. But in England, and in most other countries, the term 'Comparative Law' has become so firmly established that it must be accepted, even if it is misleading, and tends, as we shall see hereafter, to obscure the real nature of the functions which the comparative method of study is called on to discharge, and the purposes for which it exists.

1 Lee, 'Comparative Law and Comparative Lawyers', *Journal of the S.P.T.L.* (1936), p. 1. Cf. Randall, *Journal of C.L.* (3rd Ser.), vol. XII (1930), at p. 189.

The unfortunate use of the word 'law' in this connection is reflected in the various attempts which have been made to solve the problem of definition by re-christening the subject. It is sometimes referred to as 'Comparative Jurisprudence',[1] and sometimes as 'Comparative Legislation'. Both these terms are open to the charge of obscurity, but they escape the criticism arising from the confusion created by the use of the word 'law' in this context. The use of the phrase 'Comparative Jurisprudence' is an expression of the belief that the main purpose of the comparative method of study is to aid the historian or the analytical jurist in tracing the origin and development of concepts common to all systems of law. The term 'Comparative Legislation', which, as a learned writer has observed, is in the nature of a 'subterfuge',[2] seems to have been devised in order to emphasise the practical as opposed to the academic aspects of comparative legal research, and stresses two features of the results which may be obtained by the use of the comparative method. The first of these is the collection and distribution of information as to foreign law; the second is the utilisation of the experience gained in other systems of law for the purpose of law reform. The purpose underlying the reference to 'legislation' rather than to 'law' or 'jurisprudence' seems to have been to conciliate the large and influential body of legal opinion which, in all countries, shows its dislike of a purely theoretical approach to the law. It has a 'useful and practical sound', and it was thought that it might serve to disarm hostility.[3] Although we may discard both these terms, in view of the fact that they have not succeeded in displacing the term 'Comparative Law', they cannot be ignored. The Corpus Professor at Oxford holds a Chair of Historical and Comparative Jurisprudence, and the French and English Societies which were founded for the promotion of comparative studies are both styled 'Societies of Comparative Legislation'. These variations in nomenclature are, however, of no great importance save in so far as they illustrate the tendency to define comparative law in the light of the functions which it may be called on to discharge.

Legal definitions are notoriously unsatisfactory and apt to lead to controversies which are often barren of result. This, in particular, is the case when any attempt is made to define 'Comparative Law' as law, since the subject-matter, being non-existent, is one which defies definition. The consequence is that the definitions which have been framed do not deal

1 E.g. Maine, *Village Communities* (3rd ed.), p. 3; Pollock, 'The History of Comparative Jurisprudence', *Journal of C.L.* (N.S.), vol. v (1903), p. 74.

2 Randall, 'Sir John Macdonnell and the Study of Comparative Law', *Journal of C.L.* (3rd Ser.), vol. XII (1930), p. 189.

3 Randall, *loc. cit.* Lambert also uses the term 'comparative legislation' but in a somewhat special sense. See *post*, p. 6.

with the nature of comparative law but only with its objects. The author of the definition has, in each case, focused his attention on the particular function which, from his standpoint, characterises the employment of the method of comparison. The *Vocabulaire Juridique*, for instance, defines comparative law as a branch of legal science whose object it is to bring about systematically the establishment of closer relations between the legal institutions of the different countries.[1] In this definition we hear the voice of the unificationist who regards comparative research as of little importance except in so far as it operates to promote the movement in favour of international uniformity of law. The earlier comparative lawyers identified comparative law with comparative legal history, or treated it as ancillary to analytical jurisprudence. Kohler regarded *Universale Rechtsgeschichte* and *Vergleichende Rechtswissenschaft* as interchangeable terms,[2] whilst Pollock observed that 'it makes no great difference whether we speak of historical jurisprudence or of comparative jurisprudence or, as the Germans seem inclined to say, of the general history of law'.[3] Holland puts the matter in this way: 'Comparative Law collects and tabulates the legal institutions of various countries, and from the results thus prepared, the abstract science of jurisprudence is enabled to set forth an orderly view of the ideas and methods which have been variously realised in actual systems.'[4] Maine's attitude is different; he states that 'the chief function of Comparative Jurisprudence is to facilitate legislation and the practical improvement of law'.[5]

These restricted views of the nature of comparative law began to widen as the many-sided character of comparative law gained recognition. Bryce, writing in 1901, distinguished between the purely scientific aspect of the subject and its more practical side. The first aspect he describes as 'the comparative science of jurisprudence', which, like Pollock, he identifies with the 'historical study of law in general'. The second aspect has a 'palpably practical aim'. It sets out by ascertaining and examining the rules actually in force in modern civilised countries, and proceeds to show

---

1 'Branche de la science du Droit ayant pour objet le rapprochement systématique des institutions juridiques des divers pays' (*Vocabulaire Juridique*, sub tit. 'Droit Comparé'). Cf. Lévy-Ullmann's definition: 'Branche spéciale de la science juridique qui a pour objet le rapprochement systématique des pays civilisés' (*Droit Mondial du XXe Siècle*).

2 *Encyklopädie der Rechtswissenschaft* (6th ed.), p. 1.

3 'The History of Comparative Jurisprudence', *Journal of C.L.* (N.S.), vol. v (1903), p. 74.

4 *Jurisprudence* (9th ed.), at p. 8. This view is also held by Allen, who identifies comparative jurisprudence with 'the study of racial origins and early social institutions' as an aid to analytical jurisprudence (*Law in the Making* (3rd ed.), pp. 21 and 22).

5 *Village Communities* (3rd ed.), p. 3.

by what means these rules deal with problems substantially the same in those countries.[1] Salmond defines comparative jurisprudence as 'the study of the resemblances and differences between different legal systems'. He says that it is not a separate branch of jurisprudence '...but merely a particular method of that science... we compare English law with Roman law... for the purpose of historical jurisprudence in order that we may better understand the course of development of each system'.[2]

Enough, perhaps, has been said to illustrate the difficulties encountered in any attempt to frame a satisfactory definition of comparative law. Present-day writers appear to recognise this and, following the example set by Bryce, they subdivide the subject before defining it. Wigmore distinguishes between *Comparative Nomoscopy*, i.e. the description of other systems of law, *Comparative Nomothetics*, i.e. the assessment of the relative merits of the rules under comparison, and *Comparative Nomogenetics*, i.e. the study of the development of systems of law in relation to one another.[3] Rabel divides Comparative Law into Ethnological Jurisprudence, Historical Comparison and Systematic-Dogmatic Comparative Law.[4] The last-mentioned phrase calls for explanation. It refers to the comparison of the rules of present-day systems of law viewed not in isolation but as part of the systems to which they belong, and corresponds to the second limb of Bryce's definition. Lambert[5] adopts the division into Comparative Legal History and Comparative Legislation.[6] Hug[7] and Sarfatti[8] accept the dichotomy of the subject into that part of it which deals with the laws of the past and with primitive law, or so-called ethnological jurisprudence, and the part which relates to law actually in force in civilised communities at the present time.

The problem of definition is closely involved with another question, namely, the much-debated claim of comparative law to be regarded as a 'science'. There are, more particularly in the civil-law countries, two schools of thought, one of which maintains that comparative law is merely

1 *Studies in History and Jurisprudence*, vol. II, p. 188.
2 *Jurisprudence* (7th ed.), p. 8, note (*b*).
3 'A New Way of Teaching Comparative Law', *Journal of the S.P.T.L.* (1926), p. 6; *A Panorama of the World's Legal Systems.*
4 'Aufgabe und Notwendigkeit der Rechtsvergleichung', *Münchner Juristische Vorträge*, Heft 1 (1925). See also the valuable discussion of Rabel's theories in 'Comparative Law and Conflict of Laws in Germany' by Rheinstein, *Chicago L.R.* vol. II (1935), p. 232.
5 *La Fonction du Droit Civil Comparé*, see post, p. 6, note 1.
6 *Op. cit.* p. 914. The term 'Legislation' is used by Lambert as denoting the sum total of the laws written or unwritten which are in force in any relevant system.
7 'The History of Comparative Law', *Harvard L.R.* vol. XLV, p. 1030.
8 'La Comparazione storico-etnologica del Diritto ed il Diritto Comparato propriamente detto', *Introduzione allo Studio del Diritto Comparato* (1933).

a form of legal technique,[1] whilst the other insists on its scientific nature and classifies it as a distinct branch of legal learning.[2]

The question appears to resolve itself into a somewhat arid logomachy which centres round the interpretation of the terms 'science' and 'method'. As a learned writer has observed: 'how vague and interchangeable these expressions are, so far as legal terminology is concerned, may be seen from the fact that there exists an essay entitled "the methods of legal science" as well as a book styled "the science of legal method". It may well be left to philology to disentangle this problem.'[3] Neither this nor the kindred problem of the relation of comparative law to other branches of learning and, in particular, to legal philosophy[4] and to ethnology,[5] need detain us: they must be left to others to determine if they can. The issues involved are purely academic and, in any event, of doubtful importance. A method of study does not lend itself to definition otherwise than by an indication of the purposes for which it may be employed, and the essential problem is not—What is comparative law? The question of real importance is—What is its purpose?

The first serious attempts to formulate the functions and aims of comparative law were made at the International Congress of Comparative Law held in Paris in 1900, the most noteworthy being those made by Saleilles and Lambert. Saleilles, under the influence of Stammler's school of legal philosophy, considered it to be the function of comparative law to ascertain the principles which are common to all civilised systems of law. He treated these principles as universal, but not immutable, and as constituting a model law, the so-called 'law of nature with variable content' (*droit idéal relatif*).[6] Lambert's attitude was somewhat different. He considered that comparative law had two purposes. One is purely scientific, namely, the discovery by means of a process of comparison of the causes which underlie the origin, development and extinction of legal institutions, or, in other words, comparative legal history. In this case

1 De Francisci (*Rivista Internazionale di Filosofia del Diritto*, vol. I (1921), p. 246) writes, 'una scienza particolare del diritto comparato non esiste ne puo esistere'. Cf. Kaden, *Rechtsvergleichendes Handwörterbuch* (vol. VI, p. 11): 'Der Begriff der Rechtsvergleichung bezeichnet nichts anders als eine Methode.'

2 Rabel, *Aufgabe und Notwendigkeit der Rechtsvergleichung*; Sugiyama, 'Essai d'une Conception Synthétique de Droit Comparé', *Recueil Lambert*, vol. I, p. 50; Otetelisano, 'Les Conceptions de Lambert sur le Droit Comparé', *Recueil Lambert*, vol. I, p. 39; and, see generally, Schmitthoff, 'The Science of Comparative Law', *Cambridge L.J.* vol. VII (1939), at p. 95.

3 Schmitthoff, *loc. cit.*

4 See Del Vecchio, 'L'Idée d'une Science de Droit Universel Comparé', *Revue Critique de Droit et de Jurisprudence*, vol. XXXIX, p. 486.

5 Sauser-Hall, *Fonction et Méthode de Droit Comparé*, p. 97; Adam, 'Modern Ethnological Jurisprudence in Theory and Practice', *Journal of C.L.* (3rd Ser.), vol. XVI (1934), p. 216.   6 See Allen, *Law in the Making* (3rd ed.), p. 25.

the comparison extends both to time and space. The second domain of comparative law, i.e. comparative legislation, has, according to Lambert, a practical aim and is not a science but a form of legal technique. Its purpose is to create an 'International Common Law' consisting of rules which are applicable to the needs of such communities as have attained the same standard of civilisation.[1]

So far as the views held by these two famous jurists were based on the existence of certain principles common to all systems of law, they rest on a somewhat flimsy foundation and appear to have been abandoned to a very large extent at the present day. Nevertheless, the 'universalist' view of law has exercised a marked influence on the development of modern comparative law. It formed the starting-point for the wave of unificationary enthusiasm which swept over Europe in the years following the war of 1914–18, and it still provides a motive for much of the comparative study and research which is carried on at the present time. It has also found expression in Article 38 of the Statute of the Permanent Court of International Justice, which directs the court to apply, among other rules, 'the general principles of law recognised by civilised nations'. It has been suggested, moreover, that a search for 'common principles' conducted on analytical lines may result in a solution of the problem which is created in the domain of private international law by the varying interpretation given in different jurisdictions to the same legal concept, a problem which is known as that of 'Qualification', 'Classification' or 'Characterisation'.[2] It is, however, doubtful whether the universalist theory can be regarded as more than a pious aspiration founded, partly, on the need for collaboration between the nations in the legal as well as in other spheres, but, in the main, on a belief in the essential unity of mankind. If this view of the matter is put to a test in the conditions of everyday life, it is apt to break against obstacles created by differences in national mentality, by habits deeply rooted in tradition, and by variations in the structure of legal institutions and legal technique from country to country.

Although the 'universalist' theory may still be invoked in aid of projects for the unification of private law, it is no longer regarded as explaining

1 Lambert's views have been modified since the publication in 1903 of *La Fonction du Droit Civil Comparé*. See *Encyclopaedia of Social Sciences*, vol. IV, p. 127 and *Acta Academiae Universalis Jurisprudentiae Comparativae*, vol. II (1) (1934), p. 600.

2 Rabel, *Zeitschrift für Ausländisches und Internationales Privatrecht*, vol. V (1931), p. 267; Beckett, 'Classification in Private International Law', *British Year Book of I.L.* vol. 15 (1934), p. 46. For an application of universalist theories to private international law in general see Lévy-Ullmann, *La Doctrine Universaliste en Matière de Conflit des Lois* (Extrait du Cours de Doctorat), reproduced in Barbey, 'Le Rôle du Droit Comparé dans le Droit International Privé', *Recueil des Cours de l'Académie de D.I.* (1937).

the necessity for the employment of the comparative method. At the present day the tendency is to stress the value of the method by indicating the different purposes which may be served by its employment, and this has led to various attempts to classify comparative law in accordance with the objects which can be attained by its utilisation. Allusion has already been made to Wigmore's division of comparative law into Nomoscopy, Nomothetics and Nomogenetics.[1] Lambert classifies the subject into Comparative Legal History, Comparative Legislation and Descriptive Comparative Law.[2] Kantorowicz speaks of geographical, material and methodological comparison.[3] Kaden draws a distinction between formal comparison (*formelle Rechtsvergleichung*) and dogmatic comparison (*dogmatische Rechtsvergleichung*). He uses the term 'formal' to denote the comparative investigation of the sources of law, e.g. the weight given in different systems to statute law, case law and custom, and the application of differing methods of legal technique in such respects as the interpretation of statutes. Dogmatic comparison is concerned with the various solutions which have been found for the same legal problem in different systems of law.[4]

It may, however, be doubted whether much is gained by the classifications which have been mentioned. The comparative method is sufficiently elastic to embrace all activities which, in some form or other, may be concerned with the study of foreign law. As Wigmore has pointed out, 'no one scholar to-day can hope to compass it completely'.[5] There is, perhaps, a broad distinction to be drawn between comparison instituted for the sole purpose of obtaining information as to foreign law, and comparative research carried on with some other aim in view. The first of these can be classified as *Descriptive Comparative Law*, whilst the second is sometimes known as *Comparative Legislation*[6] but would seem to be more accurately styled *Applied Comparative Law*.[7] This distinction is one which has found general acceptance, and it is useful in so far as it brings into relief the fact that comparative law includes a great deal more than a mere description of the laws of a foreign country.

3 'Probleme der Strafrechtsvergleichung' (*Monatschrift für Kriminelle Psychologie* (1907), Part IV). Geographical comparison implies the parallel investigation of the general structure of the law in several systems. Material comparison is the comparative investigation of rules relating to a given subject-matter. Methodological comparison is that form of the process which is not purely analytical but leads to a synthetical view of the subject-matter.
4 *Rechtsvergleichendes Handwörterbuch*, vol. VI, p. 17.
5 *A Panorama of the World's Legal Systems.*   6 See *ante*, p. 2.
7 The term 'Applied Comparative Law' was first suggested to me by Sir Arnold McNair. It is also used by Schmitthoff, *op. cit.* Rheinstein distinguishes between 'functional comparison' and 'synoptic comparison': 'Teaching Comparative Law', *Chicago L.R.* vol. V (1938), p. 615.

Descriptive Comparative Law. This is a term which is somewhat loosely
employed and embraces many types of comparative work of varying
degrees of merit. There is a noticeable tendency to treat any investigation
into foreign law as coming under this heading, but such an extension of
the meaning of the term is unjustifiable. We may at once dismiss any such
claim, so far as it relates to a mere compilation of facts concerning a single
legal system, because in such a case there cannot be any comparison. Nor
is such a claim enhanced merely because the compilation takes the form
of a parallel or tabular statement of facts relating to several systems, which
leaves it to a reader to discover for himself what differences may exist.
But any statement of divergences between two or more systems would
seem to be admissible under this heading, even though it may be pedestrian
in character and unworthy of being dignified as legal research.

Descriptive comparative law differs from applied comparative law
because it is confined to an analysis of variations between the laws of two
or more countries, and is not directed to the solution of any problem either
of an abstract or a practical nature. The comparison has no other aim than
that of furnishing information, and it is no concern of the person undertaking it to ascertain what use will be made of the result of his investigations. A typical instance of research of this character is to be found in the
inquiry instituted in 1937 by the League of Nations into the laws which
regulate the civil status of women.[1] A committee of legal experts was
appointed by the Council of the League with instructions to carry out
their work on purely objective lines, the purpose of the inquiry being to
collect data concerning the legal position of women in different countries,
and to ascertain where the highest level had been reached, and where it
was still low. The scope of the inquiry was to include 'the application of
the law', a somewhat ambiguous phrase which was intended to broaden
the basis of the committee's work and to extend it to cover the operation
of rules of law in practice whilst excluding any matters which might be
merely of speculative or sociological interest. It was clearly not the duty
of the committee to express an opinion on the question whether the law
in any particular country is such as to call for amendment or to formulate
projects for law reform. Any use that might be made hereafter of the
information thus collected was a matter which was to be decided upon
by the League of Nations; it was no concern of the committee or of
the persons working under its direction.

'Descriptive' comparative law is open to the same criticisms which
have been levelled at similar work in other branches of learning, e.g.

[1] For an account of the circumstances in which the inquiry was instituted see the
Report on the Work of the League, 1937–8, pp. 178–81 (Part I of Document A.6.1938).

'descriptive economics', but much of it is of definite value, and the short-comings which afflict it are due, more often than not, to faulty technique in the employment of the method.

Applied Comparative Law. The use of the comparative method with a definite aim in view, other than that of obtainmg information as to foreign law, may conveniently be called 'Applied Comparative Law'. The aim in question need not be of a practical nature: it may, for instance, take the form of a comparison carried out either to enable the legal philosopher to construct abstract theories of law, or in order to assist the historian in tracing the origins and evolution of legal concepts and institutions. The distinguishing feature of this form of comparison is that it does not consist of a mere description of the differences which exist between the concepts, rules or institutions of the laws under examination, but probes more deeply into the matter with a definite purpose in view. The investigator must, first of all, ascertain how far these differences are fundamental or merely accidental; secondly, he must determine the causes underlying such differences and their relation to the general structure of the system in which they arise; and, finally, where modern law is concerned he must examine the operation of the rules in practice having regard to the legal and social environment in which each of the systems is called upon to function. The comparison must be based on a careful and accurate analysis of the foreign laws under investigation, but its most important aspect is the construction of a synthesis, founded on the results of the analytical process, which is intended to elucidate some problem either of an abstract or utilitarian character. The purpose of the comparison may be purely scientific as, for instance, when the evolution of a rule of law or of some legal institution is traced through several systems with the object of throwing light on the historical development of the same kind of rule or institution in another system. This is also true of comparisons instituted by analytical jurists in aid of attempts to ascertain the concepts and principles which are to be found in all civilised systems of law. But for the most part applied comparative law has a practical aim in view, such as law reform or the unification of divergent laws, and it is this form of comparative research which is the most vigorous and fertile in output.

Abstract or Speculative Comparative Law. The suggestion has been made that there is a third form of comparative law which Rabel[1] has termed 'pure' comparative law. This is said to consist of comparison carried out with no other object than that of increasing the sum total of our knowledge of the law. But it is, to say the least of it, doubtful whether any such category of comparative research is more than a mere abstraction which has no real

---

1 *Loc. cit.*

existence. It is, no doubt, theoretically possible to conceive of a comparison carried out *in vacuo* which is not 'descriptive', because it is not solely informative in character, and is not 'applied', because it has no particular aim other than that of scientific curiosity. In any event research of this kind must be so rare as to be virtually non-existent. If it is confined to an analysis of the differences between systems of law it would seem to fall under the category of 'descriptive' comparison: on the other hand, if the differences are regarded in the light of the historical development of the law or of social purposes for which the law exists, then the comparison is likely to lose its abstract character and to assume the guise of 'applied' comparative law. Moreover, the difficulties involved in comparative research and its arduous character are such as to act as a deterrent unless the research is necessary either to secure information as to foreign law or to achieve some other purpose.

The Unity of the Comparative Method. Comparative law is, however, not fragmentary in nature; it does not consist of a patchwork of various types of legal research, possessing an independent existence of their own, which are swept up into a common receptacle because they all involve some degree of investigation into more than a single system of law. The fundamental characteristic of comparative law, viewed as a method, lies in the fact that it is applicable to any form of legal research. The method is equally at the services of the legal historian, the analytical jurist, the judge, the practitioner and the teacher of law. It covers the domain both of public and private law; its resources lie open to the economist and to the sociologist, as well as to the lawyer. It may render useful service to the statesman, the administrator and the man of business. Not the least of its merits is its flexibility, and there is a danger that its scope might be restricted if it were partitioned off into categories which are artificial in nature and lacking in clear lines of demarcation. Not only does it yield results of importance in a material sense but it may also provide the background of law, viewed as a whole, which is absent if national systems of law are studied in isolation. It can throw light on the obscurities of rules or institutions which do not appear to rest on traditional or logical foundations; it may furnish the test by which it can be judged whether any rule of law is the best solution of the particular problem with which the rule is designed to deal. In circumstances such as these any efforts which may be made to compile a systematic, orderly and detailed classification of the purposes for which the comparative method can be employed are likely to prove unconvincing and unremunerative. In any event, the comparative method is on trial; it is still in the experimental stage, and any classification of its functions cannot, therefore, be regarded as final.

Chapter II

THE ORIGINS & DEVELOPMENT OF
COMPARATIVE LAW

COMPARATIVE LAW, in the sense in which we are employing the phrase, is essentially modern in character, although there have been many efforts to trace its origins back into the mists of the past. The supposition—for it is little more—is that the comparative method of legal study has been evolved from a spirit of inquiry into foreign law which existed among the jurists of antiquity.[1] But, however valuable the results of such investigations may be to legal historians, they can have little bearing on the question of the nature and functions of comparative law at the present time. Our knowledge of the conditions in which it was possible at an early date for the rules of one system of law to come to the knowledge of the lawyers of another system will, in all probability, always be of a meagre description. The environment of Roman law was unfavourable to the study of foreign law, and even the more important elements of the *Jus Gentium* were, in essence, Roman and were not the result of any process of comparison with foreign law.[2] In the Middle Ages, when resort to foreign rules of law became necessary, a ready instrument lay at hand in the highly developed Roman system. Any gaps which existed could be bridged over in this way, and the dominating influence in the development of medieval law on the continent of Europe was the 'masterful and all-pervasive stream of Romanic influence emanating from the juristic schools of Italy'.[3] In the early post-Renaissance period the influence of humanism created a desire to inquire into the laws of other systems, but the exclusive

---

1 'Le droit comparé est une discipline qui a des parchemins', Cornil, 'La Complexité des Sources du Droit Comparé', *Recueil Lambert*, vol. I, p. 358. The early history of comparative law is dealt with in detail by the following writers: Pollock, 'History of Comparative Law', *Journal of C.L.* (N.S.), vol. V (1903), p. 74; Wigmore, *A Panorama of the World's Legal Systems*; Hug, 'History of Comparative Law', *Harvard L.R.* vol. XLV, p. 1027; Lambert, *La Fonction du Droit Civil Comparé*; Sauser-Hall, *Fonction et Méthode du Droit Comparé*; Sarfatti, *Introduzione allo Studio del Diritto Comparato*. See also Kaden, title 'Rechtsvergleichung' in *Rechtsvergleichendes Handwörterbuch*, vol. VI, p. 20 *passim*, and the numerous monographs in *Recueil Lambert*.

2 Buckland and McNair, *Roman Law and Common Law*, pp. 18, 19.

3 Hazeltine, 'The Renaissance and the Laws of Europe' in *Cambridge Legal Essays*, p. 139. Perhaps the first instance of comparative legal research in the sense in which the phrase is understood at the present day was the *Collatio Mosaicarum et Romanarum Legum*, a work of the fourth century A.D. which contains interesting comparisons between Roman and Jewish law. See Volterra, *La Collatio Mosaicarum et Romanarum Legum*; Hug, *op. cit.*

devotion of the civilians to the tradition of Roman law was hostile to any serious comparative study.[1] England, with its common-law system, offered a more promising field to the comparative student, and it is here that we meet with the first signs of interest in foreign law, but the jealousy of the English lawyers, which forbade any encroachment on the common law by the civilians or the canonists, created an atmosphere in which comparative research could not be expected to make much headway.[2] It is not until a later date that we find a development of the idea that comparative legal studies have a part to play in the general scheme of the science of the law. Leibnitz, writing in 1667, planned a complete survey of the laws of the civilised world, but this project failed to materialise.[3] The eighteenth century marks a further and more active stage in the development of the comparative method of research. Vico[4] and Montesquieu were the sponsors of the now generally accepted view that the legal principles and institutions of the world can, as a whole, be the subject-matter of profitable study. Montesquieu, in particular, has a claim to be considered as the founder of comparative law, since it was he who first realised that a rule of law should not be treated as an abstraction, but must be regarded against a background of its history and of the environment in which it is called upon to function.[5] In *De l'Esprit des Lois* he attempted a detailed and scientific inquiry into the laws of the world, thus putting into effect the ideas which were first conceived by Leibnitz. But he attempted too much, and his work is disconnected, unsystematic and marred by eccentricities. Great as was the success of *De l'Esprit des Lois* it was not the means of placing comparative legal research on a lasting foundation. The materials used by Montesquieu were inaccessible to the writers and students of his time, and the impetus which he undoubtedly gave to the study of foreign law failed to carry with it the general body of thinkers in his own and other countries. The lead which he gave was not followed up; in fact, the efforts of the continental jurists of this period were largely devoted to the establishment of the law of nations on the foundations laid by Grotius, a task demanding an attitude of mind not wholly favourable to comparative studies, because the effort to secure recognition for the law of nature carried with it a tendency to slur over the differences existing between the laws of individual nations and to belittle their importance.[6] We are, therefore, driven to the con-

---

1 Hazeltine, *loc. cit.*   2 See *post*, p. 14.
3 *Nova Methodus discendae docendaeque Jurisprudentiae.* See Pollock, *op. cit.* at p. 83.
4 See Del Vecchio, 'La Communicabilité du Droit et les Doctrines de G. B. Vico', *Recueil Lambert*, vol. II, p. 591.   5 Sauser-Hall, *op. cit.* p. 35.
6 Pollock, *op. cit.* p. 85. For a discussion of the influence of the 'natural law' school of thought in this connection see Kaden, *op. cit.* p. 23 and Sarfatti, *op. cit.* p. 14.

clusion that, so far as its dynamic effects are concerned,¡ the life of comparative law barely exceeds the limits of living memory¦, and that, as we now know it, it dates at the very earliest from the middle of the nineteenth century. Progress was, indeed, much hampered at first by certain influences which operated during the opening years of that century. The theory of the historical school of thought that law proceeds from the common consciousness of a nation, and that its growth must, therefore, not be checked by the importation of alien elements, was inimical to the study of foreign law.[1] This period was also the era of codification, and the fear of the codifiers lest their achievements should be imperilled by the efforts of commentators also created hostility to research into the rules of foreign systems. Still, in spite of these obstacles the notion of the importance of comparative research continued to make ground. In Germany its value to the legal philosopher was insisted on by Feuerbach,[2] Gans and Thibaut, and in 1829 Mittermaier and Zachariae founded the first legal review devoted to the encouragement of the study of foreign law.[3] In France the most noteworthy events were the foundation of the Chair of Comparative Law at the Collège de France in 1832 and of a Chair of Comparative Criminal Law in the University of Paris in 1846.[4] In the United States of America the formative period of the law was tinged by hostility to all that was English, with a consequent trend in the direction of natural law which was sought for mainly in the writings of the French jurists. The result was a 'conception of an ideal of comparative law as declaratory of natural law, a conception which is especially manifest in the writings and judgments of Kent and Story'.[5] In any event, the progress made up to the middle years of the nineteenth century was due to the influence of a handful of distinguished men, and with their passing away a period of stagnation followed which lasted until it was broken by the rise of the doctrine of evolution with the stimulus thus afforded to all branches of learning.

It is perhaps remarkable that it was in England, the reputed home of legal isolationism, that much of the pioneering work in the domain of comparative law was carried out. Holdsworth has pointed out that

1 See, for instance, Savigny, *System des römischen Rechts*, vol. I, p. 14.
2 Radbruch, 'Anselm Feuerbach, Précurseur du Droit Comparé', *Recueil Lambert*, vol. I, p. 284.
3 *Zeitschrift für Rechtwissenschaft und Gesetzgebung*.
4 At a later period other Chairs were founded in the University: in 1892 a Chair of Droit Civil approfondi et comparé and a Chair of Droit Commercial Comparé, and in 1905 a Chair of Législation Civile Comparée (Lévy-Ullmann, *Journal of the S.P.T.L.* (1925), p. 16).
5 Pound, 'Comparative Law in the formation of American Law', *Acta Academiae Universalis Jurisprudentiae Comparativae*, vol. I (1928), p. 183; see also 'The Influence of French Law in America', by the same author, in *Illinois L.R.* vol. III, p. 354.

although early English law was 'fundamentally unlike that of the Continent, it was sufficiently akin to render possible a science of comparative law'.[1] It is clear that our law has been influenced by comparison with the ideas and rules of the civil and canon law, though to what extent is a matter of conjecture.[2] Bracton made use of doctrines derived from Roman sources, and St Germain's *Doctor and Student* is a comparative exposition of the canon law and the common law. But at no time in the early history of English law do we find any 'critical investigation of the foreign rules or any real attempt to construct a synthesis. Foreign principles may have been taken and adapted to an English environment, but there was no reception in detail of foreign law.'[3]

The *Lex Mercatoria* is sometimes referred to as an instance of rules based on a process of comparison, but, so far as it is possible to draw any conclusions as to the origin and nature of this branch of medieval law, it is doubtful whether it was a blend of the mercantile usages of Europe or was a body of customary law of Italian origin imposed on medieval traders by the predominance in European commerce of the Italian merchants.[4]

The first mention of comparative law, in the modern sense of the term, by any English author, seems to have been by Bacon at the beginning of the seventeenth century. King James I was anxious to take advantage of the Act of Union for the purpose of unifying the rules of English and Scots law and sought Bacon's advice. This was tendered in a cautious spirit, which illustrates the attitude of the English lawyers of the time towards comparative law. Bacon suggested that the lawyers of England and Scotland should collaborate in the preparation of a digest in which the laws of the two countries 'may be collated and *compared and that the diversities may appear and be discerned of*'.[5] He also warned King James that

1 *History of English Law*, vol. IV, p. 289.

2 A complete account of the influence of the doctrines of the civil and canon law on the growth of English law still remains to be written, but it was, probably, much greater than is commonly assumed. Bracton's work furnished the excuse, if any were needed, for resort to the civilians in questions to which the common law furnished no answer. Some, at least, of the English law libraries were well equipped with the necessary books. Senior, 'Roman Law MSS. in England', *L.Q.R.* vol. XLVII (1931), p. 339; see also *Doctors' Commons* by the same author, and Oliver, *Cambridge Legal Essays*, p. 243, and *post*, p. 16.

3 Holdsworth, *History of English Law*, vol. IV, p. 289. See also Lee, 'L'Étude du Droit Comparé en Grande Bretagne', *Recueil Lambert*, vol. I, p. 344.

4 See Macdonnell, in the introduction to *Smith's Mercantile Law* (13th ed.), p. 1, *passim*; and cf. Bewes, *The Romance of the Law Merchant*; Holdsworth, *History of English Law*, vol. V, p. 103 *passim*; Plucknett, *A Concise History of the Common Law*, p. 587 *passim*.

5 'Certain Articles or Considerations touching the Union of the Kingdoms of England and Scotland', *The Works of Lord Bacon* (Bohn's ed.), vol. I, p. 157. This appears to be the first time that the phrase 'comparison' was employed in this connection.

jus privatum should not, as a rule, be meddled with because 'men love to hold their own as they have held'. But in order that the King should be in a position to decide as to the expediency of the proposal he suggests that, first of all, 'a book of two columns' should be compiled by the lawyers of either nation containing brief summaries of the rules of both laws. He declares, however, that so far as he is concerned his participation in the enterprise must be limited strictly to English law. 'Although', he says, 'I have read, and read with delight, the Scottish statutes, and some other collections of their laws; with delight, I say, partly to see their brevity and propriety of speech, and partly to see them come so near to our laws; yet I am unwilling to put my sickle in another's harvest, but to leave it to the lawyers of the Scottish nation; the rather, because I imagine with myself that if a Scottish lawyer should undertake by reading the English statutes, or other our books of laws, to set down positively in articles what the laws of England were, he might oftentimes err, and the like errors I make account, I might incur in theirs.'[1] No one is likely to quarrel with this eminently sane and common-sense point of view, one which is unhappily too often disregarded by comparative lawyers, but nothing seems to have come of Bacon's proposals, and, even at the present day, no complete study exists of the divergences between English and Scots law and of the importance to be attached to them.[2]

In any case down to the end of the seventeenth century 'the nearest approaches to comparative criticism were made by Englishmen'.[3] In this connection one might mention the names of Fortescue,[4] St Germain,[5] Fulbecke,[6] Cowell,[7] Selden[8] and Smith.[9] One of the earliest works in the English language, in which the comparative method of legal research is employed, was Thomas Wood's *New Institute of the Imperial or Civil Law*, published in 1704. The author's object was to prove that the law of England had absorbed many of the rules of the civil law.[10] The eighteenth century was undoubtedly a period of some activity in certain branches of comparative research. Lord Mansfield, the greatest of our native com-

1 'A Preparation for the Union of Laws', *The Works of Lord Bacon* (Bohn's ed.), vol. 1, p. 642.
2 Lord Mackenzie's *Studies in Roman Law with Comparative Views of the Laws of France, England, and Scotland*, published in 1861, seems to be the only work of this kind and it merely deals in outline with certain topics.
3 Pollock, *op. cit.* pp. 81 and 82.
4 *The Governance of England* and *De Laudibus Legum Angliae*.
5 *Doctor and Student*.
6 *Parallel or Conference of the Civil Law, the Canon Law, and the Common Law of the Realm of England*.   7 *Institutiones Juris Anglicani*.
8 *History of Tithes and Titles of Honour* and *De Successionibus ad Leges Ebraeorum in Bona Defunctorum*.
9 *De Republica Anglorum*.   10 Lee, *op. cit.*

parative lawyers, was enabled to lay the foundation of English commercial law by his studies in the laws of other countries.[1] John Ayliffe, who died in 1792, was the author of a single volume published posthumously of a work planned on a large scale and entitled the *New Pandects of the Roman Civil Law*, which included comparisons between English law and the civil and canon law.[2] The works of foreign jurists, in particular those of Pothier, enjoyed a wide circulation in England,[3] and exercised a definite influence on the development of our law.

The first half of the nineteenth century was not marked by much growth in comparative studies, but a beginning was made with the application of the comparative method to the more practical aspects of law by the publication in 1838 of Burge's *Commentaries on Colonial and Foreign Laws*, a treatise designed to assist the practising lawyer, and by Leone Levi's attempt at a later date to bring about an international movement for the codification of commercial law.[4] John Austin, although much under the influence of legal ideas instilled into him during the course of his studies in Germany, only makes a passing reference to comparative jurisprudence.[5] It may, perhaps, be conceded that English lawyers during this period were, as a body, hostile to the study of foreign law, but it would be incorrect to regard England as wholly isolated during this time from the growing interest in comparative law.

The origin of modern comparative law was, however, not due to any impulse coming from within the law but was a by-product of the new school of creative thought which derived its impetus from the idea of evolution. Comparative law began to follow the other comparative sciences, such as comparative anatomy,[6] and its aim was to find in law 'the equivalent of correlation of structure in anatomy, i.e. like structures performing like functions'.[7] From this time onwards, comparative research, both on the Continent of Europe and America, no longer consists in the inspired but isolated efforts of a few men of genius, but takes its place as a recognised instrument for the development of the law. So far

1 See Holdsworth, 'Lord Mansfield', *L.Q.R.* vol. LIII (1937), p. 221. Fifoot, *Lord Mansfield.*   2 Lee, *op. cit.*

3 Plucknett, *op. cit.* pp. 265, 266. Blackstone, who can hardly be described as a comparative lawyer, explains the institution of Borough English by a reference to the practice of the Tartars, Comm. II, Ch. 6.

4 Leone Levi, *The Mercantile Law of Great Britain as compared with Roman Law and the Codes and Laws of 59 other countries* (1850–52). As to the part played by Leone Levi in the movement for unification, see *post*, p. 146.

5 *Fragment on the Uses of the Study of Jurisprudence.* See Pollock, *Journal of C.L.* (N.S.), vol. V (1903), p. 74.

6 Amari, *Critica di una scienza delle legislazione comparate* (1857), appears to have been the first writer to indicate the analogy between comparative law and comparative anatomy and philology.

7 Randall, *Journal of C.L.* (3rd Ser.), vol. XII (1930), at p. 199.

as England is concerned the turning-point was the publication in 1861 of Maine's *Ancient Law*.[1] On the Continent the recognition of comparative legal studies, in their modern form, may be said to date from the foundation in Paris of the Société de Législation Comparée in 1869.[2] In 1876 the French government established a Committee on Foreign Legislation attached to the Ministry of Justice,[3] and in the same year a bequest by Sir Richard Quain, a judge of the Queen's Bench Division, made it possible to establish in 1894 the Quain Professorship of Comparative Law at University College, London. It is of interest to record that this generous benefactor received a part of his education at the University of Göttingen, and this probably explains his desire to promote comparative legal study and research. The Institut de Droit International, founded in 1873, began, in its early days, under the influence of Asser, Rolin-Jacquemyns and Westlake, to employ the comparative method in the investigation of the problems of private international law which came within the sphere of its activities. In 1895 the English Society of Comparative Legislation was founded, thus bringing the lawyers of Great Britain into line with those of the Continent.[4]

Comparative law may, therefore, be said to have secured definite recognition as a branch of legal study during the latter half of the nineteenth century. The outward manifestation of the position which was thus secured is to be found in the publication of periodicals devoted, either wholly or in part, to the promotion of the study of the subject. In 1869 in France, the Société de Législation Comparée commenced the issue of its *Bulletin*, which throughout its long career has come to be regarded as one of the leading sources of knowledge on the subject. In 1872 the Society added to it the *Annuaire de Législation Comparée*, which contains a brief annual summary of the statute law enacted throughout the civilised world.[5] Other publications of the same kind followed the example thus set: in 1869 the first number appeared of the *Revue de Droit International et de Législation Comparée*, and in 1878 the *Zeitschrift für vergleichende Rechtswissenschaft* was published at Stuttgart under the aegis of Kohler,[6]

1 Maine was also the first occupant of the Corpus Chair of Historical and Comparative Jurisprudence at Oxford. The date of his appointment was 1869. Lee, *op. cit.* at p. 345.
2 Pollock, *Procès Verbaux du Congrès International de Droit Comparé*, vol. I, p. 258.
3 Reconstituted by decree dated 21 July 1910. *Journal of C.L.* (N.S.), vol. XII, (1911), p. 175.
4 For details of the foundation of the Society, see *Journal of C.L.* (N.S.), vol. IX (1908), p. 14.
5 Goulé, 'La Société de Législation Comparée'. *Recueil Lambert*, vol. I, p. 696.
6 For an account of the early history of the comparative movement in Germany see Rheinstein, 'Comparative Law and Conflict of Laws in Germany', *Chicago L.R.* vol. II (1935), p. 232.

whilst the *Rivista di diritto internazionale comparato* and the *Rassegna di diritto commerciale e straniero* represented the contribution of Italian scholars to the growth of periodical literature of a comparative nature.

The various activities which have been referred to were animated by the enthusiasm which characterises all innovations in any branch of learning, but the votaries of the new science were not in accord as to the object to be attained. Several cross-currents were in evidence. For some the value of comparative legal studies consisted in their practical aspect, the underlying assumption being that a nation can profit from a careful study of new legislation enacted by foreign countries, and that the knowledge thus acquired can be turned to good account in the reform and development of the law. This attitude found its expression in the phrase 'Comparative Legislation' as opposed to 'Comparative Law',[1] and it accounts for the name which is borne by the only English society which is concerned with the promotion of comparative studies and for the title of the journal which it publishes. Another view was that comparative legal research has as its object the discovery of the abstract notions which underlie all systems of law and can be utilised to build up a common system of jurisprudence, as it would be termed by an English lawyer, or legal philosophy, in the language of continental law. For others, comparative studies were only of value in a historical sense as illustrating the tendencies which mould the growth of the law in all systems or as casting light on the development of a national system in its earliest stages. The belief, however, was gaining ground that all modern systems of law are based on certain common principles which constitute the 'natural law with variable content' of the legal philosophers. Comparative lawyers, therefore, began to aim at an analysis of conflicting rules of law and the construction of a synthesis which would enable a world-wide code of private law to be framed acceptable to all the nations. Sacrifices would, no doubt, be called for, and in some cases the process envisaged would encounter difficulties which could not be surmounted. But it was held that on a broad view of the matter the objective of comparative lawyers should be the ultimate unification of private law, and the creation in this way of a form of international common law. This line of thought found expression at the First Congress of Comparative Law held in Paris in 1900, which is regarded by many as the occasion on which modern comparative law first came into being. The chief exponent of this ideal was Professor Édouard Lambert of Lyons, whose magisterial treatise, *Fonction du Droit Comparé*, gave the widest publicity to the views of this school of thought. The times were, however, not ripe for the translation into action of the conception of

1 See *ante*, p. 2.

world-wide law, and unification rested—with the exception of certain aspects of maritime, commercial and private international law—on an academic plane until it was drawn into the sphere of practical politics by the post-war spirit of internationalism. The movement towards unification, which will be dealt with more fully hereafter,[1] has promoted a great deal of comparative legal research with a practical end in view which has been carried out, in part under the aegis of the League of Nations, in part by Government departments concerned in the negotiation of private-law conventions, and in part by learned societies and commercial organisations. The activities arising out of this movement have resulted in the collection of a vast quantity of material, much of which is of permanent value to comparative lawyers, irrespective of the fact that the attempts to secure unification have not always been successful. An outward and visible sign of the growing recognition of the importance of comparative studies in the international sphere was also furnished by the establishment in Rome, as a subsidiary organ of the League of Nations, of the International Institute for the Unification of Private Law, on the initiative of the Italian government, which made itself responsible for the housing and maintenance of the Institute.[2]

A notable achievement which belongs to this period was the foundation of the International Academy of Comparative Law at the Hague. This body, which owed its origin very largely to the enthusiasm and unflagging efforts of Professor Elemer Balogh, inaugurated the holding of a series of international congresses of comparative law which attracted lawyers in large numbers from all parts of the world. The Academy has placed the question of unification in the forefront of its programme, but it is also concerned with the other aspects of legal comparison.[3]

The growth of interest in comparative legal studies during the early part of the twentieth century cannot, however, be explained solely on the ground of the importance of comparison as a factor in the movement for the unification of private law. Another motive force was also in operation, namely, a change of attitude towards the more general question of the value of the study of foreign law. This arose from the realisation of the dangers attendant on a policy of legal isolationism which separates the lawyers of the different countries from one another, and induces a

1 See *post*, Chapters XI and XII.

2 *Ibid.*; see also Sarfatti, 'Costituzione dell' Istituto per l' unificazione del Diritto Privato', *Rivista Internazionale della Filosofia del Diritto*, Anno V, fasc. 1°; David, 'The International Institute of Rome for the Unification of Private Law', *Tulane L.R.* vol. VIII, p. 406.

3 See *Acta Academiae Universalis Jurisprudentiae Comparativae*, vols. I and II, for a full statement of the policy and aims of the Academy.

complacent attitude of mind and a stagnation of thought with a resulting
reluctance to adapt existing rules of law to changing conditions in the
social and economic spheres. Lawyers were beginning to appreciate the
fact that foreign law may be studied for the lessons to be learned from it,
and that comparison was not merely an artifice to enable foreign rules
to be introduced surreptitiously into a national system of law. It was also
becoming evident to the University Faculties of Law that comparative
research might go far to provide a solution of the difficult problem of
finding subjects for advanced study and research which are not confined
to legal history or the philosophical aspects of the law.[1] In some countries,
notably in France, Germany and Italy and to a lesser degree in the English-
speaking countries, some considerable progress has been made towards
the recognition by the Universities of the value and importance of the
comparative method. This has been, for the most part, the result of the
efforts of a small band of scholars, who, in face of indifference and, sometimes, of a certain under-current of hostility, have kept the claims of
comparative law alive.

Experience has shown that comparative law, from the academic point
of view, is in the main a post-graduate subject, and this has led to the
concentration of comparative studies to a large extent in Institutes, some
of which are attached to Universities, such as those at Lyon, Paris, Strasbourg and Toulouse, whilst others have been established on an independent basis, as in the case of the Institute of Foreign and Private International
Law at Berlin and the Institute of Legislative Studies at Rome.[2] The
proposals for the foundation of an Imperial School of Law in London
have not materialised up to the present, but, in the United States, the
Tulane University of Louisiana has been recognised as the centre of comparative study, and the *Tulane Law Review* is largely devoted to the
publication of articles of interest to comparative lawyers. Certain other
American Universities[3] have also taken steps to promote legal training
on comparative lines, but it would seem that in most of them little or
nothing has been done up to the present.[4] The American Bar Association
has displayed marked activity in the field of comparative study. In 1908
a Bureau of Comparative Law was established which for some years
published an annual *Bulletin*. This, however, became moribund when the

1 See *post*, Chapter x.   2 *Ibid.*
3 E.g. Chicago University—where the Pam Chair of Comparative Law is held
by a distinguished comparatist, Dr Rheinstein—and the University of Michigan which
is the headquarters of research in Inter-American law. See an article by Professor
Hessel E. Yntema in 43 *Michigan L.R.* (1944), p. 549.
4 See the *Columbia L.R.* vol. XLIII (May 1943), p. 473; Pound, 'The Revival
of Comparative Law', *Tulane L.R.* vol. v, p. 1; Hug and Ireland, 'The Progress of
Comparative Law', *Tulane L.R.* vol. VI, p. 68.

Association commenced the publication of its *Journal*. In the meantime, the Bureau had also published translations of the Argentine Civil Code, the Visigothic Code and the Sietes Partidas. In 1932 the Association, at the initiative of Dean Wigmore, organised a special section on Comparative and International Law, which holds meetings for the discussion of questions of interest to comparative lawyers. The American Foreign Law Association also came into being in 1925 and published a number of working bibliographies on foreign law and monographs on comparative topics. A 'Special Committee on Private International Law' was also formed which co-operated with the bodies which have been mentioned. The U.S. Department of Commerce publishes the 'Comparative Law Series', which contains a review of changes in foreign law affecting American commerce.[1] The Law Library of Congress has published a useful series of bibliographies of the laws of foreign countries,[2] though no steps appear to have been taken to keep them up to date. The Association of American Law Schools has made a valuable contribution to comparative studies in the shape of the 'Modern Criminal Science Series', the 'Continental Legal History Series', the 'Modern Legal Philosophy Series' and the 'History of Continental Civil Procedure'.

Great Britain emerges badly from a contrast with the situation elsewhere; in fact, it has been said with force and also with justice that the position is 'positively shocking'.[3] The Chair of Historical and Comparative Jurisprudence founded at Oxford in 1869 is still—as it has, in reality, always been—devoted to the general theory of the law. Cambridge stands alone in possessing a Chair of Comparative Law, but this is personal to the holder,[4] though it is intended that it should, if possible, be established on a permanent basis in the future. The Quain Professorship of Comparative and Historical Law at University College, London, which has been held by a succession of distinguished comparative lawyers, including Sir John Macdonnell and Sir Maurice Amos, has been diverted to other purposes. Comparative research has been undertaken in the University of Manchester under the guidance of Dr Wortley, and a beginning has been made at Oxford towards the formation of a collection of foreign law books with a view to comparative study. Scotland has lagged behind,

1 See *Comparative Law Series*, 1937 (issued by the Department of Commerce, Washington D.C.), p. 2.

2 *Guides to the Law and Legal Literature of Germany* (1912); *Spain* (1915); *Argentina, Brazil and Chile* (1917); *France* (1931); the *Central American Republics* (1937) and *Cuba, the Dominican Republic and Haiti* (1944).

3 Lee, *Journal of the S.P.T.L.* (1936), p. 1.

4 Sir Arnold McNair, K.C., Fellow of Gonville and Caius College, Cambridge, formerly Whewell Professor of International Law, held this chair until he vacated it on his recent appointment as one of the judges of the International Court of Justice.

somewhat surprisingly in view of its close connection with the countries
of the civil law, but proposals are on foot for the institution of courses
of lectures on comparative topics in the University of Edinburgh. The
crying need is for the books which are the comparative lawyer's raw
materials, many of which are either non-existent or difficult of access in
this country, but steps have been taken and will, no doubt, be taken in
the near future to remedy this.[1]

The general situation must not, however, be regarded as discouraging.
Comparative law has not only arrived but has undoubtedly come to stay.
The atmosphere of suspicion and indifference in which it was formerly
shrouded has been dissipated to a considerable extent though, perhaps,
not entirely. But in any event comparative law has established its claim
to be recognised as a branch of legal technique and as an integral factor
and a living influence in the study and development of the law, and this
is no mean achievement for a branch of learning which has yet to celebrate
the centenary of its birth.

A comparative lawyer is, however, in no way called upon to apologise
for his subject or to defend it. The tragic events of the last half-century
have emphasised the need for more effective collaboration in the international sphere and for a pooling of the resources of the world for the
benefit of mankind in general, not merely as regards material things, but
also in the domain of science and learning. As Lord Macmillan has said:
'There is no anchorite's cell or hermitage for a nation in which it can
isolate itself from other countries....Nations have to live together, and
the best method of overcoming distrust and want of confidence and of
breaking down walls and barriers lies in the promotion of means of
sharing our intellectual interests with other nations. If this were done
many political and economic differences would tend to disappear in an
atmosphere of friendliness and trust. You are not likely to quarrel with
a person if you share with him his intellectual interests, and there is no
better foundation than this for other and perhaps more material intercourse.'[2]

1 See *post*, Chapter x.
2 *Journal of C.L.* (3rd Ser.), vol. xviii (1936), p. 8.

Chapter III

THE VALUE OF COMPARATIVE LAW

COMPARATIVE LAW has been described as the 'Cinderella of the Legal Sciences'. It has gained a foothold in the domain of the law, but its position is by no means secure, and comparative studies must often be carried on in an atmosphere of hostility or, at best, in a chilly environment of indifference. The English Universities have been stimulated into action which takes the form of the encouragement of comparative research, and the rendering of such other support to the subject as is possible, in view of the limited financial resources available for the purpose. But most practitioners in England,[1] as elsewhere, view comparative law with doubt and suspicion, and their attitude towards comparative lawyers is summed up in Lord Bowen's famous pleasantry that 'a jurist is a man who knows a little about the law of every country except his own'.

So far as lack of interest in the subject is concerned its causes are not far to seek. A busy practising lawyer cannot, as a rule, be expected to pay much heed to other systems of law. His main concern is to make himself master of the rules of law which are the subject-matter of his vocation; he will, for the most part, have neither the leisure nor the inclination to embark on a course of study which is more than usually exacting, and unlikely to prove profitable in the professional sense.[2] It is commonplace among lawyers of all jurisdictions to declare that life is too short to acquire a profound and exhaustive knowledge of a single system of law, and that to add to the normal toil of everyday existence an additional burden in the shape of the study of foreign law is to demand more than is either possible or desirable. This attitude of mind is one which cannot be regarded unsympathetically, because it is undoubtedly true that modern legislation, with its 'innumerable decrees, principal and subordinate, of an administrative character',[3] casts a very heavy burden on judges and practising lawyers. The results of this atmosphere of indifference are, nevertheless, purely

---

1 A notable exception is to be found in the generous support given to the Society of Comparative Legislation by the Inns of Courts. This has taken the form both of financial assistance and of placing the resources of their libraries at the disposal of visiting comparative lawyers who are introduced and recommended by the Society.

2 'Having entered on his career as an advocate, if he acquires extensive practice, the high road which he follows has too many objects of honourable ambition before and on each side of it to induce him to stray into the less inviting path of foreign jurisprudence.' Burge, *Commentaries on Colonial and Foreign Laws*, Preface to the 1st edition.

3 Amos, 'Have we too much law?' *Journal of the S.P.T.L.* (1931), p. 1.

negative and must not be confused with opposition to comparative
studies which rests on other and more formidable grounds. Comparative
lawyers are unfortunately only too familiar with the spirit of hostility,
generally veiled, but often openly expressed, which has sometimes hampered the growth and development of comparative studies. All systems
of law are to some extent rooted in tradition, and this traditional aspect
of national law has, in all countries, produced an intransigent attitude
towards any attempts to promote the study of foreign legal institutions
and foreign rules of law. In his heart of hearts the average English lawyer
is in agreement with the sentiments expressed by Junius, when he com-
plained bitterly of Lord Mansfield's treachery in corrupting the noble
simplicity and free spirit of our Saxon laws by importing into the court
over which he presided such elements of pollution as the Roman code,
the laws of nations and the opinions of foreign civilians. The explanation
of this aspect of our English legal mentality is to be found, as Maitland
has said, 'in our very complete and traditionally consecrated ignorance'
of foreign law. It must not be thought, however, that this attitude of
mind is confined to Englishmen because it exists more or less in every
country. In any event it is difficult to understand: law as a branch of
learning stands alone in this respect. In the case of letters, natural science,
economics, music, art, and even in the case of vocational subjects such as
engineering and medicine, there is not, and never has been, the same
reluctance to cross national frontiers. Even Anglican theologians, who
are reputed to be most nationalistic of all divines in their outlook, have
never adopted this attitude of extreme insularity. What would have been
the fate of the art of healing if our physicians and surgeons had disregarded
the research of foreign workers in the same field? It is inconceivable that
a surgeon should hesitate to carry out a particular type of operation merely
because it emanates from the hospitals of Paris or Vienna. What would
our opinion be of a pathologist who declined to employ certain materials
or specimens solely on the ground that they were imported from
abroad? Even if we admit that law does not present a strict analogy
to other branches of learning, what are the reasons which act as a
bar to any attempt to inquire into any solutions which have been
found in other jurisdictions for the problems which arise in every system
of law?[1]

---

1 'It has often been remarked with regret or surprise that while the learned in
the exacter sciences abroad and in England have the most perfect sympathy with each
other—while the physician or the mathematician in London is completely at home
in the writings of the physician or the mathematician in Berlin and Paris—there is
a sensible, though invisible and impalpable, barrier which separates the jurists',
Maine, *Village Communities* (3rd ed.), p. 341.

The grounds upon which prejudices are based must always be a matter for conjecture, but in this case the most potent influence at work would seem to be a dread of the polluting or disruptive effects which it is feared might result from the infiltration of legal ideas from abroad. Lawyers are prone to regard the institutions and the rules of the legal system in which they have been trained, not necessarily as perfect, but as affording the best solution which can be arrived at in the conditions in which rules of law are called upon to function in a workaday world. Lawyers are, consequently, apt to resent criticisms which may be passed either on the law itself or on the manner in which it is administered, and to adopt an attitude of antagonism towards any proposals for law reform which are not solely aimed at the removal of anachronisms or manifest injustice. In this respect legal opinion is apt to lag behind that of the general public and, more particularly, of the commercial community. This is perhaps not unnatural, since the man of affairs is not interested in the maintenance of the technical aspects of law, whilst, on the other hand, the far-reaching effects which changes in the law may entail are more evident to the lawyer than to the layman. But the result is that the introduction of new ideas into the law becomes a slow process, and this difficulty is much enhanced if it is suspected that any revisionist movement is inspired by a desire to import foreign concepts of law into a national system. It is not surprising, in such circumstances, that many lawyers view comparative law with hostility or, at best, with considerable doubt or dislike, and this attitude of mind will persist until the legal community, as a whole, is satisfied, not only that their fear of the disruptive consequences of comparison is unfounded, but also that comparative studies are able to make a contribution of real value to the development and expansion which is essential unless law is to fall into disrepute and decay.

What then is the value of comparative law? The answer to this question cannot be given off-hand; it involves an examination of the whole field of law in an attempt to arrive at an estimate of the results of appreciable value which can be secured if the comparative process is applied to legal study and research in its various departments. In some directions comparison yields results which are mainly useful to scholars, as, for instance, when it is applied in the domains of analytical jurisprudence, legal philosophy, or legal history. Elsewhere its object may be severely practical, as in the case of the comparative study of commercial law. In between lie many fields of research, some of which are the province of the legislator and the law reformer, whilst others are to be found in the worldwide sphere of international relationships. It may be conceded that any endeavour to classify comparative activities along these lines would be unsatisfactory, because research carried out with a particular object in view may well prove to be equally valuable—or even more valuable—for some other purpose. Moreover, if the comparative process is to meet with success it is eminently desirable, if not essential, that its employment should not be hampered by confining it to specified categories, more particularly when English law is in question, with its ill-defined boundaries to the various departments of the law. Comparison is an instrument of research which is both flexible and capable of extension to any kind of problem which may be under investigation.

There is, nevertheless, an urgent need for an understanding of the purposes served by comparison now that comparative law is slowly beginning to emerge from the mists of misunderstanding and prejudice in which it has for so long been enveloped. This would appear to justify an attempt, however imperfect it may be, to undertake a general survey of the results which may reasonably be expected from the process of comparison in relation to the various spheres of research in which it may be employed. The value of comparison can only be seen in its true perspective if an effort is made to visualise its operation in dealing with the problems which arise in connection with the various forms of human activity in which law is called upon to play its part. Some of these can be characterised as 'lawyer's law', whilst others are concerned with questions of interest to the community at large both in a national and in an international sense. With this end in view it is proposed to examine the nature and extent of the results which the comparative process is likely to secure when applied to the various departments of the law which are conventionally, though perhaps not authoritatively, recognised in all legal systems.

Comparative Jurisprudence

'Comparative Jurisprudence' is a term which has been employed in many senses,[1] but may be taken, for our present purposes, to signify the use of the comparative method as an aid to analytical jurisprudence. How far it may be of value to utilise the method in this way is a matter which is in dispute. The controversy centres round the question whether it is possible by means of analysis to ascertain principles which are common to all systems of law. This possibility, as Maine[2] observed, 'is not universally admitted', but it has found support in certain quarters.[3] The

---

1 See *ante*, p. 2.
2 *Village Communities* (3rd ed.), p. 4. Cf. Pollock, 'The History of Comparative Jurisprudence', *Journal of C.L.* (N.S.), vol. V (1903), p. 74.
3 E.g. Rabel, 'Problème de la Qualification', *Revue de Droit International Privé* (1933), p. 1; Beckett, 'Classification in Private International Law', *British Year Book of I.L.* vol. 15 (1934), pp. 58 *et seq.*

crucial point is whether the supposed analogies between the fundamental conceptions of different systems of law have any existence or whether they are merely misleading. If such universal principles exist they can, in any event, be very few in number. Legal institutions are called upon to function in so many different environments and in such different conditions that it is extremely dangerous, if not fallacious, to deduce the universality of a rule of law from its existence in all systems. But though it is undoubtedly true that deductions from supposed analogies are fraught with peril it is equally true that an analytical jurist, who founds his hypothesis on the concepts of a single system of law, may easily fall into error, unless he subjects his conclusions to verification by the experience of other systems. It is possible that enthusiasts may have exaggerated the value of the comparative method in providing a means for the determination of abstract principles, but its importance for the purposes of analytical jurisprudence cannot be denied. If the claims of ethnological and psychological jurisprudence to be regarded as independent disciplines are admitted, it is obvious that they also must rest on conclusions to be drawn from the analysis of such traces of law or custom as are to be found in primitive communities. The border-line between analytical research in the strict sense and historical comparison is, however, somewhat faintly marked, and it is, on occasion, difficult to assign the employment of the comparative method to pure analysis or to historical investigation as the case may be.

Comparative Legal History

It is generally recognised that the comparative method can yield results of great value when applied to historical research, but it is strange that this should have been denied by no less an authority than Maine, who refused to admit that comparative law had any purpose other than 'to facilitate legislation and the practical improvement of the law'.[1] At the same time he was prepared to concede that the comparative method is 'not distinguishable in some of its applications from the historical method'.[2] As Pollock observes, 'it is curious to see how far the master still was, ten years after the publication of *Ancient Law*, from realising the importance of his own work. If there is anything we have learnt from Sir Henry Maine, it is that intimate alliance between comparative and historical research is not only natural and desirable, but necessary for either branch of work being efficiently done.'[3]

The terms Comparative Jurisprudence, Comparative Legal History,

---

1 *Village Communities* (3rd ed.), p. 4.
2 *Ibid.* p. 6.   3 Pollock, *loc. cit.* at p. 75.

Historical Jurisprudence and General History of the Law have been used
interchangeably, but this is not, in itself, a matter of any great moment.
To quote Pollock once more, it is the method that is important and not
the name.[1] Legal historians of all countries and of all schools of thought
employ the method freely; it is only necessary to glance at Sir William
Holdsworth's *History of English Law* to appreciate the frequent use which
is made of the method by a great master of his craft.[2] In some quarters
there is a tendency to confine Comparative Legal History to research into
the early institutions of mankind.[3] Maine, for instance, describes the
employment of the method in the following words: 'We take a number
of contemporary facts, ideas and customs and we infer the past form of
those facts, ideas, and customs, not only from the historical records of
that past form, but also from examples of it which have not yet died out
of the world and are still to be found in it.'[4] It must, however, be remembered that Maine was inspired by the rise of new ideas connected with the
theory of evolution, and that the intellectual movement in which he played
so prominent a part was concerned with the development of entities,
whether legal or otherwise, from their earliest forms. The application
of the comparative method to the study of the history of the law does
not necessarily involve research of an antiquarian or ethnological character.
Much of modern commercial law can, for instance, only be appreciated
in all its bearings if due regard is paid to the course of its development
within living memory.[5] Many of the ideas which are now permeating
the law of obligations are of recent origin. It is only necessary to mention,
in this connection, such doctrines as those of Unjustifiable Enrichment
and the Abuse of Rights. The time has, perhaps, not yet arrived for profound historical investigation into the course of changes in contemporary
law, but such developments cannot be correctly appreciated or seen in
their proper perspective without some knowledge of the causes which
have led to an alteration of rule or, as the case may be, to the abolition
of existing legal institutions or the creation of new ones. In any event,
research on historical lines is one of the indispensable tools of a compara-

1 Pollock, *loc. cit.* at p. 76.
2 Holdsworth says of the comparative method that it is 'necessary both to students
of legal history and modern law', *History of English Law*, vol. XII, p. 161.
3 E.g. Salmond, who regards it as 'the history of the first principles and conceptions of the legal system', *Jurisprudence* (7th ed.), p. 6. Cf. Schmitthoff, *op. cit.* p. 102.
4 Maine, *loc. cit.* p. 7.
5 It would be possible to multiply illustrations, but a single instance may suffice;
namely, the Carriage of Goods by Sea Act, 1924, which owes its origin to a simul-
taneous movement for law reform emanating from the maritime countries of the
world and created by economic causes. See Gutteridge, 'Contract and Commercial
Law', *L.Q.R.* vol. LI, at p. 91.

tive lawyer whether he is concerned with questions of an academic nature or is utilising the comparative process with a practical aim in view.

Constitutional and Administrative Law

If we accept the conventional definition of constitutional law as being the law which relates to government, inclusive of so-called local government or administrative law, it is clear that it offers a wide field for comparison. The extent to which the comparative process may yield results of value is, however, open to some doubt, particularly when problems of political significance are under investigation. So much depends on the mentality of the 'governors' and those whom they govern; on the social, political or economic phenomena which may induce the 'governed' to submit to a regime which they might, in other circumstances, be disinclined to accept. Tradition also plays an important part in the matter, and unless full weight is given to all these considerations, it is highly probable that any conclusions which may be drawn from comparison will be fallacious. On the other hand, there would seem to be considerable scope for the comparative investigation of problems which are essentially of an administrative character. Rules of law relating to such matters as the control of public utilities, the provision of public services which do not fall under this heading, and the relations in general between central and local authorities and the citizen offer many opportunities for comparative study. In particular, the problem of the balance which must be struck between administrative efficiency and individual rights is one which appears to lend itself in a marked degree to comparative study.

Criminal Law

The application of the comparative method to the law of crime may appear, at first sight, to call for justification. It has been argued that social, religious, political and economic conditions vary from country to country to such an extent that comparison cannot be expected to yield results of any very great value. It is, of course, true that the historical development of the law of crime has not been the same in all countries, and that standards of wrongdoing and of the means to be adopted for its prevention and repression are by no means uniform in character. But the suggestion that this branch of the law does not lend itself to comparison appears to be inspired by the 'unificationist' view of comparative law according to which the main purpose of comparative law is to furnish materials for the drafting of unified codes of law. This being a purpose which cannot be said to exist in the case of the law of crime, save in the abstract, it is argued, therefore, that little or nothing is to be gained by comparison in this instance. We may concede that the unification of criminal law is either impossible or, if possible, would be undesirable, but this does not mean that comparison is, therefore, excluded. The nations of the world have much to learn from one another when dealing with questions of penal law, and its administration, as well as in other departments of legal activity. The success or failure of a particular policy in dealing with crime has its lessons, not only for the country which has made the experiment, but for all countries which have the like problem to solve. The diffusion of knowledge of the steps which are being taken in other countries to combat crime is, consequently, a matter of urgency and importance. Comparison also serves the purpose of fixing the optimum, i.e. the standard which should be aimed at in all countries as embodying the most enlightened conceptions of criminal justice and of the best means by which those conceptions can be realised. Comparison may also save us from the perils of undue complacency. The English people are, for instance, not unreasonably proud of their criminal system, of its impartiality and its efficiency, but there is always the danger that this feeling of satisfaction may lull us into a state of somnolence which may prove hostile to efforts to improve the law and its administration. These considerations were stressed so long ago as the year 1839, when the Royal Commission on Criminal Law presented its report. The case for international collaboration in penal matters is stronger now than it was then; the increased facilities for travel and transport, due to modern scientific discoveries, have vastly extended the territorial area of certain forms of crime, and have greatly increased the difficulties attendant on the detection and prevention of other types of criminal activity.[1]

Industrial or Labour Law

Industrial law is a convenient 'omnibus' term, adopted by writers on English law, to denote those branches of our law which are concerned with the law of master and servant and the various forms of legislation which have as their object the improvement of the conditions of labour. A word of caution is necessary, because the term 'industrial' is used in the civil-law countries in a different sense from that in which it is employed in England. Its employment in those countries is confined to so-called 'industrial property', i.e. patents, trade marks, designs and trade names.[2]

1 'Memorandum of the Department of Criminal Science of the Faculty of Law, University of Cambridge', *L.Q.R.* vol. LVIII (1942), p. 107.
2 See *Vocabulaire Juridique*, p. 393, citing the French law of 1 July 1906, Article 1, or an illustration of the use of the term in this sense.

It would, therefore, seem to be preferable for the purposes of comparative law to speak of 'Labour Law' rather than of 'Industrial Law'.

Labour law is one of the fields in which the comparative process of research has been most frequently employed. In countries of a western type of civilisation, the problems which have presented themselves for solution are very similar in kind, and this has resulted in a movement on an international scale with the aim of removing certain injustices which were believed to be incidental to the development of modern industrial life. In 1900 the International Association for Labour Legislation was founded, and in 1905 and 1906 two International Conferences were held at Berne, at which conventions were drafted for the prohibition of night work for women, and the use of white phosphorus in the manufacture of matches. The movement thus begun received a great impetus from the establishment of the International Labour Office at Geneva in 1919. Since then a vast amount of comparative research in labour law has been carried out, mostly at Geneva, but also by government departments and private organisations. The necessity and value of such research depends on two considerations. In the first place a country cannot fail to benefit by the experience of other countries in dealing with labour problems; secondly, in the international sphere, it is essential that the same standard should, so far as is possible, be reached by legislation everywhere or, otherwise, the more advanced countries may be handicapped in competition for international trade.

Research of this type is usually practical in character and is thus more likely to attract the legislator or law reformer than the scientific lawyer. But since labour laws, like all legislation, must be dovetailed into the general structure of a legal system the process of comparison may indirectly yield by-products of considerable value to those who are pursuing other lines of research. Thus an examination of the *Annual Survey of Decisions in Labour Law* issued by the International Labour Office may occasionally reveal legal developments which are of interest, not only to those concerned with labour law, but also to investigators in other fields.

Family Law and the Law of Property and Succession

Although it is, generally speaking, true that the comparative method lends itself to research in almost every conceivable branch of the law, there are, nevertheless, certain aspects of private law which make only a limited appeal to the comparative lawyer. It is sometimes assumed that family law and the law of property and succession lie outside the scope of comparison, but this is a sweeping generalisation which is only partially correct.[1] Family law is so largely moulded by racial or religious and political considerations that comparison is fraught with difficulty and apt to be inconclusive, but even in this instance it may serve a useful purpose by indicating the highest standard which has been attained in practice in fixing the status of the individual. Such results as are forthcoming from this type of comparative research may, however, often be of doubtful value, except for purposes of propaganda with which lawyers are not concerned.

There is likewise little profit to be gained from an investigation of modern rules governing the ownership of immovable property, and the methods by which it can be transferred or hypothecated, though the historian or the ethnologist may obtain useful material from a comparative study of primitive forms of land tenure. But here again, so far as the alienation of immovables is concerned, comparison may be useful as serving to indicate a standard of efficiency to be aimed at as regards expedition and economy. Local conditions are, however, so closely involved in the question that research of this kind is, in the main, more valuable to legislators than to lawyers.[2]

The law of movable property offers greater opportunities for comparison, more especially in connection with the law of the sale and the hypothecation of goods, a topic which is, however, more closely associated with commercial law than with the law of property. This aspect of comparative law may be regarded as including the rules relating to certain forms of movable property of an intangible character, such as patents, trade marks, designs, and copyrights, which provide a field for descriptive comparison, though this is a matter for specialists in these branches of the law rather than for comparative lawyers.

The Law of Obligations

The law of obligations or, as an English lawyer would say, the law of contract and tort, appears to provide one of the most promising fields for comparative study and research. As Professor Lambert has observed, it deals with what he terms the 'mobile' elements in human relationships; in other words, it is the law of everyday life. Breaches of contract and tortious acts give rise to much the same kind of problems in all civilised communities, and this lends a peculiar interest to comparison in this branch of the law. The conclusions arrived at are, in general, more or less

1 The Inheritance (Family Provision) Act, 1938, is an illustration of the influence of legislation in other countries on the development of our law of succession.

2 The experience gained in working the 'Torrens' system of land registration is a case in point. See Hogg, *The Ownership and Incumbrance of Registered Land*, and *Journal of C.L.* (N.S.), vol. VII (1906), p. 287.

identical, although the method of arriving at them may differ considerably; but where a problem in the law of obligations is solved in different ways in various countries the value and importance of comparison becomes apparent.[1] It is not difficult to justify this aspect of comparative study and research. The law of contract furnishes the necessary groundwork for a comparison of the commercial laws of the world; it is also the essential prelude to any proposal for the unification of these laws. A comparative study of the laws of contract, particularly in so far as it extends to American and Dominion law, is also an element of great importance in any proposals for the reform of our existing English rules. This has become clear in connection with the reports of the Law Revision Committee on such questions as the Statute of Frauds, the Doctrine of Consideration and the rule in *Chandler* v. *Webster*.[2] Even in the realm of the law of torts, which is characteristically English, and difficult to contrast with the relevant rules of the European codes, there is ample scope for comparison. The problems arising out of the growth of motor traffic[3] furnish a case in point, and the movement for the reform of the English law of defamation, particularly in so far as it relates to newspaper libels, has been to some extent inspired by the experience of other countries. Above all, certain rules of our law of contract and tort have, as the result of traditional influences, become so rigid as to create the possibility of a failure of justice. Equity may in certain directions afford some relief, but its rules have become stereotyped, and often fail to achieve the desired result. The situation in this respect appears to be one which calls for a study of the laws of those countries which have endeavoured to mitigate it by the recognition of what Lord Dunedin has called 'super-eminent equities', such as doctrines of the Abuse of Rights[4] and Unjustified Enrichment.[5] This does not imply the acceptance of any particular solution arrived at by foreign law, but we can profit from the experience of other systems, even if we merely learn in this way how to avoid the mistakes which they may have made.

1 Sir Frederick Pollock has put this aspect of comparative law very clearly. He observed that 'with the increase of international trade and of cases dependent on international transactions it was becoming more and more important to have some kind of accurate acquaintance with the principles of continental law. It would soon be hardly possible to draw a sharp line between the study of our own law and a moderate knowledge of continental systems, especially commercial law. The days were past when on a question of foreign law an English practitioner could be content to rely on the first expert he picked up. Law was becoming more and more cosmopolitan' (*Law Journal Newspaper*, vol. CLXXX, p. 49).
2 [1904] 1 K.B. 493.
3 See the *Report of the Law Revision Committee on Contributory Negligence*, Cmd. 6032 (1939), at p. 17.
4 See 'Abuse of Rights', *Cambridge L.J.* vol. V (1933), p. 22.
5 See 'The Doctrine of Unjust Enrichment', *Cambridge L.J.* vol. V (1934), p. 204.

The law of obligations also provides the most suitable material for instruction in the use of the comparative method. It is relatively free from complicated technicalities: its terminology presents little difficulty to a student who has mastered the elements of Roman law, and it is well fitted to attract and to retain his interest in comparative study.

Comparative Commercial Law

Commercial law is, strictly speaking, merely one aspect of the law of contract, but its volume, and the importance of its subject-matter, have elevated it to the rank of an independent branch of the law in general. The value of comparison seems to be beyond doubt in this instance. Diversity of law affects commerce more sensibly than any other form of human activity, and constitutes an impediment to the free interchange of goods which is the life breath of trade. International commerce is ambulatory in nature, and transactions may often range over a very wide area, thus rendering them subject to several different systems of law. Private international law has failed to provide a remedy for this state of uncertainty, and men of business have been driven to seek their own remedies. These generally take the shape either of the use of standardised forms of contract designed to supersede or modify the legal situation, or of the communication to the business world of details of the foreign rules of law which may give rise to difficulties.[1] In either case, the value of comparative investigation of commercial law is so obvious as to make it unnecessary to labour the point. Commercial law also offers the most favourable opportunities for the process of unification which necessarily involves comparison of the relevant laws. This question is, however, one which will be discussed hereafter.[2]

Comparative Procedure

So long as jurisdiction is founded on a territorial basis it is clear that rules of procedure must vary from country to country, and even if a world state were to come into existence it would, probably, still be necessary to adapt the machinery for the legal settlement of disputes to suit local conditions and variations in the psychological characteristics of litigants.

Up to the present little attention has been devoted to this aspect of comparative law except in Switzerland, Germany[3] and Italy.[4] This is

---

1 See, for instance, the *Digest of Bankruptcy Law in the British Empire*, issued by the Federation of Chambers of Commerce of the British Empire.

2 See *post*, Chapter XII.

3 Meili, *Das Internationale Zivilprozeßrecht* (Zürich, 1906); Leske-Löwenfeld, *Das Zivilprozeßrecht in den europäischen Staaten und ihren Kolonien* (Berlin, 1913).

4 Morelli, 'Il diritto processuale civile internazionale' in vol. VII of the *Trattato di diritto internazionale* of P. Fedozzi and S. Romano (Padua, 1938).

unfortunate, because similarity of rule in two or more systems of law, in the substantive sense, may easily be nullified by divergences in procedure. The method of ascertaining the facts of a case may lead to varying results in different countries, or a claim to redress may be stultified by procedural rules which deprive a supposed remedy of any real value. It is consequently a matter of great importance for anyone who seeks to enforce his claim in a foreign court to ascertain the kind of evidence which he must adduce in support of his case, the remedy which he is likely to obtain, the extent to which he will be indemnified against the costs of the proceedings, and how he can enforce any judgment which may be given in his favour. There are, in addition, certain incidental matters which he has to consider, such as any requirement there may be as to providing security for costs. The present-day tendency to resort to arbitration in international commercial disputes can be explained in part by the suspicion which litigants entertain as to the course of ordinary legal proceedings in other countries. But even in the case of arbitration, we find wide differences in procedure, which prompted the attempt by the Rome Institute to frame an international code of the law of arbitration.[1] The comparative study of procedure has considerable value from a purely utilitarian point of view, but its importance also rests on other considerations. Procedural reforms at home, when contemplated, will often be assisted materially by a study of the measures taken in other countries to solve problems of the same kind. Questions of procedure also play a vital part in connection with the unification of private law. The drafting of a rule which is to be applied universally is not sufficient to unify the law: if unification is to possess any real value it is essential that the unified rules should be applied in practice without any impediments created by procedural difficulties. This is an aspect of the problem which has failed to receive adequate attention, largely because such unification as has taken place has not been of a nature in which the problem is urgent. It would, however, seem to be obvious that no scheme of unification can be regarded as satisfactory if proceedings in one of the participating countries are more dilatory or more expensive than in the others, or if the remedies afforded by the unified law are not the same.

Legislation and Law Reform

Many eminent authorities have regarded legislation as the field in which the comparative method can be applied to the greatest advantage. Maine[2] says, for instance, that it would be 'universally admitted by competent

1 See David, *Rapport sur l'Arbitrage* (Rome, 1932), U.D.P. Études III—S. de N. 1932—C.D. 1932; and Cohn, 'The Unification of the Law of Arbitration', *Transactions of the Grotius Society*, vol. XXIV (1939), p. 1.
2 *Village Communities* (3rd ed.), p. 4.

jurists that, if not the only function, the chief function of Comparative Jurisprudence is to facilitate legislation and the practical improvement of law'. He adds that 'by the examination and comparison of laws the most valuable materials are obtained for legal improvement. There is no branch of juridical enquiry more important than this.'

Although it may not be possible to accept Maine's opinion that the promotion of legislation and law reform is the only function of the comparative method, there are many considerations which support his views as to the importance of its employment for this purpose.

The basic principles of the law may, perhaps, have assumed a more or less settled form in all countries, and the legislator may only be concerned with them in so far as the operation in practice of these principles may require adjustment in order to ensure that justice will be done. But new conceptions of rights and duties are coming into existence, owing to far-reaching changes in the political and economic structure of society. The legislator cannot always rely on existing rules of law to meet the situation thus created; new rules must be devised, and the vast volume of legislation during the last two decades is largely directed to this end. It would, of course, be possible to ignore any action taken in other countries in regard to such developments, and to disregard the experience which has thus been gleaned; though this policy would not only be unwise, but also in contradiction of the existing practice. In the civil-law countries, and to a lesser degree in the common-law jurisdictions, the legislator turns to a comparison of laws as one of the sources of the materials which he requires.

On the continent of Europe and in the United States, official sanction has been given to the study of foreign legislation. The French government established a departmental committee charged with this task and gave material support to the Société de Législation Comparée.[1] The recent German law dealing with trading companies and partnerships was preceded by a detached comparison of the existing German laws with those of foreign countries.[2] Instances of a similar kind could be multiplied, but it appears to be obvious that no country can afford to ignore any experience gained by other countries which have proceeded farther along the road to legislative action. To put it at its very lowest, there is often much to be learned from the process of trial and error which is a feature of much of our modern legislation. In Great Britain the enactment of such measures as the Workmen's Compensation Acts and the National Health Insurance Acts was preceded by an investigation of the steps taken in other countries

---

1 Goulé, *Recueil Lambert*, vol. I (1938), p. 396 and see *ante*, p. 17.
2 See Hamburger in *Rechtsvergleichendes Handwörterbuch*, vol. II, p. 112; Hallstein, *Die Aktiengesetze der Gegenwart* (1931), and Mann, 'The New German Company Law', *Journal of C.L.* (3rd Ser.), vol. XIX (1937), p. 220.

to solve the problems which were in issue. Even as regards a subject-matter which is so purely 'English' as the law of defamation, the Lord Chancellor's Committee, charged with the duty of reconsidering the existing rules, has been at pains to ascertain the state of the law elsewhere. The Law Revision Committee has also investigated foreign rules of law whenever this appeared likely to be of assistance. It is obvious that in certain cases, such as that of the law relating to the capacity of married women, a comparison with the laws of foreign countries would have been otiose. The reports of the committee do not stress the comparative aspects of the problems entrusted to them because it was essential, in the existing state of opinion, that their labours should not be open to any suspicion that they are inspired by any ulterior motive such as the unification of English and foreign law.

There is a further aspect of this question which calls for notice. Law-reform in its initial stages is not required to wait upon the convenience of the legislature, and there appears to be no reason why certain of the most urgent problems in English law should not be the subject-matter of comparative study in an anticipatory sense. Government departments are not likely to initiate inquiries of this nature, and they must therefore be undertaken by private enterprise either with or without the assistance of the State. The foundation of an Institute of Advanced Legal Studies might provide the necessary machinery for this purpose, though it would be undesirable to clothe a body of this nature with authority or privileges which might have the effect of damping down the enthusiasm of individual researchers or would discourage the development of comparative research in the Universities.

The Value of Comparison as a Source of Law

No system of legal rules has been devised or ever will be devised which is capable of dealing with every situation of fact which might conceivably arise. Certain of the continental codes[1] envisage the possibility that there may be gaps of this kind in the law, and lay down rules to be followed by the judges in such circumstances. An English judge, on the other hand, is left to his own devices if he is unable to find a statutory rule or precedent to guide him. By virtue of a pious fiction there are supposed to be no gaps in English law, and in laying down the rule which he applies to the facts the judge must avoid any suspicion that he has borrowed his law from a foreign system. There can be little doubt that much Roman

---

1 E.g. the Swiss civil code, Article 1; see Williams, *Swiss Civil Code (Sources of Law)*, p. 34; Del Vecchio, *Riforma del Codice Civile e Principii generali di Diritto*.

law has found its way into our common-law system either directly or
through the canon law.[1] Roman law appears to have been resorted to
frequently by the judges of the Chancery Courts, 'amid whose recorded
dicta we often find entire texts from the *Corpus Juris Civilis* imbedded,
with their terms unaltered though their origin is never acknowledged',
and in the eighteenth century the works of the Dutch jurists appear to
have been studied by English lawyers and to have had 'considerable
effect' on the rulings of the Chancery Court.[2] The extent to which our
law has been influenced in this way has not yet been fully examined:
the research involved would be so prolonged and tedious that it is doubtful,
as a learned writer has observed, whether it would repay the labour of
investigation.[3] If confined to a more restricted area it might be worth
while. English commercial law is largely derived from foreign sources,
partly owing to its descent from the *Lex Mercatoria* of the Middle Ages,
and partly by reason of the fact that it was moulded at the critical stage
of its development by the genius of Lord Mansfield, perhaps the greatest
of English comparative lawyers. Research in this direction might yield
results which would not only be of interest in themselves from the historical standpoint but might also help to dispel the erroneous belief
widely held in other countries that the law of England is so ultra-national
and particularistic in character as to render comparison either impossible
or of very little value.

Roman law has been invoked in aid of a number of recent cases, the
latest leading case—if we except the *Cantiare San Rocco* case[4] which concerned Scots and not English law—being *Keighley Maxted and Co.* v.
Durant.[5] The tendency at the present day is, however, to resort to modern
systems of law, and, more particularly, to those of the English-speaking
countries. It is only natural that the Anglo-American system should take the
place of Roman law as a general guide to the English courts, whenever
they desire such guidance, and that to-day English judges should refer to
American and Colonial cases where their predecessors resorted to the
Corpus Juris.[6]

The citation of foreign authorities is, however, not encouraged as a rule
by the English judges. In *Manton* v. *Brocklebank*,[7] the Master of the Rolls,
when dealing with references made by counsel to the law of other

1 Oliver, 'Roman Law in Modern Cases in English Courts', *Cambridge Legal
Essays*, p. 244.   2 Maine, *Ancient Law* (7th ed.), p. 44.
3 Oliver, *op. cit.*   4 [1924] A.C. 226.
5 [1901] A.C. 240.
6 Schmitthoff, 'The Science of Comparative Law', *Cambridge L.J.* vol. VII (1939),
p. 10. Cf. Pollock, *First Book of Jurisprudence*, p. 326.
7 [1923] 2 K.B. at p. 218. Cf. *Card* v. *Case* (1848), 5 C.B. 622.

countries, said: 'It must not be forgotten, however, that these other systems of jurisprudence are relevant only so far as they throw light on our law.' In *Donoghue* v. *Stevenson*,[1] Lord Buckmaster, referring to the citation of an American case,[2] expressed the view that 'such cases can have no close application and no authority is clear, for though the source of the law in the two countries may be the same, its current may well flow in different channels'. On the other hand, in the same case Lord Atkin stated his opinion[3] that 'it is always a satisfaction to an English lawyer to be able to test his application of fundamental principles of the common law by the development of the same doctrine by the lawyers of the Courts of the United States'. In referring to 'the illuminating judgment' of Cardozo J. in *MacPherson* v. *Buick Motor Co.*,[4] Lord Atkin says: 'he states the principles of the law as I should desire to state them, and reviews the authorities in other states than his own. Whether the principle he affirms would apply to the particular facts of that case in this country might be a question for consideration if the case arose.' In *Haynes* v. *Harwood*,[5] where the effect of the assumption of risk in relation to the principle of *volenti non fit injuria* was under discussion, Greer L.J., after alluding to the scarcity of authority in this country, said: 'There is, however, a wealth of authority in the United States, and one of the cases, which is quite sufficient to show what the American law is, has been cited to us—namely, *Eckert* v. *Long Island Railroad Co.*[6] The effect of the American cases is, I think, accurately stated in Professor Goodhart's article to which we have been referred on "Rescue and Voluntary Assumption of Risk" in *Cambridge Law Journal*, vol. v, p. 192.' The learned Lord Justice then referred to Professor Goodhart's summary of the American rule,[7] and concluded by saying: 'In my judgment that passage not only represents the law of the United States, but I think it also accurately represents the law of this country.' The present-day position seems to be that the English judges do not resort as they did in the nineteenth century to the Roman law[8] and the writings of Pothier,[9] but that there is a distinct tendency on their part to lend a willing ear to the citation of American

---

1 [1932] A.C. at pp. 576, 577.   2 *Thomas* v. *Winchester*, 6 N.Y. 397.
3 *Ibid.* at p. 598.   4 217 N.Y. 382.
5 [1935] 1 K.B. at p. 156.
6 43 N.Y. 502. See also the observations of Lord Wright in *Beresford* v. *Royal Insurance Co.* [1937] 2 K.B. at p. 216.
7 *Cambridge L.J.* vol. v (1934) at p. 192.
8 The English cases in which the principles of Roman law have been considered in modern times in the English courts are very ably discussed by Oliver, *loc. cit.* See also Schmitthoff, *loc. cit.* at pp. 104–7. *Acton* v. *Blundell* (1843) 12 M. and W. at p. 353 and *Taylor* v. *Caldwell* (1863) 32 L.J.Q.B. at p. 166, furnish typical instances of the consultation of the *Corpus Juris* by the English Courts.
9 *Hodgson* v. *De Beauchesne* (1858) 12 Moore P.C. 285.

authorities. They do so, however, more by way of testing the soundness
of their conclusions than in reliance on the foreign decision.

Scottish and Irish cases are frequently cited in argument before the
English courts and have great persuasive force. Dominion and Colonial
case law is not utilised to the same extent, but this is to some extent due
to the fact that English text-book writers and encyclopaedists persist in
ignoring these sources. This is regrettable, but it is only fair to add that
the relevant law reports are often inaccessible or difficult to procure—a
matter which should be remedied at the earliest opportunity. The Canadian
law reports, in particular, are not resorted to as frequently as they might
be, and the law reports of South Africa, Australia, New Zealand and
British India contain material which is often valuable but is overlooked.

At some future date more extensive use will, no doubt, be made of
foreign law for the purpose of assisting our judges to fill the gaps that are
still to be found in our own law. The manner in which such sources can
be utilised to advantage is illustrated by the judgment in *Bechervaise* v.
Lewis,[1] and, in particular, by the judgment of Kotze C.J. in *Lewis* v. *The
Salisbury Gold Mining Co*.[2] There is, moreover, another aspect to this
question—namely, the importance, when international co-operation is
called for, of ensuring that no element of complication or uncertainty
should be introduced into the matter by contradictory decisions emanating
from the courts of the countries which are concerned. The Gold Clause
in International Loans is an instance of the confusion which may be
created in this way, and there have been occasions on which the intention
underlying international treaties has been defeated by the different interpretations given to them by the courts of the contracting countries.[3] If
unification of law is to be anything more than a pretence it would seem
to be essential that the courts of the countries concerned should endeavour
to secure uniformity in their decisions so far as is reasonably possible.[4]

International Law and International Relations

The functions which comparative law may be called on to discharge
in the sphere of international law and international relations are, obviously,
of such importance as to require careful consideration, and they will,
accordingly, be dealt with in more detail hereafter.[5]

---

1 (1872) L.R. 7 C.P. 372.   2 (1894) 11 C.L.J. 137.
3 See Schmitthoff, 'The Gold Clause in International Loans', *Journal of C.L.*
(3rd Ser.), vol. XVIII (1936), at p. 266; Wortley, 'The Gold Clause', *British Year Book
of I.L.* vol. 17 (1936), p. 112.
4 See *post*, p. 106.
5 See Chapter IV ('Comparative Law and the Conflict of Laws'), and Chapter V
('Comparative Law and the Law of Nations').

Chapter IV

COMPARATIVE LAW & THE CONFLICT OF LAWS

COMPARATIVE LAW and private international law have much in common because the two disciplines converge on the same focal point, namely, the necessity for international collaboration in matters of private justice. But this does not presuppose an identity of purpose or a similarity of method between these two departments of the law. The fact that both have originated from the existence in the world of many different systems of law, and that both are concerned with foreign law, has resulted in a certain blurring of the border-line between the two, which is not, in itself, a matter of great importance, but has led to the belief in certain quarters that comparative law is mainly concerned with the removal of the causes of the conflict of laws—a belief which has profoundly influenced the development of comparative law in directions which have not been altogether to its advantage.

The kinship between comparative law and private international law is, of course, closer than that which exists in the case of the law of nations or public international law; nevertheless, it is more apparent than real. Both subjects are concerned with the differences which exist between the legal systems of the world, and both stand apart from any of the accepted schemes of the classification of law according to its subject-matter.[1] The analogy cannot, however, be said to extend very far beyond this point, because the two subjects not only differ intrinsically, but exist for widely different purposes. Private international law is 'law' in the full sense of the word: comparative law is merely a convenient label attached to a particular method of study and research. If a dispute contains a foreign element, private international law intervenes to select the jurisdiction which is competent to decide it and the system of law by which it is to be governed. This process is selective and not comparative; the judge is not called on to examine the foreign law and to compare it with his own law. Comparative law, on the other hand, is not concerned with the selection of appropriate jurisdictions or with the choice of law. The task which it has to perform covers a far wider area and does not depend

---

1 Dr Baty's distinction between the two subjects appears to rest on a misapprehension of the functions of comparative law. He refers to it as a 'deeply interesting academic study' which lacks the 'interest of reality' found in private international law (*Polarised Law*, p. 6). This view of the matter ignores the fact that comparative law has repeatedly given proof of its practical value, more especially in the domains of maritime and commercial law.

on the existence of disputes; it is not confined to conflicts of jurisdiction or law. To a comparative lawyer similarities of rule may, indeed, be of equal or perhaps even greater interest than differences. It might even be argued that private international law and comparative law are, in a sense, antagonistic, because private international law has the effect of stabilising a situation of conflict, whereas comparative law—so far as it may be concerned with conflict—does not act as an umpire between competing jurisdictions or rules of law but envisages a solution which will do away with conflict once and for all.

But even if we assume that the comparative lawyer and the private international lawyer are not engaged in a common task, it is, nevertheless, beyond dispute that the two disciplines are in very close contact with one another. Every comparative lawyer must of necessity also be a private international lawyer, for otherwise he can never hope to gain a true appreciation of the extent to which differences in law constitute a barrier to intercourse between the nations. It has also been said that every private international lawyer must be a comparative lawyer. This generalisation is incorrect if it means that a private international lawyer necessarily engages in a comparative study of the rules of conflict of his own system and the corresponding rules of other systems of law. So long as private international law continues to be regarded as being essentially a part of the municipal or internal law of a country it is quite possible and, indeed, usual for a private international lawyer to refrain from concerning himself with foreign rules of conflict unless he is compelled to do so, as, for instance, when questions of 'renvoi' or 'qualification' arise. On the other hand, the mere fact that a private international lawyer deals with issues of law and fact which contain a foreign element means that he must inevitably come into contact with the concepts and institutions of other systems, and so acquire some knowledge of foreign law though, possibly, only to a limited or superficial extent.

The importance of 'Comparative Private International Law', as a branch of legal study, is beyond doubt, both as regards private international lawyers themselves and the growth and development of collaboration in matters of justice between the nations. If, as private international lawyers, we regard the matter subjectively it must be conceded that comparison broadens our outlook and keeps us in touch with current movements and developments in other countries. It will teach us that the true significance of rules of conflict is not always to be ascertained by the consultation of codes and text-books, but depends on a variety of elements which go to build up a branch of the law which is still so hesitant and vacillating that it may be difficult to extract with confidence the

governing principle on which any rule of conflict is based.¹ Thus we may
hope to learn of the dangers to be encountered and seek to avoid the many
pitfalls which lie in the path of those whose studies lead them into new and
unfamiliar paths. 'Comparative Private International Law' also holds out
great possibilities as an element in advanced legal education and study.
But by far the most important aspect of the comparison of the various
systems of the rules of conflict is to be found in its bearing on the future
of private international law.

Two questions appear to be involved. The first is whether the results
of comparison can be regarded as a source of private international law,
in the sense that they can be made available to fill any gaps which exist
in our own and other systems of the rules of conflict. The second question
concerns the nature and extent of the assistance which can be rendered by
comparison to those who are endeavouring to find a cure for the many
ailments from which private international law is suffering in all jurisdictions. This is a question of very great importance because the unhappy
condition in which private international law finds itself at the present day
constitutes one of the major failures in the sphere of international collaboration in matters of justice. It is one which would merit careful consideration
in connection with any plans for post-war legal construction, more particularly if the proposals which have been made for a federation of the
European countries should hereafter enter the realm of practical politics.

Comparison as a Source of the Rules of Private International Law

How far can the results of comparison be regarded as a source of private
international law? The answer to this question is not in doubt. Private
international law, as Dr Cheshire points out, is still in the formative stage.
'It is at the moment fluid not static, elusive not obvious; it repels any
tendency to dogmatism, and, above all, the possible permutations of the
questions that it raises are so numerous that the diligent investigator can
seldom rest content with the solution that he proposes.'² Private international lawyers in general will find themselves in agreement with this
dictum of Dr Cheshire's. They have many difficulties to contend with
which are peculiar to this branch of the law. New problems are constantly arising; existing rules may have to be adapted to deal with situations either of law or of fact which are unfamiliar to them because they
emanate from abroad. Foreign legal concepts must somehow or other

---

1 Cheshire, *Private International Law* (2nd ed.), p. 21. See also Schmitthoff, 'The
Science of Comparative Law', *Cambridge L.J.* vol. VII (1939), p. 94.
2 Cheshire, *op. cit.* Preface to the 1st ed.

be brought within the categories of institutions and relationships recognised by the lawyer's own law. No system of private international law is complete; it may contain gaps which have been bridged over by other systems. In such circumstances comparison cannot fail to be of value; it must, indeed, be regarded as indispensable.

The importance of comparison has been recognised by the leading American and English text-book writers. Story, Beale, Westlake, Dicey, Foote, and Cheshire all turn to foreign sources for the elucidation of problems for which no solution can be found in English case law. The English judges have also sought enlightenment in the same quarter. The early history of the English rules of conflict lies outside the scope of our present inquiry, but it appears to be well established that these rules were largely built up, in the first instance, on the doctrines of the Dutch jurists of the seventeenth century—notably on Huber's *De Conflictu Legum*.[1] These doctrines were known to and applied by such great lawyers as Lord Mansfield[2] and Lord Hardwicke,[3] though it was mainly through the instrumentality of Story's *Commentaries on the Conflict of Laws* that they ultimately became absorbed into the common law.[4] In the early part of the seventeenth century the English judges frequently resorted to foreign sources when laying down the rules of conflict, as, indeed, they were compelled to do owing to the paucity of material in our own law.[5]

English private international law is, however, passing out of the formative stage, and a body of case law has come into existence which establishes its main principles. This development has combined with the cleavage between the common-law and civil-law systems on the subject of the weight to be attached to domicile and nationality respectively to lessen the frequency with which foreign authorities are consulted, with the exception of the case law and doctrinal writings of the United States which are being resorted to by English judges and practitioners as freely as before.

It is regrettable that civil-law sources should not be utilised to the same extent, but this can, no doubt, be explained by linguistic difficulties, and by the fact that the technique of continental legal authors is apt to be

---

1 Westlake, *Private International Law* (7th ed.), p. 8; Llewellyn Davies, 'The Influence of Huber's *De Conflictu Legum* on English Private International Law', *British Year Book of I.L.* vol. 18 (1937), p. 52; Sack, 'Conflicts of Law in the History of English Law', *Law, a Century of Progress*, vol. III, p. 342.

2 See *Robinson v. Bland* (1760), 1 W.Bl. 1.234, at p. 256 and the other cases referred to by Llewellyn Davies, *supra*.

3 *Ex parte Burton* (1744), 1 Atk. 255.

4 Beale, *Conflict of Laws*, vol. III, p. 1904.

5 Llewellyn Davies, *supra*, cites the following observation by Grant M.R., in *Potinger v. Wightman* (1817) 3 Mer. 67, as regards the law of domicile: 'we are obliged to resort to the writings of foreign jurists for the decision of most of the questions that arise'.

baffling to one who has been trained in the methods of approach of the common law. There is also, in the background, a feeling that, since the rules of conflict must be considered to be part of the common law, there is little help to be derived from civil-law sources. This unfortunate attitude not only fails to recognise the importance of ensuring that similar problems in the conflict of laws should not receive different solutions in different jurisdictions, but it also ignores the fact that problems of conflict often assume the same form in all systems of law. This was pointed out by high authority when Lord Wright said, in dealing with the construction of 'gold clauses' in agreements for international loans,[1] that 'it would be a very serious matter' if these clauses were interpreted in different senses in different countries. When delivering a dissentient judgment in a recent case[2] Scott L.J. made the following observation: 'I now come to the jurists. Although Private International Law is a branch of English Law their opinions are of great weight.' The learned Lord Justice followed up this remark by a discussion of the opinions of Savigny, Lafleur and Von Bar on the point at issue (a question of legitimation by declaration), thus reverting to the admirable precedent set by English judges of an earlier epoch.

The fact remains, however, that the opinions of foreign legal authors and the decisions of foreign courts do not receive the attention in this country which is due to them. This is, perhaps, only natural up to a point, because it would be too much to expect of our judges that they should all be comparative lawyers. The burdens imposed on them are already sufficiently heavy without the addition of a further requirement that they should engage in a profound study of foreign law. This is a plea, however, which should not be available to those who practise in the courts. If they themselves have not the qualifications to enable them to place before the court an accurate synopsis of solutions which have been arrived at or proposed in other jurisdictions it is their duty to consult others who are in a position to supply the information which is needed. The situation is not improved by the difficulty of access in this country to more than a limited number of foreign law books, including books on American law. This is a matter which might well engage the attention of those responsible for the maintenance of our law libraries, since the body of foreign literature relating to matters of private international law, though voluminous, is not so large as to involve a prohibitive expenditure of library funds or the allocation of an excessive amount of shelf room. Much might be done by co-operation between the libraries; it should be possible to assign the literature of a certain country or of a particular subject to each of the

1 *Rex* v. *International Trustee* [1937] A.C. at p. 515.
2 *In re Luck's Trusts* [1940] 1 Ch. at p. 914.

libraries, thus avoiding overlapping and unnecessary expense. A central catalogue would enable the books to be traced and consulted without undue delay or inconvenience. Some progress has, nevertheless, been made. At the moment there is in the Squire Law Library at Cambridge, for instance, a good working library of foreign books and periodicals dealing with private international law; it is, of course, in no sense complete, and contains gaps which should be filled and would, for the most part, have been filled by now if obstacles had not arisen to the import of books from abroad.

Further difficulties are created by the rules in force in this country with regard to the proof of foreign law.[1] It is, in reality, incorrect to say that a foreign rule of law is one of the facts in a case; on the contrary, it is provided by statute[2] that questions of foreign law must be determined by the judge and not be left to the jury. But the judge cannot deal with such a question *ex officio*; he must be furnished with proof of the nature and content of the foreign rule relied upon, and in default he must assume that the foreign law is the same as English law although he may be perfectly well aware of the existence of the foreign rule. In a recent case of *Hartmann* v. *Konig*[3] the question at issue was one of the interpretation of a contract which was in the German language and was governed by German law. The court of first and second instance acted on their knowledge of the continental methods of interpretation, of which no proof had, however, been given by the expert witnesses. The Master of the Rolls said: 'I think we are entitled, particularly as we are now considering German law and a German contract, to look at the surrounding circumstances with a more liberal interpretation of that term than is permitted under English law. I think it is commonly known that continental jurists adopt a wider interpretation of surrounding circumstances than we allow for the purpose of a contract in England.' But when the case went to the House of Lords the absence of any expert evidence to support the conclusions of the Master of the Rolls, correct though they were, was treated as fatal. Lord Buckmaster in his speech laid it down that 'it is impossible to rely on knowledge that may be possessed by expert lawyers here, but which has never found expression in any evidence, to interpret a contract made in a foreign country'. Quite apart from any other changes in the existing law which may be desirable it would seem that

---

1 For a general discussion of this question see Dicey, *Conflict of Laws* (5th ed.), p. 859; Westlake, *Private International Law* (7th ed.), pp. 423–8; Cheshire, *op. cit.* p. 129; Halsbury's *Laws of England* (Hailsham ed.), vol. XIII, p. 614; Kuhn, *Comparative Commentaries on Private International Law*, p. 97.
2 Supreme Court of Judicature (Consolidation) Act, 1925, s. 102.
3 (1933) 50 T.L.R. 114.

there is a strong case for a relaxation of the rule which forbids a judge to go outside the four corners of the expert evidence presented to the court.[1]

Proof must take the form of the evidence of an expert in the foreign law concerned, and may be tendered in the form of an affidavit though it is normally given in open court in the same way as evidence in general. If the experts disagree, as may well happen, the English judge finds himself in the unfortunate position of being called upon to decide between them. How difficult this may be can be seen by referring to such cases as those of *The Colorado*,[2] in which experts in French law were unable to agree as to the nature and effect of a *hypothèque* on a ship, or the *Russian Bank* cases,[3] where serious differences of opinion arose as to the consequences of the decrees of nationalisation of the Soviet government. It would seem that once proof is tendered, but not otherwise, the English judge may, if he so choose, pursue his own inquiries into the sources of foreign law and draw his own conclusions, and there is no reason to doubt that he does do so on occasion.[4] The difficulties attendant on any investigation of this kind may, however, be such as to deter him, for few of our judges are likely to possess the knowledge of foreign law and foreign legal terminology required for the task. In many cases the court has to make the best of a difficult situation and arrive at such conclusions as appear best suited to do justice. It may happen that the point before the English court has already been decided by a foreign court, and although the foreign judgment does not bind the English judges,[5] it is unlikely that they will incur the responsibility of overruling the foreign decision, except in a case where there has been a manifest error. There is at least one instance of a foreign judgment being dissented from by an English court. In *Guaranty Trust Co. of New York* v. *Hannay and Co.*,[6] the Court of Appeal examined a decision of the courts of the State of New York in the light of the American case law on the point, and the opinions of American text-book writers, and held that the decision was obviously incorrect and could not be treated as binding on an English court. On the other hand, it would obviously be undesirable for an English court to place a construction on a foreign rule of law which would run counter to the interpretation of it given by the highest foreign court, or to ignore

1 I am greatly indebted to Dr Kauffmann for calling my attention to this case.
2 [1923] P. 102.
3 See *Lazard Brothers and Co.* v. *Midland Bank* [1933] A.C. p. 289, and in particular pp. 298 and 299; cf. *Russian Commercial and Industrial Bank* v. *Comptoir D'Escompte de Mulhouse* [1925] A.C. 112.
4 Dicey, *op. cit.* at p. 861; Westlake, *op. cit.* p. 426; *Kolbin and Son* v. *Kinnear and Co. Ltd.* (1930) S.C. 724 at p. 737, and see the authorities cited in the preceding note.
5 *Bankers and Shippers Insurance Co.* v. *Liverpool Marine and General Insurance Co.* (1925) 24 Ll.L.Rep. 85.   6 [1918] 2 K.B. 623.

the implications of the *jurisprudence constante* or *Rechtsprechun* of a foreign country.

As I understand it, there is a division of opinion with regard to the matter on the Continent of Europe, though the attitude is less rigid there than in England.[1] So far as the German courts are concerned the judges appear to have a free hand: they may demand the production of evidence by the parties as to the foreign law or they may avail themselves of other sources of information. In any event the German judge cannot fold his hands and leave the question to be dealt with by the parties; he must take it up himself and pursue the matter on his own account.[2]

Our concern is, however, not so much with the rule which requires foreign law to be proved as a fact as with the legal technique which is employed in giving effect to the rule. One may well ask oneself if the process of eliciting information as to a foreign rule of law by means of the examination in open court of an expert witness is the method best adapted to secure satisfactory results. The expert is, in a certain sense, both an advocate and a witness, save that he has not the right to address the Bench. But, quite apart from this, it may be extremely difficult for him to explain his conclusions by means of answers to questions put to him by counsel who may only have a perfunctory knowledge of the point at issue. If the expert is unaccustomed to the trial methods of our courts he may, without realising it, be induced to qualify his evidence, and to obscure its effect, by skilful cross-examination, and it is sometimes extremely difficult to repair the damage so done by means of re-examination of the witness.[3]

It is also open to doubt, for other reasons, whether the process of question and answer in open court always results in the giving of satisfactory evidence on a point of foreign law. Let us assume that the foreign law on a given question is to be proved in an English court. One or more foreign lawyers are to enter the witness box and give evidence, and, as they do not speak English, an interpreter is in attendance who knows the language but not the law of the expert's country. Counsel on either side have been primed, in conference or consultation, with as much foreign law as is deemed necessary to enable them to examine their witnesses, and to address the court on the point of foreign law. Can it be suggested that this is the procedure best adapted to ensure that a foreign rule of law, if held to be applicable, will be applied correctly?

1 See Kuhn, *op. cit.* p. 101; Frankenstein, *Internationales Privatrecht*, vol. 1, pp. 291 and 294; Arminjon, *Précis de Droit International Privé*, nos. 139 *passim*.
2 Code of Civil Procedure, Art. 293.
3 The position appears to be the same in the United States. See an extremely interesting and valuable discussion of this question (to which I am much indebted) in Moses, 'International Legal Practice', *Fordham L.R.* (May 1935), at p. 27.

The interpreter may be perfectly competent, so long as he is dealing with questions of fact, but it may easily happen that he will distort the effect of the expert evidence, since he will almost certainly be unfamiliar with the legal terminology used by the experts, and will not appreciate the background to the answers given by them. The foreign expert, unless he is an old hand, may be too ready to assume that the general principles of his law, and the environment in which they are called on to function, are so well known as not to require elucidation. The combined effect of these factors may easily be to confuse the issue or to cloud the real purport of the expert evidence. The situation is much the same if affidavit evidence is substituted for evidence given in open court. Sir Frederick Pollock has put the matter very clearly in the following way: 'As a matter of fact you cannot begin by asking questions of a foreign lawyer in the right way until you know something about the general ideas and methods of his system. It is quite probable that if you address him in the language of your own law he will not know what you are talking about. But if he is a very wise man it may seem to him that he does not know and there will have to be further explanations. But if he is an ordinary learned man he will just interpret your questions in the way of his own thinking and he will give you an answer which will be quite misleading. And the more correct it is in the terms of his own system, the less likely it is to have any bearing on yours.'[1]

A further complication may arise if the foreign expert cites authorities in support of his opinion. So far as references to the provisions of codified law are concerned this is a simple matter, but if—as may happen—the codes do not supply the answer to a problem of foreign law, the expert will have to rely on the decisions of the foreign courts or on *doctrine*, that is to say, on the opinions of foreign text-book writers. Unless the expert explains fully the precise degree of authority possessed by each of these sources an English judge may easily be misled and may fail to recognise the persuasive effect of *doctrine* or may attach undue importance to the foreign case law. An expert witness who is unfamiliar with the structure of our law may not realise the necessity for such explanation, nor may counsel whose duty it is to examine him in chief.

It is, of course, true that the present method of obtaining proof of foreign law possesses many advantages. The presence of experts in court at the hearing of the case may sometimes be of assistance to the judge who can obtain from them, there and then, such further explanations as to the foreign law as he may require. The liability to cross-examination may also exercise a restraining influence on experts who might otherwise

---

1 *Proceedings of the American Foreign Law Association*, no. 9, pp. 7 and 8, cited by Moses, *supra*.

be tempted to give rein to views and opinions which they believe to be correct but are not accepted by other lawyers in the foreign country. It is also fortunate—at least in the case of the main systems of law—that expert witnesses are generally available who understand our trial methods and can be relied on to see that the court is properly informed as to the issues of foreign law. It is, nevertheless, sometimes difficult to obtain expert evidence as to the law of certain other countries, or with regard to certain highly specialised branches of foreign law, without incurring great expense which may well prove to be prohibitive.

The situation cannot therefore be described as satisfactory. That this is so is, in fact, admitted by our courts in applying the rule as to proof of foreign law; the rigidity of the rule has sometimes been relaxed where hardship would have resulted, and the courts have on occasion accepted the evidence of witnesses with no qualifications or doubtful qualifications, such as government officials,[1] or professors of law.[2] The need for some alternative method of proof has also been recognised by the enactment of two statutes, i.e. the British Law Ascertainment Act, 1859,[3] relating to proof of the law of British Overseas Territories, and the Foreign Law Ascertainment Act, 1861,[4] which deals with proof of the law of other countries. In both instances the prescribed procedure is to request a foreign court to give an opinion, but in the case of countries other than those embraced in the British Commonwealth of Nations this procedure is only available when it has been sanctioned by an appropriate convention between the United Kingdom and the country whose law is to be the subject-matter of proof. In practice little use appears to have been made of these statutory provisions.[5]

It is not easy to suggest remedies for the existing situation. It would, no doubt, be possible to raise the status of experts in foreign law to that of assessors and so remove them from the witness box. Or it might be frankly recognised that an expert is, in reality, often an advocate and allow him to address the court on behalf of his clients. But it is at least doubtful if either of these expedients would be preferable to the present practice. The substitution of an assessor or assessors for expert witnesses is, at first sight, an attractive solution, but it would always be difficult and, sometimes, even impossible to obtain the services of foreign lawyers of the

1 *In the Goods of Prince Oldenburg* (1884) 9 P.D. 234.
2 *Bailey* v. *Rhodesia Consolidated Ltd.* [1910] 2 Ch. 95.
3 22 and 23 Vict. c. 63.   4 24 and 25 Vict. c. 11.
5 See Dicey, *Conflict of Laws* (5th ed.), p. 862; *The Annual Practice*, note to R.S.C. Order xxxvii, Rule 5; the power of an English court to apply to a foreign court for its opinion may, perhaps, exist independently of statute, but this seems to be doubtful. See *Phosphate Sewage Co.* v. *Molleson* (1876) 1 A.C. 780, per Lord Selborne at p. 787.

required standing. Nothing would, in my opinion, be gained by treating foreign experts as advocates rather than witnesses, and the objections to this expedient are obvious.

The only alternative which would function in practice appears to be to make use more freely of the discretionary powers possessed by the English courts to obtain advisory opinions from foreign courts. This expedient presupposes, of course, that the foreign countries concerned have made provision for the adoption of this procedure, and it by no means follows that they would be willing to do so. In any event this form of procedure is one which should not be adopted normally: it should only be resorted to in cases of complexity or grave doubt.[1] International collaboration in matters of justice has not yet reached such a pitch of cordiality that applications of this nature would be welcomed by the judicial authorities of the countries concerned, and, if the request for an advisory opinion has to be forwarded by the usual diplomatic channels, the result is to cause very considerable delay. A possible solution of the problem might be to provide, by common international action, for the establishment in each country of a panel of eminent lawyers who would, when requested to do so by a foreign court, give an advisory opinion on such questions as might be submitted to them. The advantage of this procedure would be that it would avoid the infliction on already overworked tribunals of the additional duty of furnishing opinions for the benefit of their foreign colleagues, and would avoid the necessity for filtering requests for such opinions through the Foreign Offices and the Ministries of Justice of the two countries concerned.

If we assume that the present procedure for the proof of foreign law before an English court is to remain as it is, then the remedy for the present shortcomings lies very largely in the hands of those whose duty it may be to give expert evidence on foreign law. It is, I think, too much to hope that all judges and barristers will become comparative lawyers, but an expert witness on foreign law should always be prepared to make use of the comparative method if the necessity should arise. If he is familiar with the law of the country of the court, as well as with his own law, he will often be able to prevent misunderstanding by calling attention to fundamental points on which the two systems differ. He will also be in a position to avoid the pitfalls created by any assumption that the elementary principles of his own law are axiomatic and need not be referred to. He will also realise the need there may be for an explanation of the

---

1 A somewhat similar situation has arisen in the case of the Permanent Court of International Justice. See Jenks, 'The Interpretation and Application of Municipal Law by the Permanent Court of International Justice', *British Year Book of I.L.* vol. 19 (1938), at p. 10.

precise weight to be attached to any authorities that he may cite, or
that may be cited against him by experts on the other side.

It must, of course, always be borne in mind that a comparative lawyer
cannot enter the witness box in that capacity. This follows from the rule
that, save in exceptional circumstances, a witness can only be admitted
to give proof of foreign law if he is able to show that he has carried on
practice in the country concerned or has held some position which is the
equivalent.[1] In *Bristow* v. *Sequeville*[2] an attempt was made to assist the
court by calling a comparative lawyer to prove that the law in force at
Cologne, on all material dates, was the Code Napoléon. It may well be
that he himself was largely responsible for the rejection of his evidence,
because he described himself as a 'jurist' (a fatal term to employ where
English judges and lawyers are concerned!). He had studied law at the
University of Leipzig and was legal adviser to the Prussian Consul in
London, but had never practised at Cologne. It is somewhat difficult to
see why his evidence was excluded but in so doing Alderson B. made the
following observations: 'If a man who has studied law in Saxony, and
has never practised in Prussia, is a competent witness, why may not a
Frenchman, who has studied the books relating to Chinese law, prove
what the law of China is?'

There are, no doubt, good reasons in a normal case for preferring the
evidence of witnesses who have experience of the application of foreign
law in practice, but if the dictum of the learned judge means that in no
circumstances shall a witness be permitted to testify unless he is so qualified,
the result would be to exclude comparison from consideration when it
becomes a question of laying down a new rule of conflict. When a gap
in our existing rules has to be filled it is difficult to understand why the
court should not be entitled to receive expert evidence, given by a witness
who has studied the matter comparatively, for the purpose of ascertaining
whether the point has arisen in other jurisdictions and, if so, what are the
solutions which have been arrived at. As our rules of evidence now stand
this is impossible, and the court may be left to come to a conclusion as
best it can. It seems strange that a judge who may consult a text-book
on Chinese law written by a Frenchman, who has merely studied that
law but not practised it, is compelled to exclude the same Frenchman
from the witness box if his evidence is tendered as that of an expert. The
moral to be drawn is that the rules as to proof of foreign law should be
treated as flexible and should not be applied in a hard and fast manner.

1 The rule has been relaxed in certain cases apparently on the ground of possible
hardship resulting from its enforcement. See the instances given in Dicey, *op. cit.*
at p. 860, and Cheshire, *op. cit.* at pp. 131, 132.
2 (1850) 19 L.J.Ex. 289.

It has been found necessary to relax them when their enforcement would mean that no evidence could be given owing to difficulty in complying with the rules. It would seem worth while to consider, at least, whether the rules could not also be relaxed at the discretion of the court when a problem of a novel character has to be solved and no assistance is forthcoming either from existing case law or the pages of 'Dicey' or other English or American writers.

Comparison as a Remedy for Defects in the Rules of Conflict

The complexities and uncertainties which in practice characterise the operation of the rules of private international law at the present time have done much to prejudice its position as a solvent of conflicts of law and jurisdiction. A branch of the law which exists for the purpose of doing away with conflict has developed within its own bosom a mass of inconsistencies and ambiguities which have resulted in conflict being piled on to conflict.[1] Private international law has become enveloped in a cloud of abstract theories, some of them of great intricacy and difficulty, which flourish in the atmosphere of the lecture room, but create serious embarrassment to judges and practitioners. An illustration of this is to be found in the uncertainty which prevails when the rights of parties turn on the question whether the doctrine of *renvoi* is accepted by the law of a foreign country or not—a state of affairs which has been stigmatised by high authority as unsatisfactory because it depends in some instances on the doubtful and conflicting evidence of foreign experts.[2] It is a matter of common knowledge that the manner in which a clash between two competing systems of law will be solved may turn on the success or otherwise of a manœuvre for position by the parties in order to obtain a hearing in the courts of the particular country whose rules of conflict are most favourable to the one side or the other. The boycotting of courts of law by men of business and the drifting away of commercial litigation into the hands of arbitrators is, to no small extent, the result of a marked disinclination to run the risk of becoming involved in the mesh of rules of conflict which are so complicated and obscure that neither the merchant nor his legal advisers can foresee their effect on the rights of the parties with any reasonable degree of certainty. Moreover, the law which will prevail when there is a conflict may ultimately be determined by some event which is purely fortuitous, or relatively trivial. Thus in the much-discussed case of *Vita Food Products Inc.* v. *Unus Shipping Co.*[3] English law

1 'A conflict between the laws that solve a conflict of laws is an absurdity' (Mendelssohn-Bartholdy, *Renvoi in Modern English Law*, p. 83).
2 See per Maugham J. *In re Askew* [1930] 2 Ch. at p. 278.
3 [1939] A.C. 277.

was held to be the proper law of the contract because the master of a small coasting vessel had framed the contract of carriage on an obsolete printed form of bill of lading which we may assume was not read either by him or the cargo owner. It is quite certain that if the signatories to the Brussels Maritime Convention of 1923 had realised that the rules of private international law might have the effect of rendering their efforts nugatory, steps would have been taken to prevent this from happening.

The remedies for this unhappy state of affairs can be sought in two directions. The first remedy consists in the unification of private law, which would go to the root of the matter by removing the causes of conflict altogether. The second remedy takes the form of the codification of private international law, a method which leaves the state of conflict untouched but aims at the establishment of universal rules of the conflict of laws which would get rid of the present situation of conflicts within conflict. In addition to these two remedies it has also been suggested that the malaise from which private international law is suffering is largely if not entirely due to the existence of certain specific ailments which can be cured with the aid of comparative law. The ailments which have been specified are the following: *renvoi*, the conflict of qualifications, the overriding effect of national rules of public policy or *ordre public*, and the uncertainty which prevails as regards the right of the parties to a contract to choose their own law.

The unification of private law represents a noble ideal which is the embodiment of the spirit of international collaboration in its highest form and, if successful, possesses the very great advantage of causing conflicts to disappear entirely. But this question is one which lies outside the scope of our present discussion and will be dealt with hereafter.[1] The process of unification, in any event, represents a long-term policy which would be of little avail in solving the urgent problems with which we are concerned.

The codification of private international law,[2] on the other hand, does appear to offer a reasonable prospect of finding a remedy for the present situation. It will not be an easy task or one which can be carried through rapidly because it will not consist in the mere technical process of embodying the existing rules of conflict in a systematic form but will also involve the revision or reform of many of those rules. It must also be admitted that the results obtained by the attempts which have been made hitherto to codify the rules of conflict are not such as to furnish much ground for

---

1 See *post*, Chapter XII.
2 See the observations of Brierly on the use of the term 'codification' in this connection, 'The Future of Codification', *British Year Book of I.L.* vol. 12 (1931), at pp. 3 and 8.

encouragement. All efforts of this kind encounter special difficulties due to the imperfection of the international machine which is necessary to the working of the process and to the admixture of political considerations which have become infused into the material with which that machine will be called upon to deal. But it would be wrong to adopt a defeatist attitude, and the attempts hitherto made should be renewed. They may, perhaps, not meet with immediate success, but it will, at least, have been worth while to make them.

The duties to be discharged by a comparative lawyer in this connection are twofold in character and consist, in the first place, in the provision of materials required for the purpose, and secondly in the scrutiny of the proposals of the codifier with a view to the discovery of any elements which might render such proposals unworkable either because of the phraseology which is employed or because the proposals themselves cannot be fitted into the general scheme of any of the national systems of law concerned.

The collection of the necessary materials is essentially a matter for comparative lawyers. No one would seriously deny the importance of this preliminary stage of the enterprise involved in codification, although there is, in some quarters, a tendency to belittle it, and to assume that much of the materials in question can be procured, almost mechanically, by means of questionnaires addressed to governments, and such-like expedients. But those who have had practical experience of the working of what may, perhaps, be called the 'questionnaire' process will be well aware of its limitations; more is needed than a mere series of answers to questions, however detailed and carefully framed these may be. Divergences of rule must, for example, be considered in the light of the causes which may have brought them into being, apparent similarities must be rigidly scrutinised and tested with a view to ascertaining whether they are real or conceal hidden divergences. Above all, codification can only be carried out successfully if it is based on a synthetical statement of the situation which emerges from a study of the divergences and similarities between different systems of the rules of conflict.

Much work of this kind has already been done though the results are scattered. It is, however, satisfactory to know that an organised and systematic attempt to explore the ground is being made in the United States. The Restatement of the Conflict of Laws has been taken as the basis for a comparative survey of the common-law and civil-law systems of the rules of conflict and a series of studies by Dr Rabel is now being published under the aegis of the American Law Institute and the University of Michigan.

In addition, the comparative lawyer may also be called upon to render services of a consultative character whilst the work of codification is in progress. He is not directly concerned in the drafting of the codified rules because—as Dr Schmitthoff observes [1]—his role is that of a diagnostician and not that of a clinical expert. But questions will frequently arise as to whether the phraseology of the code is appropriate. 'Terms of art', as a common lawyer would say, do not always possess the same meaning in all systems of law, and the draftsman of an international code may use phraseology which is incapable of being translated correctly into other languages. This particular difficulty was not encountered by the framers of the only code of private international law which can be said to have met with any success, namely, the Codigo Bustamante, but it provides a serious problem when multi-lingual codes are being drafted.

Everything will, of course, turn on the readiness of the nations concerned to make sacrifices and to abandon the pronounced national features which characterise private international law at the present time. The discordance between the various systems of the rules of conflict is too marked to be ignored; in fact, there is little or no agreement of a general nature on the fundamental principles of this branch of the law. It has been suggested that there are certain principles which can be described as 'rules of international conflict of laws' and are to be found in the decisions of the international tribunals set up at the close of the last war.[2] It is true that these courts referred on occasion to certain principles of conflict alleged to be recognised by all civilised nations, but the existence of such principles is open to very grave doubt, except in the few instances where a principle compels universal recognition because it is the only one which would function in practice. Thus, in the case of the principle of *locus regit actum* and of the principle that rights in immovable property depend on the *lex rei sitae*, the unanimity which exists is not due to international consensus but to the inescapable necessity for the application of these principles if any positive result is to be achieved.

It is this absence of universal agreement on fundamental questions which constitutes the main impediment to codification of the rules of conflict, and it is difficult to believe that any real progress can be made until they are surmounted. The thorniest problem of all will, of course, be to bridge over the gulf between the rival claims of domicile and nationality as the basis of the personal status of individuals. The Codigo Bustamante was, to some extent, rendered nugatory by failure to reach agreement on this

---

1 'The Science of Comparative Law', *Cambridge L.J.* vol. VII (1939), p. 94.
2 Lipstein, 'Conflict of Laws before International Tribunals', *Transactions of the Grotius Society*, vol. XXVI (1941), pp. 175, 176.

question, the obstacle being one of a political character, namely, the desire of countries of immigration to retain domicile as the test of personal law whilst the other countries were unwilling to surrender the principle of nationality. The solution of this and similar problems is not the task of the comparative lawyer, but comparative law may, perhaps, be of value in so far as it enables an appreciation to be made of the operation in practice of the two competing systems of national and domiciliary law. Each of them possesses certain merits and is also open to certain objections, so that the balance between them is somewhat delicately poised. In these circumstances it may, conceivably, be possible to arrive at a compromise such as that suggested by a comparative lawyer, the late Dr Asser, which would for the purposes of the rules of conflict treat a period of habitual residence in a given country as the equivalent of nationality of that country. This period of residence would, of course, have to be of sufficient duration to eliminate any temptation there might be to effect a change of residence with the sole intention of obtaining a change of law.

In any event, it would seem that comparative law has a definite part to play in connection with any proposals for the codification of private international law. There remain the other claims which have been advanced for its value in other directions. One of these, at least, seems to demand more than a mere passing reference, namely, that comparative law may assist in finding a solution for the problems which have been epitomised under the heading of conflicts of qualifications. The theory of 'qualifications'—or 'classification' or 'characterisation' as it has been variously styled—has not so far received judicial notice in our courts. Dicey only refers to it very briefly, though Cheshire deals with it at some length.[1] It consists of a statement in reasoned form of a problem which is encountered in every system of private international law, and arises from the fact that a legal relationship may be placed in different categories by the two systems of private international law which happen to be in collision. One system may, for instance, classify the issue between the parties to a dispute as a matter of matrimonial law, whereas the other treats it as a question of testamentary law, and the ultimate decision of the court may depend in which of the two categories the issue is to be placed, because a different national law is applicable in the case of each category. There is no agreement, either within the systems or internationally, as to the law which should govern the process of categorisation. The problem has always been there, but it is only in recent years that it

---

1 See Dicey, *op. cit.* p. 43; Cheshire, *op. cit.* p. 24; Balogh, 'Le Rôle du Droit Comparé dans le Droit International Privé', *Recueil des Cours de l'Académie de D.I.* (1937), Ch. II.

has attracted the attention of the jurists, which rather suggests either that
it is not of such importance as is sometimes asserted to be the case or—
which is more probable—that the *lex fori* has been applied in such cases
with results that have not been unsatisfactory in practice. The alternative
solutions of the problem are to qualify or classify the issue in a dispute
either according to the *lex fori* or the *lex causae* or according to the principles of general jurisprudence, and it is with this last alternative that
we are concerned, because it implies the use of the comparative method.
It rests on the belief that there are certain concepts of private international
law which are distinct from those of internal or domestic law and are of
universal application. These concepts can—it is said—be ascertained 'by
the study of comparative law, which extracts from this study essential
principles of professedly universal application—not principles based on
or applicable to the legal system of one country only'.[1]

This view of the matter cannot fail to make a strong appeal to a comparatively minded lawyer, but it is, nevertheless, one which it is difficult
to accept. To begin with, no one appears to have attempted to indicate
any principles of this nature, and it would seem that if they exist they are
few in number. Nor, if these principles can be ascertained, is it clear to
what extent they would help to solve the problem of 'qualifications'.
In any event it does not appear to be feasible to insist on a solution which
would demand from judges and practitioners a knowledge of analytical
jurisprudence and an experience of the working of the comparative method
which few of them are likely to possess. A well-known private international lawyer expressed the opinion that 'if the contribution comparative
law has recently offered to the question of qualification or classification
in private international law is to be taken as a test it might even be
found that the confusion has been considerably increased'.[2]

It also seems to be more than doubtful whether comparative law has
any contribution to make towards the solution of the vexed question of
renvoi.[3] Private international lawyers are divided in opinion as to the
merits or demerits of this doctrine, but in all probability most practitioners

---

[1] Beckett, 'Classification in Private International Law', *British Year Book of I.L.*
vol. 15 (1934), p. 59; see also Rabel, 'La Problème de la Qualification', *Revue de
Droit International Privé* (1933), no. 1, p. 1. Cf. Robertson, *Characterization in the
Conflict of Laws*, pp. 38–43; Falconbridge, 'Characterisation in the Conflict of Laws',
L.Q.R. vol. LIII (1937), pp. 235, 537; Unger, *The Place of Classification in Private
International Law* (Bell Yard, 1937), p. 3.

[2] Mendelssohn-Bartholdy, 'Delimitation of Right and Remedy in the Case of
Conflict of Laws', *British Year Book of I.L.* vol. 16 (1935), p. 20.

[3] See also Cohn, 'The Unification of the Law of Commercial Arbitration',
Transactions of the Grotius Society, vol. XXIV (1939), p. 1. See *contra*, Balogh, *op. cit.*
Ch. III.

and judges would welcome its disappearance. In these circumstances it is difficult to appreciate the value of any assistance which comparative law could provide in mitigating the uncertainty and inconvenience which is undoubtedly caused by the absence of any general agreement as to the scope and nature of the doctrine. If a remedy is required it will call for more drastic measures than a comparative investigation of *renvoi* in all its various aspects.

The same considerations would appear to apply to the further sugges- tion[1] that comparative law can be relied upon to furnish some relief from the difficulties created by the tendency to resort to national rules of public order when the rules of conflict are deemed in some way or other to be contrary to national interests. This particular problem is one which is not limited to private international law, but forms part of a very much wider question, namely, of the limits which should be assigned to general principles or *clausulae generales* which can be used as a supereminent or overriding force to control the operation of the rules of private law. That national rules of public policy or order constitute a serious menace to international collaboration in the field of the conflict of law is beyond doubt. Even if agreement can be reached to apply an identical rule of conflict in all jurisdictions, the result thus achieved can at any moment be rendered of no avail if the courts of one of the contracting parties should decide that the internationally agreed rule constitutes an infringement of the national public policy rules of the court.[2] Public policy and public order are concepts of a fluctuating character, and are, therefore, a source of great uncertainty. They cannot be measured by any fixed standard, and like all the *clausulae generales* are subject to sudden transformation in obedience to current ideologies. In countries under democratic rule the governing factor will be public opinion; in totalitarian states the standard is of an arbitrary nature and depends on the caprice of a dictator or ruling clique. National rules of public policy are moulded by in- fluences which lie outside the law, and this, coupled with the fluid character of the rules, is sufficient to deprive a comparative study of the rules of any real or permanent value. Even the most learned and industrious of comparative lawyers can hardly hope to acquire the insight into the political and social mentality of other countries which would enable him to give a complete and accurate synopsis of the international situation.

This does not mean, of course, that the comparative method can be disregarded when such concepts as those of *renvoi*, 'qualification' or 'public

1 Balogh, *op. cit.* Ch. IV.
2 Nolde, 'Codification du Droit International Privé', *Recueil des Cours de l'Académie de D.I.* (1936), p. 117.

order' are placed under scrutiny. The international regulation of the problems presented by these concepts would be an impossible task without a realisation of the extent to which they impede the normal operation of the rules of conflict. But the task of finding a cure does not devolve on the comparative lawyer.

In conclusion, the value of comparative study to the private international lawyer himself is self-evident, because without it he cannot be said to be adequately equipped or trained for his duties; nor would anyone deny the value of comparison in filling any gaps there may be in the rules of conflict. Comparison is also an indispensable preliminary to any project of codification, but, as Professor Brierly has pointed out, the codification of rules which are to function in the international sphere means more than the reduction of known and accepted principles into a systematic form so that they can be adopted in all jurisdictions.[1] It necessarily involves the reform and development of the law, and is, therefore, not a purely technical task, but is to a large extent political in character. The process of comparison may furnish the materials from which a policy of development and reform can be shaped, and so make possible the first steps towards that end, but the task of determining what those steps shall be is not for the comparative lawyer but for others.

The present state of private international law appears to be such as to give rise to serious misgivings. A branch of the law which calls for a very high degree of international collaboration is subject to the constant menace of discordance of rule created by rival concepts of the basis upon which it rests and by many competing measures for the solution of conflicts. These disturbing factors are too often ignored or else viewed with complacency or even approval because of the absence of the communion of thought which alone can indicate the existence of discordance and point the way towards its removal. The comparative method of study and research has many tasks to perform, but not the least important of these is the service which it may be able to render in bringing about a common understanding of the many difficult problems which the private international lawyer has to face and thus pave the way for action which will result in general agreement as to the basic principles upon which all systems of the rules of the conflict of laws should be founded.

1 Brierly, 'The Future of Codification', *British Year Book of I.L.* vol. 12 (1931), pp. 4 and 5.

Chapter V

COMPARATIVE LAW & THE LAW OF NATIONS

IF by the law of nations or public international law we understand the principles of justice, which, by the common consent of mankind, should govern relations between states or nations, the employment of the comparative method would, at first sight, appear to be excluded, because rules which are avowedly universal in character do not lend themselves to comparison. So far as it exists at all, any relationship or kinship between comparative law and the law of nations must, therefore, be of a very shadowy nature, and the only possible link between the two disciplines is to be found in the extent to which the comparative study of private law can be regarded as an instrument to be employed in promoting the growth and development of the law of nations.

The publicists[1] have devoted a certain amount of attention to this question, but they have concentrated for the most part on the controversial topic of the admissibility of private-law rules as a source from which the law of nations may be developed. They are more concerned with this problem than with the discussion of the manner in which, or the extent to which, the comparison of private law rules can be utilised for the purpose. The approach of a comparative lawyer is of a different nature because the controversial aspects of the matter are of little interest to him, and he will be content to accept the realities of the situation which make it clear that whatever the sources may be from which gaps in the law of nations should, in theory, be filled it is an indisputable fact that resort is very frequently had to private-law sources and analogies as an aid to the settlement of international disputes. It is immaterial to a comparative lawyer whether this practice involves the general recognition of private-law rules as a source of international law or whether it is merely an expedient adopted in particular instances, with the consent of the parties to a dispute, for the purpose of bridging over any gaps in the international rules which might give rise to difficulties. The resort to private-law principles is in both cases limited to those which can be described in such terms as 'general', 'universal' or 'common to civilised nations' and the like, and an inquiry into the existence of these principles and into the manner in which they are to be ascertained constitutes the link which binds the two disciplines in a common task.

---

1 Notably Lauterpacht, *Private Law Sources and Analogies of International Law* and *Function of Law in the International Community.* See also Gihl, *International Legislation* and *post* p. 71, note 2.

The first question which would occur to a comparative lawyer is the need for some definite agreement as to the meaning of 'private law' when the phrase is employed in this context. The basis on which the law of nations rests is made up of concepts taken from the civil law of Rome—however much these concepts may sometimes have been disguised in the garb of custom, reason or the law of nature. Moreover, many modern systems of private law are founded on Roman law, though, perhaps, not to the extent that is generally believed. This has led to the assumption, conscious or unconscious, by many publicists that it is to Roman law that we must look in the search for principles common to all nations. It is, of course, true that the law of nations, as we now have it, is predominantly Romanistic in character. On the other hand, the position must be faced that something like one-half of mankind is living at the present time under a regime of law which is of a different character, namely, that of the common law of England. If voting power is to be determined by nations without regard to the population of a country, as has been the international practice hitherto, the situation is otherwise; the Romanistic systems are in an overwhelming majority, and the common law may be pushed into the background. This is a factor in the scheme of international legal collaboration which may create misunderstanding and even friction. The common-law nations are exposed to the danger of being 'voted down' in international assemblies summoned to deal with legal matters. International tribunals are for the most part manned by jurists whose legal training and outlook is that of the Romanistic systems and have little or no knowledge of common-law principles. It is as well to be frank on this point, because it may afford the real explanation of the abstention on certain occasions of the common-law countries from many of the efforts made to secure international collaboration in matters of justice. If we regard the problem of the development of the law of nations in the light of present-day conditions, there seems to be no justification for an attitude which would regard Roman law and the modern civil-law systems as the sole source of the principles which can be utilised in order to fill in gaps in international law.[1]

In any event, it is eminently desirable that we should clarify our minds as to the meaning of the phrase 'Roman Law' in this connection. Do we mean the classical law of Rome as taught at the Universities, or the *usus modernus* developed by the Pandectists which consists to a considerable extent of principles which have nothing to do with Rome or the Romans?[2]

[1] Lauterpacht, *Private Law Sources and Analogies of International Law*, p. 178.
[2] Buckland and McNair, *Roman Law and Common Law*, p. 9. The authors refer, by way of illustration, to the *Willenstheorie* of modern German law which is not derived from Roman law but from the philosophical writings of Kant.

As Maitland has remarked, 'Englishmen have often allowed themselves phrases which exaggerate the practical prevalence of Roman law on the continent'[1] of Europe. The law of Rome was only one of the sources from which the modern European codes have been built up. It may well be that there is sometimes 'less difference between the approach of a common lawyer to a problem and that of a French jurist than between the approach of a French and a Spanish jurist'.[2] Maine, writing in the latter half of the nineteenth century, failed to appreciate the extent to which non-Roman elements have percolated into modern continental law, and it is not improbable that Maitland had Maine in mind when he alluded to the tendency to attach undue weight to the existence of Roman principles in modern law.[3]

It would seem that this question of the meaning to be attributed to the phrase 'Roman law' is one which does not admit of any ready answer. If the formulation of an entirely new rule of international law becomes necessary, the position is somewhat different from that which arises when an international judge is merely called upon to give an extensive interpretation to a rule of international law which is already well established. In the former case Roman law must mean the *usus modernus* embodied in present-day systems of law as well as Roman law in the strict sense, because it would clearly be wrong to hark back solely to earlier forms of Roman law for the purpose of ascertaining whether a principle can be regarded as recognised or not by modern law. On the other hand, if an established rule of the law of nations, derived from the classical texts, is to be adapted to new circumstances, it may be necessary to concentrate on the source from which the rule was originally absorbed into the law of nations, and to emphasise the classical law of Rome for this purpose. The truth of the matter appears to be that international lawyers have used the phrase 'Roman law' in a loose sense. At times it means the law as expounded in the texts of the *Institutes* and the *Digest*; at others it is merely a 'portmanteau' phrase which serves to indicate that existing systems of law have adopted a principle which is based on the *usus modernus*. Subject to this the importance of the part which Roman law plays in the international sphere is beyond doubt, and it becomes possible to agree with Maine's verdict that a knowledge of Roman law and its history 'are equally essential to the comprehension' of international law. These considerations apply with special force to international lawyers whose training has been confined to the common law, for without some

1 *English Law and the Renaissance*, p. 65, note 37.
2 Deák, 'The Place of the "case" in the Common and the Civil Law', *Tulane L.R.* vol. VIII, p. 337.
3 See Maine, *Village Communities* (3rd ed.), p. 351, *passim*.

acquaintance with the concepts and terminology of Roman law they will be met at every point by 'a vein of thought and illustration which their education renders strange to them'.[1]

It would, however, be indefensible to treat Roman law, including the *usus modernus*, as the only source from which materials are procurable for the development of the law of nations. To do so is to place a meaning on the phrase 'principles recognised by civilised nations' which fails to correspond to the new situation which has arisen since the age of Grotius, when the law of Rome was the basic element in almost the whole of the law of Europe and was universally regarded as the standard by which justice should be measured. Nor can we afford to ignore the contribution which the common-law systems are in a position to make towards the filling of gaps in the law of nations. Such concepts as those of estoppel, of the trust and of the strict and punctual performance of contractual obligations may, in the future, have an important part to play in the development of international law.

If the phrase 'private law' is to receive this wider meaning then the next question is that of the attributes which a principle of private law should possess in order to qualify it for adoption by an international tribunal. It is at this point that comparative law and the law of nations are in close contact, because the absence of any international body of a legislative character has thrown the duty of filling in the gaps in international law on the international tribunals charged with the settlement of disputes between states or nations. This is a duty which cannot be evaded, and, unless its discharge is to be left to the uncontrolled discretion of international judges or arbitrators, the only alternative is that they should be furnished with some criterion of the sources to which they are to be permitted to resort. A test which has been widely adopted in the past is to refer, among other sources, to such principles of private law as are held in common by all civilised systems of law. This practice was recognised in Article 38 (3) of the Statute of the Permanent Court of International Justice which refers to the general principles of law recognised by civilised nations. As Professor Lauterpacht observes, 'that which had hitherto been done on the initiative of individual arbitrators or laid down in individual arbitration conventions has, in this way, received the sanction of the family of nations'.[2]

The words 'general', 'universal' and 'recognised' do not, however, furnish any clear indication of the kind of legal principle which can be

---

1 *Village Communities* (3rd ed.), p. 353.
2 *Private Law Sources and Analogies of International Law*, pp. 67 and 68. See also Gihl, *op. cit.* pp. 82 and 83.

regarded as conforming to the requirements for its adoption by an international tribunal. Is it essential that it should, for this purpose, be one which exists in identical form in every system of civilised law? Or, will it suffice if it can be found in substance in the majority of such systems? It would seem that the more generous of these criteria is to be preferred, because to insist on precise similarity of rule in all systems would be to demand the impossible and so to destroy or, at least, seriously diminish the value of resort to private-law sources. This conclusion is supported by the wording of Article 38 (3) of the Statute of the Permanent Court of International Justice which does not require a recognition by *all* systems of civilised law as would have been the case if identity of rule is to be the criterion. If any real meaning is to be given to the words 'general' or 'universal' and the like, the correct test would seem to be that an international judge before taking over a principle from private law must satisfy himself that it is recognised in substance by all the main systems of law, and that in applying it he will not be doing violence to the fundamental concepts of any of those systems.

The next question is whether the employment of the comparative method for this particular purpose presents any features which distinguish it from its use for other purposes. The answer is that it does not, except in so far as the importance of the subject-matter calls for the exercise of an even higher degree of care than usual. In particular, it is unwise to draw hasty conclusions from the *litera scripta* of any system of law, because the provisions of a code or a statute which lay down a principle may be misleading unless they are read in the light of judicial interpretation or are considered together with other principles. So far as case law is concerned, it is possible to attach undue weight to a particular precedent, as is sometimes done in the case of English law by continental jurists who are not familiar with the method by which the *ratio decidendi* of a decision is ascertained and the processes by which apparent precedents are often 'distinguished' by English judges on various pretexts. Above all it must be remembered that the importance of a principle may vary in the different systems according to the political or economic structure of society in the countries concerned, so that its meaning may have to be ascertained in the light of each of the political and social systems in which it is employed.[1]

It is not possible to enumerate the principles of private law which can be regarded as 'general' principles which are 'recognised by civilised nations'. But it would seem that such principles must be rare, partly

1 Friedmann, 'Social Security and Developments in the Common Law', *Legal Theory*, p. 320.

because there is little or no scope for the employment of any save the main principles of law for this purpose, and partly because such exploration of the field as has been attempted appears to indicate that there are few principles of this description. Writers on international law who have dealt with this question have addressed themselves, for the most part, to an examination of the extent to which the existing rules of international law can be regarded as having a private-law origin, but they suggest, by way of illustration, that there are certain other principles of private law which could be employed for the purpose of the further development of the law of nations. Reliance has been placed, for instance, on the principles of private law dealing with the impossibility of the performance of contracts, on the doctrine of the abuse of rights and on the principle which finds expression in the common-law doctrine of estoppel. It may, perhaps, be helpful to examine, from the angle of comparative law, the claim for the recognition of these particular principles by international tribunals. It is not suggested that an examination of this kind will furnish an answer to the problem with which we are dealing, but it may serve to stress the need for caution before the seal of recognition is placed by international lawyers on any given principle of private law, and also to indicate the limits within which such recognition should be granted.

The principle of *pacta sunt servanda* is one which is held in common by international and private law, but, in both cases, the same problem has arisen, namely, how far a supervening change in circumstances may be treated as releasing the parties to an agreement from any further obligation to fulfil their promises. The doctrine of *clausula rebus sic stantibus* has been proposed as the solution of this problem, but it would seem that the doctrine has never been recognised and is, therefore, inadmissible in international disputes.[1] On the other hand, it appears to be admitted that there is scope in international law for a different rule which would enable a contracting party to obtain relief from treaty obligations which it would be oppressive to enforce and would be 'comparable to the legislative or judicial interferences which modify the obligations of private contracts in the interests of social order'.[2] Reliance is placed for this purpose on such principles of private law as the English doctrine of the frustration of contracts, the theory of *imprévision* evolved by the *Conseil d'État* in France, and the application by the German *Reichsgericht* of the principle of good faith (*Treu und Glauben*) to the catastrophic conditions brought about by monetary inflation. But whether it is possible to dis-

---

1 See Brierly, *The Law of Nations* (3rd ed. 1942), pp. 204–7; Lauterpacht, *Private Law Sources and Analogies of International Law* (1927), pp. 170, 171; Friedmann, *op. cit.* pp. 314, 315.   2 Brierly, *loc. cit.*

cover in these doctrines some underlying principle which is common to all these attempts to solve the problem, and whether such principle, if it exists, could be adapted to the settlement of international disputes, appears to be a matter of grave doubt. It is, of course, obvious that the environment in which such a principle would be required to function is not the same in the international as in the private sphere. This is so, not merely because the element of duress which so often accompanies the conclusion of international agreements rarely enters into the formation of private-law contracts, but because the problem as it arises in private law has an economic background which is very different from the political considerations which surround it in international law. The circumstances which can be regarded as excusing the further performance of a bargain entered into between individuals relate almost entirely to the rendering of services, the occupation of land or the transfer of proprietary rights. But quite apart from this a comparison of the various private-law solutions of the problem does not hold much hope of the discovery of a principle which is recognised by all systems\or even by a majority of them. The question was considered at some length by the Committee of the Rome Institute, which prepared a draft international code of the law of sale for submission to the League of Nations, and the conclusion arrived at was that any solution which could be reached for international purposes would have to rest on a basis different from that adopted by any of the systems of private law.[1] It was felt that the efforts of these systems to reconcile the formula of *pacta sunt servanda* with the demands of justice had only resulted in the resort to principles either of a fictitious nature, such as that of the implied condition in English law, or to artificial concepts, of limited scope, such as those of *imprévision*, which it was impossible to define. It may well be that in the international sphere, as well as in that of private law, it is necessary that the courts should have power 'in some form or other to take cognizance of the change of conditions subsequent to the creation of the obligation'.[2] If so, it may be best, in both cases, to leave the matter to the discretion of the courts to be dealt with in accordance with their view of the demands of justice in the particular circumstances. This may, it is true, lead to varying results because judges do not always take the same view of the inferences to be drawn from facts of a similar nature. But the prospects of injustice would appear to be even greater if we were to try to 'mechanise the law where a certain amount of pliability in its

---

1 *Rapport sur l'activité de l'Institut International de Rome pour l'unification du droit privé* (1938–9), p. 10.
2 See *Hirji Mulji* v. *Cheong Yue S/S Co.* [1926] A.C. per Lord Sumner at p. 510; *The Fibrosa Case* [1943] A.C. per Lord Wright at p. 70.

application is essential'.[1] In any event the problem of the difficulties created by the *clausula rebus sic stantibus* is not one which can be solved by invoking the aid of private law, except in so far as a moral can be drawn from the failure of private law to arrive at any solution which is common to all systems.

As regards the doctrine of the abuse of rights, some writers, notably Lauterpacht,[2] rely on the doctrine as a general principle of private law which lends itself to employment in the international system. This doctrine has attracted a good deal of attention of late on the Continent of Europe, and has undoubtedly been recognised in varying degree by the laws of France, Germany, Switzerland, and Soviet Russia.[3] It has also been referred to with approval by the Permanent Court of International Justice on two occasions.[4] In spite of this it is difficult to accept it as a principle common to civilised nations. The doctrine is still in a formative stage, and its implications are by no means clear. It is rejected by Italian law, and the trend of judicial opinion in England is against its recognition as a general principle. Further, the doctrine is one which demands great caution in its application because of its possible subservience to ideological aims and the facility with which recalcitrant debtors can utilise it to escape from their obligations. It has on at least one occasion been put forward as an argument justifying the repudiation of international indebtedness incurred towards an ally in time of war.[5] If the doctrine is to be absorbed into the law of nations it may be that this decision is not one which a comparative lawyer would be justified in challenging, but it is submitted that he is entitled to lodge an objection against the description of the principle as one common to civilised nations. A comparison of the rules of the various private-law systems can only have the result of proving that this is not the case.[6]

An aspect of the law of nations which, at first sight, may appear to present a promising field for the application of the results of comparative research is that of the law of treaties. But it would seem that comparative law is, in this instance, only called upon to play a very modest part, and that certain features of the private law of contract are inadmissible for the purpose. International law has its own rules with regard to the form of

1 Professor Winfield in *Pollock on Contracts* (11th ed.), at p. 235.
2 *The Function of Law in the International Community* (1933), Chap. XIII. See also Friedmann, *op. cit.* p. 316.
3 See Gutteridge, 'Abuse of Rights', *Cambridge L.J.* vol. v (1934), p. 22, and the authorities referred to there.
4 Judgment No. 7 concerning German interests in Polish Silesia, Series A, No. 7, p. 30; Order of 6 December 1930 in the Free Zones Case, Series A, No. 24.
5 See Gutteridge, *op. cit.* p. 25, note (11).
6 *Contra*, see Lauterpacht, *The Function of Law in the International Community* (1933), Chapter XIII.

treaties and the capacity of the parties and their representatives. Theoretically, the private-law rules relating to reality of consent may have some bearing on the formation of international agreements, but it is significant that these rules have never been resorted to by international tribunals, and little or no reliance is placed on them by writers on international law. It would, in any event, be difficult to derive very much in the nature of principles which are generally recognised from a comparison between the common-law rules dealing with mistake and misrepresentation and the civil-law rules as to error and *dolus*. As regards the discharge of contracts, reasons have already been given for thinking that the private-law doctrines of frustration, *imprévision*, etc., will be of little, if any, assistance in the solution of the problem presented by the doctrine of *clausula rebus sic stantibus*. The private-law rules relating to remedies for breach of contract (e.g. the question of the measure of damages and of the payment of interest) appear to stand on a somewhat different footing, and it is possible that a comparison of private-law rules might, in this instance, provide material for the development of international law. This, however, is a matter which demands a more detailed and careful investigation than is possible in this brief survey of the position.

The most interesting question which arises in the sphere of the law of contracts is whether international law can derive any help from private law in regard to the interpretation of treaties. There are, no doubt, certain principles of interpretation which are common to both systems, e.g. the governing principle that an agreement is to be construed in accordance with the intention of the parties. There are also certain maxims of interpretation which are found in both systems, e.g. *generalia specialibus non derogant*. But there would seem to be little or no scope for the employment of the comparative process in this connection. The drafting of international agreements is carried out in conditions which make it desirable that the draftsmen should not be fettered by meticulous rules of interpretation, and such agreements should be construed in as large and liberal a spirit as possible. Even if it were desirable to resort to private law for the purpose there would appear to be very little to be gained by so doing. The divergences between the different systems of private law are such as to negative the existence of more than a very few rules which could be regarded as generally recognised. This is not the place in which to examine these divergences, but the situation may be summed up by saying that comparison reveals a 'difference of psychological attitude and conception of the duty of the interpreter' in the various systems of private law.[1] In some systems the rules of interpretation are far more rigid than in others,

---

1 Amos, 'The Interpretation of Statutes', *Cambridge L.J.* vol. v (1934), at p. 174; see Allen, *Law in the Making* (3rd ed.), at p. 436.

so that greater importance is attached to the literal meaning of words. *Travaux préparatoires* may be resorted to by the judge in some systems; in others he is precluded from so doing. The judge is bound in some systems by precedents of interpretation, in others he has a free hand. In these circumstances it is obvious that the search for principles which are generally recognised will not carry the investigator very far. Comparison of private-law rules may, it is true, be useful to the interpreter of a treaty in so far as it throws light on any 'terms of art' which may have been used by the draftsman, but this appears to be an emergency measure to deal with a situation which should never have been allowed to arise rather than an expedient to be adopted for general use.

The submission has already been made that if the phrase 'general principles recognised by civilised nations' means that an international judge must not resort to a principle of private law, unless it is one which is universally applied, then the contribution which comparative law can make to the development of the law of nations is bound to be of a meagre character. There are, no doubt, certain principles of this kind. Estoppel is a case in point, because it appears in all systems of civilised law either under its common-law designation or as an instance of the *exceptio doli* of Pandectal law.[1] It is also possible that the growth of more intimate intercourse and exchange of ideas between the lawyers of different jurisdictions may lead to a communion of thought which will have its repercussions in the international sphere and so ultimately prove to be the greatest service which comparative law can render to the development of the law of nations. There does not, however, seem to be any reason to believe that the framers of section 38 of the Statute of the Permanent Court intended their language to be construed in any rigid sense. The situation which they had in mind resembles that in which a Swiss judge is placed by Article 1 of his civil code which directs him in case of need to fill a gap in the law according to the rules which he would lay down if he had himself to act as legislator, but with due regard to legal doctrine and judicial decisions. The object seems to be the same in the case both of Swiss law and of the Statute of the Permanent Court, namely, to provide the judge, on the one hand, with a guide to the exercise of his 'choice of a new principle', and, on the other hand, to prevent him from 'blindly following the teaching' of the jurists with which he is most familiar 'without first carefully weighing the merits and considering whether a principle of private law does in fact satisfy the demands of justice' if applied to the particular case before him.[2] In other words a judge sitting in an international tribunal must not forget that he is an international

1 Friedmann, *loc. cit.*   2 Williams, *Swiss Civil Code (Sources of Law)*, p. 64.

judge, and before making use of a principle of private law on which to base his decision he must test it by ascertaining whether it is one which finds acceptance in the main systems of civilised law. If this be the correct view of the purpose of the reference in the statute to general principles recognised by civilised law then comparative law is not merely a mechanical process placed in the hands of the international judge in order to aid him in the discovery of principles of private law which can be used for the purpose of filling gaps in the law of nations. It also furnishes him with an objective test by which he can measure the justice of a principle which he believes to be the correct one and proposes to apply to the facts of a particular case when the existing rules of the law of nations do not furnish him with the materials for a decision.

It is submitted that the value of the assistance which comparative law may be in a position to render in developing the rules of the law of nations cannot be measured solely with reference to its possible use as a means of discovering such principles of private law as are held in common by all systems of law and are, therefore, to be regarded as ripe for absorption into international law. It depends above all on its employment as a corrective to any tendency there may be on the part of international judges or lawyers or on the part of the draftsmen of treaties to employ concepts or rules which either belong exclusively to a single system or are only to be found in a few of such systems. The possible consequences of any such tendency have been summed up in the following words by the writer who has devoted most attention to the question of the part to be played by private law as a source of the law of nations: 'To attribute to one system of a particular time and space the qualities of a universal law and to see in it a vehicle of the development of international law, may well result in checking that development.'[1]

If comparative study furnishes a means by which this danger can be avoided its value as an instrument for the development of the law of nations is undoubted, quite apart from any other services which the comparison of private-law rules may be in a position to render to the cause of international collaboration in the field of justice.[2]

[1] Lauterpacht, *Private Law Sources and Analogies of International Law* (1927), p. 178.
[2] A strong affinity exists between comparative research in the case of private law problems and the research which must precede any attempt to codify the law of nations. See Oppenheim, *International Law (Peace)*, 5th ed. by Lauterpacht (1937), pp. 51–8, and the Memorandum of the Columbia University Research in International Law in McNair, *Law of Treaties*, App.

Chapter VI

THE PROCESS OF COMPARISON[1]

IT is, for many reasons, impossible, in an introductory work, to deal exhaustively with all the problems which may arise when an approach is made, for the first time, to the comparative study of law. The many-sided nature of comparison, the width of the area within which it can be employed, and the variety of the purposes which it may be called on to serve, all combine to make it difficult and, in many respects, unsatisfactory to attempt a summary description of the working of the comparative process, or to deal with more than a few of the obstacles which must be surmounted if the comparison is not to result either in a waste of effort or in conclusions which may be entirely misleading. There are, however, certain features of the process and also certain characteristics of foreign law which must be appreciated before the task of comparison can be undertaken, and it is with these that it is proposed to deal in this chapter. Experience alone will enable the comparative student to avoid the more subtly concealed pitfalls which lie in his path, but something, at all events, will be gained if the more serious of the obstacles which he is likely to encounter are indicated.

Such questions as these will arise: Does a given problem of law lend itself to comparative investigation? Where are the relevant rules of foreign law to be found? What weight is to be attributed respectively to statute law, customary law, judge-made law and the opinions of legal text-book writers? What means can be adopted to ensure that the literature which is available gives the actual state of the law and is not obsolete or otherwise misleading? Are there any special features of the foreign laws about to be examined which, if not known to him, might lead an English lawyer astray? There are, of course, many other questions, some of which are of a very special character and only concern particular forms of comparative research and cannot be dealt with here. It must be remembered that the potential field of comparison is so vast that the technique to be employed cannot be standardised. A method which would give good results in relation to a particular system of law, or a particular purpose, may well prove to be a failure if applied in other directions. Subject to this the following would appear to be the main questions calling for consideration.

---

1 The questions dealt with in this chapter are confined to the comparison of English and continental law. A comparison of our law with that of the other English-speaking nations obviously stands on a different footing.

The Subject-matter of the Comparison

It is, of course, true that the scope of comparison is not infinite, and that in every system of law there are certain topics unsuited to comparison, usually because of peculiarities in the social, economic or political life of the countries concerned. But, broadly speaking, the subject-matter of comparison is not, in itself, a matter of paramount importance. This is also true as regards the number of systems which it may be proposed to compare.

Comparison must not, however, be indiscriminate if it is to yield valuable results. The classic instance of illusory comparison is to be found in Montesquieu's occasional excursions into exotic fields of research. However picturesque or entertaining they may be it is clear that enterprises of this nature cannot be expected to lead to conclusions of any real importance. It is quite feasible, for instance, to compare the law of the ancient races of the East with modern European law, but, as Pollock observes, such comparison 'can lead to nothing but ludicrous if not dangerous misunderstanding'. Like must be compared with like; the concepts, rules or institutions under comparison must relate to the same stage of legal, political and economic development. To quote Pollock once more: 'Ulpian would have stared and gasped alike at a strict settlement and at a debenture payable to bearer, but for wholly different reasons. If, again, Papinian could have been transported from York to India he would have found millions of men living under systems of family law so ancient that only faint vestiges of a corresponding stage could be found in Roman traditions and forms.'[1] It is, nevertheless, evident that chronological sequence is not material if the laws to be compared are in the same stage of development; the mere order of time has next to nothing to do with the matter.[2] Institutions may be widely separated in point of time but may be sufficiently akin to make comparison fruitful and also valuable. If any proof of this be needed it will be found in the pages of Professor Buckland and Professor McNair's comparative study of the principles of Roman and English law.[3]

So long as the subject-matter lends itself to comparison its nature and extent may be left to the discretion of the investigator. The ground to be covered may comprise the whole of two or more systems of law, or it may be confined to some particular branch of the law, or even to a single concept of law. Everything depends on the purpose which the investigator may have in mind when applying the process of comparison.

1 'The History of Comparative Jurisprudence', *Journal of C.L.* (N.S.), vol. v (1903), p. 74.
2 *Ibid.*   3 *Roman Law and Common Law* (1936).

It will be found, however, that the area of comparison is apt to be restricted by such considerations as the inaccessibility of materials and linguistic impediments. This is more especially the case when research extends beyond the boundaries of the principal European systems of law. Unless there are good reasons to the contrary, prudence demands that the number of systems placed under comparison should be limited, so far as this can be done without defeating the purpose of the comparison. The multiplication of the laws to be examined obviously increases the difficulties which may be encountered in any form of comparative research. It is, for instance, perilous for an investigator to pursue his inquiry into laws written in a language with which he is unfamiliar, or to rely on information derived at second hand. These difficulties may, occasionally, be surmounted by the selection of one system of law from a group of kindred systems, e.g. by treating the French *Code Civil* as the prototype of the codified law of the Latin countries or the German civil code as representing the laws of central Europe, but this is an expedient which cannot always be employed. Attempts to group the legal systems of the world are apt to be unsatisfactory, owing to the existence of cross-divisions such as are found, for instance, in the laws of British India, where the law of obligations follows the English model, whilst family law and the law of inheritance are based on Oriental law. The usual classification of law into common law, civil law, canon law and Oriental law breaks down in this and other instances. Continental law can, it is true, be divided for certain purposes into two groups, namely, the law of the Latin countries, of which the French *Code Civil* is the leading example, and the law of the central European countries which finds its expression in the German *Bürgerliches Gesetzbuch*, but this grouping, though it corresponds to certain fundamental differences in legal thought and legal technique, only indicates the actual situation in a very broad sense. In these circumstances it is, perhaps, fortunate that the value of comparison does not depend on the number of systems submitted to investigation. As a general rule comparison should not be carried beyond the extent required to bring the relevant principles of law into relief. Nothing is gained by a catalogue of all the differences of law which exist unless this should be necessary for some exceptional purpose such as the preparation of plans for the unification of the law or the compilation of information for the use of traders or other persons interested in differences of law for practical reasons.

The Sources of Foreign Law

The question—'Where shall I find my law?'—is one with which all lawyers are familiar, though the difficulties which it presupposes are greatly enhanced if the inquiry extends to foreign law. An English lawyer who engages in comparative study passes from the environment of his own law into a world governed by legal concepts which may be unfamiliar to him, and will often find that rules of law must be sought for in directions other than the sources to which he has hitherto been accustomed to resort.

Some misapprehension appears to prevail in England as to the sources of foreign law. This is largely due to a belief that the whole of continental law is to be found in the codes and that this codified law is, in substance, based on Roman law. Both these assumptions are ill founded and arise from what Maitland described as our 'traditional ignorance' of foreign law.

To begin with, the continental codes do not comprise the whole of the law in force, even when they purport to be all-sufficient. Codified law is invariably amplified, restricted or modified in its operation by a variety of factors which will be referred to in due course. For the moment it will be sufficient to emphasise the point that the provisions of a code cannot always be accepted as a complete answer to any given legal question. Secondly, it is only true in a certain sense to say that the origins of continental law are to be found in the law of Rome. The mentality of continental lawyers and their approach to legal problems are strongly tinged by Romanistic influences, but the Roman law which brings this about is not the ancient or classical Roman law studied in our Universities, but the *usus modernus juris Romani*, namely, the law of the Byzantine Empire as interpreted, and to some extent refashioned, by the Glossators and Post-glossators, and at a later date by the Pandectists. Much of it is puzzling to one who has learnt his Roman law at Oxford or Cambridge,[1] and it is dangerous to assume, as is sometimes done, that the concepts and methods of the classical Roman law have been transplanted into the modern civil law. Professor Buckland observes that 'it may be a paradox, but it seems to be the truth that there is more affinity between the Roman jurist and the common lawyer than there is between the Roman jurist and his modern civilian successor'.[2]

---

1 See, for instance, the employment of the *actio de in rem verso* by the French courts in order to give effect to the doctrine of unjustified enrichment (David, in *Cambridge L.J.* vol. v (1934), at p. 209).

2 *Roman Law and Common Law*, p. xi. To the same effect, Pringsheim, 'Relationship between English and Roman Law', *Cambridge L.J.* vol. v (1935), p. 347.

It appears, likewise, to be incorrect to assume that continental law is so closely akin to Roman law that it is permissible to treat the European countries as a unit for the purpose of comparison with Anglo-American law. The *Corpus Juris* is undoubtedly one of the sources and, possibly, the main source of modern European law, but the continental codes have drawn freely from other sources, and a Roman principle or rule which is incorporated in one of the codes may well be absent from the others or may be reproduced in a different form. In other words the modern civil law cannot be identified with the *Corpus Juris* and still less with the classical law of Rome. Certain branches of continental law—notably commercial law[1]—are to a large extent free from Roman influence. Planiol states that there is only one section of French civil law (the *régime dotal*) which is solely inspired by Roman principles.[2] There are also certain European systems of law, such as those of Hungary and the Scandinavian countries, in which Roman principles only play a subsidiary part. Maitland has reminded us that Englishmen are prone 'to allow themselves phrases which exaggerate the practical prevalence of Roman law on the continent of Europe'.[3] A knowledge of the classical Roman law must not, therefore, be regarded as the key which will open all doors leading to an understanding of foreign law. The European systems are far from homogeneous, and a famous German comparative lawyer warns us that it is not true to say that continental lawyers understand one another more easily than they understand English or American lawyers.[4] But an English comparative lawyer who is unfamiliar with the method and terminology of Roman law is only partially equipped for his task because he will undoubtedly find it difficult to appreciate the mentality of continental lawyers and to follow their line of reasoning. Further, the terminology of Roman law is a *lingua franca* which sometimes furnishes the only vehicle for the interchange of ideas between the civilians and the common lawyers however imperfect it may be for this purpose. It is, generally speaking, difficult for an English lawyer to derive much benefit from the study of continental legal treatises unless his mind has been attuned to the phraseology and modes of thought of the Roman jurists.

Although the chief source of continental law is to be found in the European codes it would be erroneous to suppose that they are the only

1 Moses, 'International Legal Practice', *Fordham L.R.* (May, 1935), p. 11.
2 *Traité Élémentaire de Droit Civil*, § 89. See as to German Law, *Rechtsvergleichendes Handwörterbuch*, vol. I, pp. 81 and 82.
3 *English Law and the Renaissance*, p. 65, note 37, and cf. Holdsworth, *History of English Law*, vol. IV, p. 11.
4 Rabel, *Zeitschrift für Ausländisches und Internationales Privatrecht*, vol. I (1927), p. 21. See also Deák, *Tulane L.R.* vol. VIII, p. 342, note 9.

sources of law. The codes are supplemented by other elements, namely, statute law, judicial precedents, custom and the opinions of commentators and text-book writers. They must also be read against a background of *Droit Common* or *Gemeinrecht* which is, in effect, modernised Roman law and may be utilised, if it becomes necessary, to fill a gap in the codes or to remove ambiguities. The provisions of the codes are, in certain circumstances, liable to be modified, or even to be superseded, by judge-made law or by the operation of the continental rules of the interpretation of statute law. The result is that the sources of continental law are much more varied than would appear to be the case. The different sources will now be considered, but the questions arising out of the weight to be attached to judicial precedents and the problems connected with the interpretation of such statutes are of such importance that they call for separate treatment.[1]

The Codes. When called on to deal with foreign law an English lawyer passes from an environment of case law into a 'world governed by codes'.[2] His first step must, therefore, be to examine the relevant provisions of the codified law, and it will be necessary for him to remember that there are certain differences between the continental codes and English codifying statutes such as the Sale of Goods Act, 1893. A continental code is intended to lay down new rules and is not conceived as resting on a pre-existing body of law. The history of a rule of continental law is, consequently, not a matter of very great importance save in exceptional cases. 'Whereas an English lawyer seeking to interpret a legal principle will look first to its pedigree, a continental lawyer will search for its policy.'[3]

The structure of the continental codes is also different from that of English codifying statutes. They are usually prefaced by an *Allgemeiner Teil* or 'General Section', which deals with the general principles of the law.[4] The remaining sections of the codes follow more or less accepted lines and, broadly speaking, group the topics under the headings of the law of persons, the law of things, the law of obligations, and the law of inheritance, but this classification is not strictly followed and the basis of division is not the same in all the continental codes. The important thing for an English lawyer to remember is that a foreign code is not arranged in accordance with the classifications with which he is familiar. There are, for instance, no divisions between real and personal property or between contracts and torts, and certain topics which he regards as substantive law

---

1 See *post*, Chapters VII and VIII.
2 Walton and Amos, *Introduction to French Law*, p. 4.   3 *Ibid.*
4 An English work compiled on similar lines to a continental code is the *Digest of English Civil Law* by Jenks and other authors. For this reason it is much favoured by continental students of English law.

appear in procedural codes and vice versa.[1] He will also have to become
accustomed to classifications with which he may be unfamiliar, such as
the distinction between movable and immovable property and the various
types of the community of goods between husband and wife.

The draftsmanship of the codes differs somewhat widely from that
employed in the case of our Acts of Parliament. It is the aim of the continental legislator to express a rule of law in as concise a form as possible,
with the result that continental statute law, in contrast to its English
equivalent, is conspicuous for brevity and clarity. This is rendered possible
by the fact that a continental code stands—at least theoretically—on its
own footing without regard to other sources of law and has been planned
both methodically and systematically. The result is to give the continental
judges somewhat wider powers of interpretation than those enjoyed by
our Bench, because the continental legislator is usually content to lay
down a principle and to leave it to the judges to work out the details.
Perhaps the most striking differences of form between English and continental draftsmanship are the following: The continental codes are replete
with cross-references which are anathema to our parliamentary draftsmen.
The relative merits of the two points of view are open to argument, but
the writer's experience, in some of the attempts which have been made
to draft international legislation, suggests that, in most cases, little is gained,
and that confusion may easily be created by a multitude of cross-references.
The continental codes are divided into 'Articles' which correspond to the
'Sections' of an Act of Parliament, but subsections are not, as a rule,
identified by sublettering (e.g. Section (1), subsection (2)), and this is
a cause of some embarrassment to English lawyers until they realise that
the continental *alinéa* or paragraph is the equivalent of the English subsection. Continental lawyers are strongly opposed to interpretation sections, and these are, therefore, rarely found in the European codes. The
motive which prompts this antagonism is the fear that provisions of this
kind may unduly fetter the judge in interpreting the phraseology of the
code, but several eminent continental lawyers have expressed an opinion
to the writer that the balance of convenience is on the side of the English
practice.

A further possible source of misunderstanding lies in the fact that it
may be necessary to refer to more than one code in order to ascertain the
state of the law. Dr Schuster observes that a disregard of this precaution
'may lead to most serious mistakes'.[2] Thus agreements for compound

---

1 Thus the rules of private international law relating to the enforcement of foreign
judgments are in German law regarded as procedural.
2 *The Principles of German Civil Law* (1907), p. 3.

interest are declared to be void by the German civil code[1] save in the case of certain specified banking transactions. On the other hand, in spite of this general prohibition, compound interest is permitted to be charged by virtue of the commercial code in respect of mercantile transactions carried out on current account.[2]

Misunderstandings may also occur owing to the existence of false analogies between the provisions of certain of the European codes. Some of the codes are to a large extent identical in their phraseology, e.g. the French, Italian, and Belgian civil codes, but it would be dangerous to assume that because the same words are used their effect is necessarily the same.[3] Difficulty may also be created in the case of multilingual legislation by variations in the text of the different versions which are all declared to be of equivalent authority. This is a question which will be discussed in greater detail when the problems presented by legal terminology are considered hereafter.[4]

Other forms of Statute Law and Regulations. Codified law cannot be all-embracing; new situations arise which were not contemplated by the codifying authority and further legislation becomes necessary. The complexity of modern life also makes it difficult for the legislature to cope with all the varied and detailed problems which must be solved if statute law is to discharge its functions efficiently. Thus in all the countries of codified law we find statutes which amend or supplement the provisions of the codes and are, in substance, treated as if they formed part of the codes. We also meet with a mass of delegated or subsidiary legislation which is designed to fill gaps in the law or to determine the detailed application of statutory provisions in particular circumstances. This delegation of legislation is nothing new to an English lawyer, who is only too familiar with its existence in his own system of law.

So far as statutes which amend the codes are concerned little difficulty will be experienced, as they are noted and dealt with in the commentaries on the codes and the text-books. Regulations of a subsidiary character present a more serious problem; but with the exception of a limited sphere of law, notably labour legislation, they will not greatly concern the comparative lawyer. This is fortunate because, however hard it may be for a lawyer to keep pace with enactments of this nature in his own system, the problem is intensified when he comes to investigate a foreign system of law. The question of the means by which and the circumstances in which legislative powers may be delegated is one of great interest from a

---

1 *Bürgerliches Gesetzbuch*, Article 248. See Schuster, *op. cit.* p. 104.
2 *Handelsgesetzbuch*, Article 355.
3 Lepaulle, *Harvard L.R.* vol. xxxv, p. 853.   4 See *post*, Chapter IX.

comparative standpoint, but it lies beyond the scope of our present inquiry.[1]

Custom. The legal term 'custom' has many different and concurrent meanings, and it is desirable that we should be clear as to its purport before seeking for analogies in continental law. It sometimes means the custom of the realm or a locality, or the term may be employed to denote the practice of a trade or locality as evidence in the light of which a contract or relation may be construed.[2] This difficulty cannot be overcome by any attempt to distinguish between 'customs' on the one hand and 'usages' on the other, because the term 'usage' may be employed in foreign legal terminology as the equivalent of the immemorial local custom of English law.[3]

In a system of codified law there should in theory be no room for custom in the first sense indicated above. The code displaces previous sources of law and can only be amplified or modified by legislation.[4] But, in practice, continental lawyers admit the existence of customary law (*Droit Coutumier* or *Gewohnheitsrecht*), although they may not be agreed as to what is to be included in the term or as to the conditions in which it comes into existence or its relationship to codified law. The Swiss civil code[5] recognises custom as a subsidiary source of law; the German civil code is silent on the question, but the leading German text-book writers accept custom as a possible source of law.[6] In France the law of 30 Ventôse, An XII (31 March 1804) abolished all general or local customs, but certain of them still survive in the *Code Civil*.[7]

It is unnecessary for us to pursue the question of the place of custom in foreign law, as it raises problems which are beyond the scope of this work. There are, however, two considerations which should be borne in mind. In the first place the term customary law may be employed by writers to indicate the unwritten law (*Gemeinrecht, Droit Commun*) of Romanistic origin which often serves the purpose of supplying any gaps there may be in the provisions of the codes. An illustration is to be found in the provisions of the French *Code Civil*[8] relating to the *régime dotal*, which only deal with the subject-matter in outline, leaving the details

1 See the discussion of the position in French law by Lambert, Pic and Garraud, 'The Sources and Interpretation of Labour Law in France', *International Labour Review* (1926), vol. XIV.
2 Salt, 'The Local Ambit of a Custom', *Cambridge Legal Essays*, p. 279.
3 See *Vocabulaire Juridique*, sub tit. 'Usage'.
4 Walton and Amos, *Introduction to French Law*, p. 5.
5 Article 1; see Williams, *Swiss Civil Code (Sources of Law)*, p. 185.
6 See Ennecerrus, Kipp and Wolf, *Lehrbuch des Bürgerlichen Rechts*, vol. I, p. 37; Schuster, *op. cit.* p. 5.
7 See Colin-Capitant, *Cours Élémentaire de Droit Civil Français* (6th ed.), vol. I (1930), § 2, no. 23.   8 Articles 1540–81; Colin-Capitant, *loc. cit.*

to be supplied by Roman law. The provisions of the German civil code relating to unjustifiable enrichment are general and are left to be worked out on the lines of the Roman *condictiones*.[1] In both these instances the supplementary provisions are sometimes referred to as customary law and sometimes as common law. Further, so far as usages of the second type mentioned above are concerned the question is not one of the application of customary law but of the interpretation of contracts. Evidence, for this purpose, is more readily admitted on the Continent than in England, and trade or professional usages do not become frozen by the operation of the doctrine of *stare decisis* with the result that commercial usages can more easily be adapted to the changing needs of the times.[2]

The Opinions of Legal Writers. Legal literature is not only more extensive on the Continent but also carries more weight.[3] Academic lawyers enjoy a degree of prestige which is the envy of their English colleagues, and is best illustrated by the French practice according to which the opinions of eminent professors prepared *ad hoc* can be submitted to the courts. Much depends, of course, on the esteem in which a particular legal author is held, and the importance of doctrinal writings would seem to lie in the fact that they constitute a subsidiary source of law which comes into play if other sources are not available or are inconclusive. The continental judges have always declined to recognise the solutions of legal writers as authoritative, and the law as laid down in University lecture rooms is frequently disregarded by the courts.[4] On the other hand, foreign legal authors criticise the decisions of the courts with much greater freedom than in England, and they do not allow their views to be shaken by judicial rulings. The fact that a continental case may at any time lose its authority gives added weight to these criticisms. An English writer who challenges a ruling of the House of Lords can only hope that Parliament may hereafter give effect to his views, but a French or German commentator can always envisage the possibility that his opinion will ultimately be accepted by the courts.

The extent to which continental legal literature can be regarded as authoritative appears to be a matter of controversy,[5] but there seems to be no doubt that commentaries and text-books are freely cited and that

---

1 Articles 812–18; see Schuster, *op. cit.* pp. 350–5.
2 See Goodhart, *L.Q.R.* vol. L, at p. 46; Chorley, *L.Q.R.* vol. XLIII, p. 51.
3 'If decided cases have less authority in France than they have in England, legal text-books and the opinions of institutional writers have distinctly more.' Walton and Amos, *op. cit.* p. 8. See also Swiss civil code, Article 1.
4 See Ancel, 'Case Law in France', *Journal of C.L.* (3rd Ser.), vol. VI, p. 1.
5 See Lambert and Wasserman, 'The Case Method in Canada', *Yale L.J.* vol. XXXIX, p. 1; Ancel, *op. cit.* p. 5.

their persuasive influence is considerable, more especially if there is no case law in point. It would, indeed, be remarkable if this were not so, having regard to the fact that the judges of all jurisdictions—even those ruled by the common law—are inevitably influenced by the views expressed in the standard treatises with which they are familiar and to which they must constantly refer.

The main differences between the status of legal doctrinal works in English and continental practice seem to be as follows. In the first place, no obstacles are placed on the Continent in the way of the citation of works by living authors. Secondly, continental case law is more contradictory in nature than ours, as will be explained hereafter,[1] and in such circumstances the opinions of the text-book writers, if unanimous, may often prove to be the decisive factor.

The Materials for Comparison[2]

So far we have been considering the various sources from which the rules of continental law are derived, and the next step must be to examine the further question of the publications to which a comparative lawyer can resort in order to procure such information as he may require with regard to the structure of foreign law or its detailed rules. It is also essential that an English lawyer should know how far he can expect to find his materials on the shelves of law libraries in this country.

In a broad sense, the materials available consist of (*a*) bibliographies, (*b*) certain works of an encyclopaedic type, (*c*) introductory works intended to meet the requirements of those interested in the nature and functions of comparative law, (*d*) codes, (*e*) law reports, (*f*) commentaries and text-books, and finally (*g*) legal periodicals. It is proposed to consider each of these materials in turn.

The only bibliographies in the English language are those published in America by the Library of Congress. They take the form of six volumes, i.e. the *Bibliography of International and Constitutional Law* (1913), the *Guides to the Law and Legal Literature of Germany* (1912), *Spain* (1915), *Argentina, Brazil and Chile* (1917), *France* (1931), *the Central American Republics* (1937), and *Cuba, the Dominican Republic and Haiti* (1944). With the exception of the last-mentioned volume these bibliographies are, however, obsolescent and must, consequently, be utilised with caution. As regards bibliographies in foreign languages, the most important of these is the

---

1 See *post*, p. 91, for the further consideration of this topic.
2 The observations which follow are confined to civil and commercial law, as a complete exploration of the whole area of law open to comparison would introduce an element of complication without serving any practical purpose, in view of the exigences of space which do not permit of more than a general survey of the matter.

Bibliographie des Sciences Juridiques of Grandin, which includes works published in French in Switzerland and Belgium. Kaden's _Bibliography of Comparative Law_[1] is the only work of the kind specially designed to meet the requirements of comparative law and contains much valuable material. But, so far as French and German law are concerned, an English reader will probably find a great many of the references which he requires in the bibliographies which are included in most, if not all, of the leading textbooks on the subject-matter with which he may be concerned.[2] The bibliographies contained in the publications of the Istituto di Studi Legislativi of Rome must not be overlooked, as they furnish a valuable guide to publications of recent date.[3]

But bibliographies, however well planned and exhaustive they may be, cannot always meet the requirements of an English reader who may need more detailed and explicit information. In this event he can consult the Society of Comparative Legislation which is prepared to use its best endeavours either to furnish the information or to put the inquirer into touch with someone who can do so.

As regards encyclopaedic works the only publication of this description in English is Burge's _Colonial and Foreign Law_ (new edition), which has never been completed and is, moreover, to some extent obsolescent. There is, in fact, only one work of this nature in any language which can be regarded as meeting the needs of comparative lawyers, namely, the _Rechtsvergleichendes Handwörterbuch_,[4] which was almost completed when war broke out in 1939. Those whose knowledge of the German language is adequate will find this work an invaluable guide to the structure of foreign law. It also includes summaries of the detailed provisions of foreign law and very useful bibliographies. It must be regarded as indispensable to any library which claims to provide for the requirements of comparative students. The _Répertoire de Droit International_, by Lapradelle and Niboyet, contains much valuable material for the comparison of the rules of private international law.

There are not many treatises of a general character designed to serve as an introduction to the study of comparative law. None exists in the English language, but Lambert's _Études de Droit Commun Législatif_, Sauser-Hall's _Fonction et Méthode de Droit Comparé_, Sarfatti's _Introduzione allo_

1 _Bibliographie der rechtsvergleichenden Literatur_, 1870–1928 (Berlin, 1936).
2 Useful bibliographies will be found in the _Rechtsvergleichendes Handwörterbuch_ under the various headings.
3 _Bibliografia Giuridica Internazionale_ (1932–9).
4 _Rechtsvergleichendes Handwörterbuch für das Zivil- und Handelsrecht des In- und Auslandes_ (Berlin, 1929–38), Franz Vahlen. Six volumes have been published covering the titles _Abandon_ to _Unsittliche Rechtsgeschäfte_. Supplements were in course of preparation in 1939 which would have brought the work up to date.

Studio del Diritto Comparato and Schnitzer's *Vergleichende Rechtslehre* are well-known and widely read works of this type. Though they do not belong strictly to this category, the Acts[1] of the Academy of Comparative Law, of which two volumes have been published, and the *Recueil*, in honour of Professor Édouard Lambert,[2] contain much material of an introductory nature.

The starting-point for any investigation of the detailed provisions of continental law must consist in an examination of the relevant code or codes. The more important of the European codes are published in many forms. Some of these publications are merely reprints of the text of the codes together with any amending statutes; others run into several volumes with extensive commentaries on each of the articles of the code. There are also editions of an intermediate type intended for those who desire a book which is not too bulky or expensive, and these usually contain short notes on controversial points of law arising out of the articles of the code. Most of the European codes in various forms are to be found in the libraries at Oxford, Cambridge and the London School of Economics and some of them in other libraries. An English reader must not, however, expect to find the codes of every country, because it has proved impossible for our libraries to cover the literature of all the legal systems of the world.[3] Translations into English exist of the French, German and Swiss civil codes,[4] but in the case of most other countries a knowledge of the particular language concerned is required.

Next in importance come the continental law reports. These exist in some countries but not in all; in fact, the only legal systems which can claim to be well equipped with law reports are those of France, Germany, Italy, Belgium and Switzerland. Elsewhere law reporting is either practically non-existent or in an undeveloped state. The leading French law reports are the series of Dalloz and Sirey; in Germany we find the *Reichsgerichtsentscheidungen* and the *Landesgerichtsentscheidungen*, in Italy the *Giurisprudenza Italiana* and the *Foro Italiano*, and in Switzerland the *Arrêts du Tribunal Fédéral (Bundesgerichtsentscheidungen)*. Most of the continental legal periodicals also devote a portion of their space to reports of such cases as are likely to be of special interest to their readers. Digests of case law such as we have in England are not published on the Continent, their

1 *Acta Academiae Universalis Jurisprudentiae Comparativae*, vol. I (1928) and vol. II (1934).
2 *Introduction à l'Étude du Droit Comparé. (Recueil d'Études en l'Honneur d'Édouard Lambert* (1938).)
3 See *post*, p. 133.
4 E.g. the translations of the French *Code Civil* by Blackwood Wright or Cachard; of the *Bürgerliches Gesetzbuch* by Chang or Loewy, and of the Swiss civil code by Dr Williams.

place being taken by Summaries or Tables of Cases which are not, as a rule, of much assistance to comparative students. This is, however, not a matter for concern because the standard commentaries and text-books give references to case law of importance. The method of citation of cases varies from country to country. It is not usual to identify a case by the names of the parties, and the method generally adopted is to state the court which is responsible for the judgment and the date on which the judgment was delivered.[1]

A comparative student will find that he must as a general rule base his reading on the foreign commentaries and text-books. To enumerate even the most important of these is the function of a bibliography rather than of a work such as this, but the following general observations may, perhaps, be of some assistance to English readers.

The foreign law books available to them are to be found almost entirely in certain libraries, namely, the Squire Law Library at Cambridge, the Codrington Library at Oxford, the Schuster Library at the London School of Economics, and the Library of the Faculty of Advocates at Edinburgh. Other books no doubt exist, but they are scattered on the shelves of certain libraries such as those of the Foreign Office, the Inns of Court, the Law Society, and the British Museum, or are in the possession of practitioners in London and elsewhere. The best of these collections is, probably, that contained in the Squire Law Library which comprises the French, German, Italian and Swiss law reports and is well provided with works on the law of obligations and private international law. Most of the books are either up to date or reasonably so, though there are gaps, chiefly due to the suspension of book imports during the war. The Schuster Library contains much valuable material, but some of the books are either obsolete or obsolescent. It cannot be said that the position of an English comparative lawyer, as regards materials for his study or research, is satisfactory at present. In some cases he may find materials in this country but may be in doubt whether he can rely on them; in other instances the materials will be unprocurable and must be sought for in foreign libraries. The question of library facilities for comparative research will be discussed more fully when we come to consider the relation of comparative studies to legal education.[2] It will be sufficient, for the present, to observe that sufficient materials can be obtained in this country for most types of comparative study, and that the foundations have been laid for the building up at some future date of adequate facilities for research into foreign law.

---

1 See Appendix which gives the abbreviations used in citing French, German, Italian, and Swiss cases. I owe this to the kindness of Dr Lipstein.
2 See *post*, Chapter x.

So far as the main systems of European civil law are concerned most
of the standard works can be found in one or other of the libraries mentioned above, e.g. the *Traités de Droit Civil Français* by Planiol-Ripert and
Colin-Capitant, the commentaries by Planck and Staudinger on the
Bürgerliches Gesetzbuch, the *Lehrbücher* of German civil law by Ennecerrus
and Cosack, the treatises of De Ruggiero and Dusi on Italian civil law,
of Manresa on Spanish civil law, and of Rossel and Mentha and Oser on
Swiss civil law.[1] If information as to other systems of law is desired the
quest may prove to be in vain, but the gaps are filled to some extent by
such works as the *Rechtsvergleichendes Handwörterbuch* or the series known
as *La Vie Juridique des Peuples*.[2]

For those who are hampered by linguistic troubles there is a very
limited number of introductory works in English such as Burge's *Foreign
and Colonial Law*, Walton and Amos's *Introduction to French Law*, Schuster's
Principles of German Civil Law, Walton's *Egyptian Law of Obligations* and
Dr Ivy Williams's books on Swiss law.[3]

The legal periodicals published on the Continent are more numerous
and enjoy a wider circulation than those issued in this country. They are
valuable to comparative lawyers because they often contain articles of
considerable importance by distinguished foreign lawyers. They also
supply the best means available of keeping up with changes in foreign
law. Some of these are available in this country, but, with the exception
of those dealing with international law, public or private, the majority
of such periodicals are unfortunately missing from the shelves of our
libraries.

It is desirable and, perhaps, necessary to utter a word of warning against
the indiscriminate use of such materials as can be found in this country.
Some of the available books are unreliable because they take the form of
early editions which are now dangerously out of date. Moreover, some
works of little or no value have found their way into our libraries—usually
by way of gift from the authors. It must be remembered that the bulk
of foreign legal literature, as evidenced by the bibliographies and booksellers' catalogues, is staggering to an English lawyer. But there is much
of it which can be disregarded. Legal authorship is considered on the
Continent to be one of the roads to success in the practice of the law, and
this accounts for a plethora of monographs of varying merit on special

1 It may be added that the standard works on French and German commercial
law are also available, e.g. Thaller-Percerou and Lyon Caen-Renault on French
commercial law, and the commentary by Staub on the German commercial code.
2 This series includes five volumes dealing in outline with the legal systems of
France, Belgium, Czecho-Slovakia, Roumania and Switzerland.
3 *The Swiss Civil Code* (1925); *Swiss Civil Code (Sources of Law)* (1923).

topics. The outpour from the continental presses of minor works by legal authors, is, however, mainly accounted for by the fact that every successful candidate for the degree of doctor of law—and there must be hundreds of these every year—is required to publish his thesis. Most of these dissertations are of no particular merit, though occasionally they may be of some assistance to the comparative lawyer in so far as they may give him the information which he requires or may indicate the sources from which it can be procured.

But if due caution is exercised and the comparative student is careful to obtain advice from the proper quarter as to the materials at his disposal, he will not only avoid much trouble and anxiety but will also be preserved from the danger that his efforts may be rendered of no avail by the employment of materials which might lead him astray.

Chapter VII

THE COMPARATIVE APPROACH TO CASE LAW

THE position occupied by judicial decisions as a possible source of law is a question which has been much discussed by comparative lawyers.[1] Its importance is undoubted because one of the most serious of the many concealed perils which await an unwary student of foreign law is the risk that he may, on the one hand, ignore or minimise the effect of a decision of the courts or may, on the other hand, attribute to it a higher degree of authority than that to which it is in fact entitled.

The problem is one of some considerable difficulty because the weight to be attached to judicial decisions varies from country to country. Generalisations are, consequently, dangerous, and it is only with great diffidence that an English lawyer can venture to express his views on the questions involved. This much, however, seems to be clear—there is an abundance of continental case law and its authority cannot be ignored, although the field within which it can be regarded as operative is much more restricted than in Anglo–American law.[2] Viewed comparatively, the following are the matters which appear to demand discussion. First of all, How does continental case law differ, in point of form, from English case law? Secondly, Where is it to be found? Lastly, How far can it be treated as authoritative? Another question which arises incidentally is that of the merits or demerits of the doctrine of *stare decisis*, but, although this problem is one which calls for comparative investigation, it is not relevant to our present inquiry and may be left to others to solve.[3]

So far as questions of form are concerned, continental case law, like our own, consists of the reported decisions of the courts, but the two bodies

1 Allen, *Law in the Making* (3rd ed.), pp. 151 *et seq.*; Goodhart, 'Precedent in English and Continental Law', *L.Q.R.* vol. L, p. 40; Deák, 'Place of the Case in the Common and Civil Law', *Tulane L.R.* vol. VIII, p. 334; Ireland, 'The Use of Decisions by United States Students of Civil Law', *Tulane L.R.* vol. VIII, p. 358; Lambert and Wasserman, 'The Case Method in Canada', *Yale L.R.* vol. XXXIX, p. 1; Ancel, 'Case Law in France', *Journal of C.L.* (3rd Ser.), vol. XVI (1934), p. 1; Lambert, Pic and Garraud, 'The Sources and Interpretation of Labour Law in France', *International Labour Review*, vol. XIV (1926), p. 1; Pound, 'The Theory of Judicial Decision', *Harvard L.R.* vol. XXXVI, p. 641; Llewellyn, *Präjudizienrecht und Rechtsprechung in Amerika*; Cohn, 'Precedents in Continental Law', *Cambridge L.J.* vol. V (1935), p. 366; Gény, *Méthode d'Interprétation et Sources en Droit Privé Positif*, vol. I, para. 145 *et seq.*; Goldschmidt, *English Law from the Foreign Standpoint*, pp. 38 *et seq.*
2 Cohn, *op. cit.* at p. 367; see also Ireland, *op. cit.*
3 See the authorities referred to in note 1 *supra*, and Holdsworth, 'Case Law', *L.Q.R.* vol. L, p. 180; Allen, 'Case Law, a Short Replication', *L.Q.R.* vol. L, p. 196.

of law differ in many respects. The characteristic feature of a continental law report, when compared with its English equivalent, is its brevity. The facts are only summarised; the arguments of counsel are not reported and the conclusions arrived at by the court are sometimes stated in a few sentences. A continental judgment is purely impersonal; it is the decision of the court as a whole, and the voice of the dissentient judge is never heard. Precedents are very rarely referred to in judgments and, in any event, they are not cited as precedents but are only mentioned as supporting or illustrating the line of reasoning adopted by the court.

The reasons for these variations in form lie, for the most part, in differences of legal technique. To begin with, continental lawyers do not search for a precedent applicable to the particular facts of the dispute with which they are concerned, but consider how far the facts are covered by some general principle or principles.[1] They are not hampered in arriving at their conclusions by the doctrine of *stare decisis*, and the elaborate discussion of precedents which is a characteristic of English judgments and legal opinion is, consequently, unnecessary. Secondly, judgments must be reduced to writing and, in some systems, must also comply with certain formal requirements which have the effect of preventing any lengthy discussion of the point or points of law involved. It may be useful to illustrate the position by reference to the form of a French judgment in a civil action.[2] The judgment begins with the *qualités*, i.e. the names of the parties, the issues raised on the pleadings and a summary of the various steps in the action preceding the judgment. The *qualités* are drawn up by the parties under the supervision of the court. Then follows the *minute* which is the work of the court itself. It contains the *motifs* or the ground on which the court has come to its decision and the *dispositif* which is the operative part of the judgment. Every French judgment must be *motivé* and must deal with all the points of law raised by the parties and state the reasons for the conclusions arrived at by the court; in default the judgment may be quashed on appeal. The result, as Dr Allen says,[3] is that 'there is much to be read between the lines', and that French judgments are 'highly compressed' and 'not always easily understood by anybody who is not familiar with the French Codes and Statute law and the method of their interpretation'. A special feature of the French

---

1 Cohn, *loc. cit.*; Moses, 'International Legal Practice', *Fordham L.R.* vol. IV (1935), p. 11.

2 See Cuche, *Précis de Procédure*, § 294 *passim*; *La Vie Juridique des Peuples*, vol. III (*France*), p. 367; Wright, 'French and English Legal Procedure', *L.Q.R.* vol. XLII, pp. 502, 503. The judgments of the German and Swiss courts approximate more closely to English or American judgments.

3 Allen, *op. cit.* pp. 168, 169.

law reports consists in the notes to the more important cases written by the *arrêtistes* who are usually well-known specialists in the subject-matter of the judgment which is in question. These comments sometimes enjoy a high degree of persuasive authority.

The next question which arises—namely, Where is continental case law to be found?—will be dealt with hereafter when we come to the consideration of the materials at the disposal of an English comparative lawyer.[1] This brings us to the most important question of all—How far can continental judicial decisions be regarded as a source of law?

Much has been written on this topic,[2] but the position may be summarised as follows. Theoretically, as we have already seen, continental case law has no binding force; 'a judicial precedent does not bind either the court which established it nor the lower courts'.[3] There is no need to labour this point, for so much is quite clear. But it is equally certain that the persuasive influence of continental case law is so great that it is only by shutting one's eyes to its existence that it can be eliminated from any general conspectus of the sources of law. How far this influence extends is, however, more open to doubt.

It is generally assumed that judicial decisions do not become a source of law on the Continent until a series or group of cases has been formed creating a practice,[4] or what a continental lawyer would describe as *usus fori*. In other words an individual decision can never be treated as a source of law. An English lawyer is, perhaps, hardly qualified to express an opinion on a question of this kind, but there appear to be grounds for thinking that this statement of the position must be accepted with some reserve. Individual cases are frequently cited both in argument before the courts and in the text-books and commentaries, and it would seem that a single precedent cannot be ignored.[5] A chain of decisions on a single question of law is frequently met with in the continental systems, but this does not necessarily mean that the first decision would not have been followed if it had stood alone. A single decision of a supreme appellate tribunal such as the *Cour de Cassation* or the *Reichsgericht* cannot be disregarded, because higher courts are reluctant to reverse their own decisions and very rarely do so. The judges of a lower degree in the hierarchy are thus forced to have regard for the authority of the higher courts even if

1 See *post*, p. 130.   2 See the authorities cited at p. 88, note 1 *ante*.
3 Lambert and Wasserman, *op. cit.* at p. 14; cf. Lambert, Pic and Garraud, *International Labour Review*, vol. xiv (1926), p. 1. Cf. Goldschmidt, *op. cit.* p. 39.
4 Goodhart, *op. cit.* p. 42 and the authorities referred to *supra*, at p. 88, note 1.
5 Goldschmidt, *loc. cit.* It is significant that one of the most controversial questions in the whole range of private international law, i.e. *Renvoi*, appears to have been settled in France by two decisions of the Court of Cassation, i.e. *Forgo's Case* and *Soulié's Case*.

only on grounds of expediency. Moreover, continental judges are not recruited from the ranks of the Bar but are members of a judicial service into which they enter at the outset of their careers and in which they hope to spend their working days. They are naturally swayed by a sense of loyalty to their service, and judges of first instance, moreover, are unlikely, save for some very cogent reason, to endanger their prospects of promotion by coming into conflict with the considered opinions of their seniors and superiors.

The bulk of foreign case law is considerable,[1] but an English comparative lawyer must resist the temptation to approach the study of a problem in continental law by way of judicial decisions. Failure to observe this precaution will often result in a sheer waste of time and may even nullify the value of the comparison. The method adopted by continental lawyers when they are finding their law has been described in the following terms: 'it is not to delve right away into the decisions with the help of elaborate digests and tables, subject indexes...and whatever other guides there are. In fact such auxiliaries hardly exist in foreign countries. What the foreign lawyer generally does to ascertain the law is, first of all, to find the statutory provisions which apply....If the matter is questionable, one or more commentaries or text-books are looked up; and, if the points involved are particularly "nice" the lawyer will read the court decisions and special literature on the question, all of which are ordinarily found by reference to them in the commentaries.'[2]

Continental case law is often contradictory, and it is no uncommon experience, more particularly in French law, to find a chain of decisions both for and against a given solution of a legal problem. The reason for this conflict of authority is to be found in the non-recognition of the doctrine of *stare decisis* on the Continent coupled with the large number of courts of appellate jurisdiction. Appeals in civil causes are not centralised as in England but are heard, in the first instance, by district courts of appeal of which there are in France, for example, no less than twenty-seven. Since these courts are not bound to follow each other's decisions they often disagree. The result might well be to produce a state of chaos if it were not for the controlling influence of the supreme courts of appeal such as the *Cour de Cassation* in France and the *Reichsgericht* in Germany. One important distinction should, however, be noted, the *Cour de Cassation* and the *Reichsgericht*, do not, like the House of Lords, deliver final judgment but are only courts of revision having no power to give a final decision in the litigation. They can only quash the judgment under

---

1 'France has just as many leading cases as England', Lambert and Wasserman, *op. cit.* p. 15.　　　　　　　　　　　　　2 Moses, *op. cit.* p. 14.

appeal if it is incorrect in law. In that event the case goes back for rehearing, generally by a different court to the district court which has given the judgment under appeal. The court which rehears the case is free to follow or to dissent from the opinion expressed by the supreme appellate tribunal. In the great majority of instances it will, for reasons which have already been mentioned, accept the views of the supreme court and give judgment accordingly. This probably ends the litigation, but it may happen that the decision of the supreme court on the point of law is not adopted and that the case will travel back once more to that court for reconsideration. If this happens the second hearing must be by the plenum of the supreme court whose judgment is conclusive in the sense that the court to which the case is remitted must accept the views of the plenum. It should be noted, however, that the ruling of the plenum does not settle the question once and for all; it may be disregarded at a future date if the question should arise once more. The German *Reichsgericht* appears to be in a somewhat different position from that of the French Court of Cassation, because of the many expedients which the German judges have devised in order to avoid a reference to the plenum of the court. It is true that the *Reichsgericht*, like the Court of Cassation, is not bound by its previous rulings (subject to a curious exception[1] which need not detain us), but it is, to say the least of it, unlikely that a Court of Appeal would persist in refusing to recognise the views of the *Reichsgericht* and continue to give decisions which are merely destined to be overruled.

Continental case law must, therefore, be approached in a cautious spirit. An individual decision, unless it emanates from the supreme appellate court, cannot be regarded as more than an expression of opinion which ranks, in a sense, with the *obiter dicta* of our judges. The decisions of district courts of appeal carry considerable weight if they all point in the same direction, but even so, they still leave the question open. Continental case law must in any event be balanced against other factors in the situation, notably the extent to which a decision is accepted as correct by the legal public and survives the ordeal of criticism to which it may be subjected at the hand of legal writers, who enjoy a freedom of comment rarely exercised by their brethren in jurisdictions where *stare decisis* prevails and the dissenting writer is traditionally required to tone down his criticism by some expression of 'respectful submission', or the like, so as to make it clear that his observations are conceived in a proper spirit of humility.

But, whatever degree of authority may be attributed to continental judicial decisions, the fact remains that the task of comparison may resolve

1 See Cohn, *op. cit.* p. 366.

itself into an examination of continental case law. Codified law may fail to provide a rule to meet a particular state of fact, or may deal with it in a manner which experience has proved to be inadequate. It then becomes the duty of the judges to find some solution of the difficulty and to frame a rule to meet the situation. Existing law may be inadequate to ensure justice, and in that event 'a strong and uniform line of decisions may modify or even completely reverse a rule of legislation'.[1] Instances of developments of this kind are numerous, but an allusion to a few of them must suffice for our present purpose. The French law of delicts or tort is founded on the very brief provisions of Articles 1382–6 of the *Code Civil*, but its substance is contained in a very large number of judicial decisions.[2] Until 1930 the French law of non-marine insurance was entirely case law. Article 1864 of the *Code Civil* merely states that insurance is an aleatory contract and refers the matter to maritime law, which only deals with marine insurance. The rules governing fire, life and accident insurance had therefore to be worked out by the judges, and so a large volume of case law came into existence which was ultimately reduced to statutory form by the law of 13 July 1930.[3]

Judicial decisions may, therefore, be regarded as an important—even if subsidiary—source of law in the continental systems and may not be neglected by a comparative lawyer. The weight to be attached to them is, however, not the same in all jurisdictions. The *jurisprudence* or case law of France is more potent in its influence than the decisions of the German courts.[4] Much depends, in practice, on the frequency with which and the extent to which judicial decisions are reported. In certain countries the law reports are of such a modest character that precedents occupy a very humble position in the hierarchy of legal sources. This means that in the case of certain countries, such as Portugal, Roumania, Spain and Greece, a comparative lawyer will not receive much assistance from case law and must rely for the most part on other sources. It is even possible in the case of certain countries that he will find no law reports to which he can resort.[5]

The Influence of Overriding or Super-eminent Principles. To an English lawyer one of the most interesting features of continental case law is that it has furnished the means employed by judges, not merely in order to fill gaps in the law, but also to mitigate hardships which may flow from

1 Allen, *op. cit.* p. 169.
2 See Mazeaud, *Responsabilité Civile* (3rd ed.) 1938–9, 3 vols., which is largely a digest of the relevant cases.
3 See the summary of the cases in Planiol, *Traité Élémentaire de Droit Civil* (12th ed.), vol. II (1932), § 2152 *passim*.   4 Deák, *op. cit.* at p. 342.
5 See Appendix, *post*, for a list of foreign law reports.

rigid adherence to the letter of the law and to prevent it from being employed as an instrument of fraud or chicanery. The continental judges have utilised the technique of 'extensive' interpretation with this end in view: that is to say, they have used their interpretative function for the purpose of enlarging, restricting or modifying the scope of statute law in order to prevent injustice. This exercise of their prerogative must be distinguished from the other aspect of the interpretation of statute law, namely, the explanation of the meaning of the phraseology employed by the legislator, a matter which will be dealt with hereafter.[1]

This process of extensive interpretation, which to some extent resembles the English method of preventing a statute from being made an instrument of fraud,[2] is sometimes described as 'Continental Equity'. The continental legal systems do not, however, recognise any such difference as that which exists in our system between law and equity and have not developed anything in the nature of a 'pretorian jurisdiction distinct from that of the ordinary courts'.[3] When a continental lawyer uses the terms *Équité* or *Billigkeit*, or their counterparts in other languages, he does not contemplate a dual system of rules one of which merely exists as an appendage to the ordinary civil law. It is, therefore, inaccurate, and perhaps misleading, to speak of 'Continental Equity', but this consideration must not be allowed to obscure the undoubted fact that the provisions of the European codes are, as a rule, subject to control by certain super-eminent or overriding principles which may—and often do—change the complexion of the codified rules to a marked degree.

These principles (*clausulae generales*) are usually stated in a general way in the introductory articles to a code, or what a German lawyer would term the *Allgemeiner Teil*, but this is not invariably the case. The most striking example of a paramount principle to which the whole of a code is subject is to be found in the first article of the civil code of Soviet Russia, which provides that civil rights must be exercised in accordance with their economic and social purpose in order to secure protection.[4] The doctrine of unjustified enrichment (*enrichissement sans cause*) in French law, on the other hand, only finds partial expression in the *Code Civil*, and its operation depends almost entirely on the principles of *Équité* which have been evolved by the judges in the course of the process of 'extensive' interpretation. The matter is, in either event, one of the exercise of judicial

---

1 *Post*, Chapter IX.
2 See Friedmann, *Legal Theory*, p. 304; *Marlborough (Duke), In re Davis* v. *Whitehead* [1894] 2 Ch. at p. 141.
3 Walton and Amos, *Introduction to French Law*, p. 12; Friedmann, *op. cit.* p. 304. Schwarz, in *Recueil Lambert*, part IV, at pp. 586 *et seq.*
4 Patouillet, *Les Codes de la République Soviétique*.

discretion. The continental judges are the guardians of the interests of the community, and in certain circumstances it may be incumbent on them to determine whether the rights of the individual must prevail or whether they shall give way to a higher conception of the requirements of justice. It is for the purpose of their guidance in the discharge of this duty that these super-eminent principles, which are necessarily of a general and elastic nature, have been laid down because it would be impossible to detail all the circumstances in which a given rule of law may have to be applied or to predict all the consequences which might result from its application.[1] To some extent these principles are of a fluid nature and are susceptible to influences which lie outside the law, such as current ideas of morality, political ideologies and economic and political changes in the structure of human society, so that their application calls for the exercise of caution to prevent them from being utilised in such a manner as to undermine or supersede the ordinary rules and bring about radical changes in the law by indirect means.[2]

The task of dealing with these principles in detail is one which lies beyond the scope of this work, more particularly in view of the fact that some of them have not found universal acceptance and may vary in form from jurisdiction to jurisdiction. It may, however, be useful to give a brief account of their nature and effect in order to illustrate the manner in which they can be employed to supplement, to modify, or even to supersede the provisions of codified law. For this purpose it is proposed to consider the following concepts, namely, *Aequitas*, as understood by continental lawyers, Good Faith, Good Morals and Public Order.

Aequitas

The continental codes contain many references to equity but do not define it.[3] An English writer is therefore on delicate ground when he seeks to discuss its nature and characteristics. It would, however, seem to be clear that *Équité* and *Billigkeit* are concepts of a somewhat vague character with an undefined sphere of application. The *Vocabulaire Juridique* defines *Équité* as follows: 'Conception d'une justice qui n'est pas inspirée par les règles du droit en vigueur et qui même peut être contraire à ces règles.' Von Tuhr regards *Billigkeit* as the yardstick which furnishes a standard of

---

1 Von Tuhr, *Der Allgemeine Teil des Deutschen Bürgerlichen Rechts*, vol. I, p. 29. These principles are supplemented by the *exceptio doli generalis* of Pandectal law which can often be made to serve the same purpose.
2 Hedemann, *Die Flucht in die Generalklauseln.*
3 E.g. Articles 565, 1135 of the *Code Civil*; Articles 315–19 of the *Bürgerliches Gesetzbuch* and Article 4 of the Swiss civil code.

justice to be adopted by a judge when called upon to exercise his discretion.[1] Dusi draws a distinction between *legge* and *equità*. The former, he says, represents a standard of justice applicable as a general rule to any given group of cases. *Equità*, on the other hand, 'è la giustizia del caso singolo' which means in effect that it is the standard which a judge must apply in an individual case if he comes to the conclusion that injustice would result from the application of the *legge* or general, or ordinary, rule to the facts of the dispute which it is his duty to determine.[2] Pothier takes a somewhat different view because he regards *Équité* as furnishing a basis for the declaration of rights and duties in general.[3] It would seem that the nearest equivalent to these concepts in our law is that of 'natural justice' which has been roughly handled in our courts but has survived, though possibly only in an attenuated form. But continental lawyers regard the concept of *aequitas* as something more than 'vague jurisprudence'[4] or 'well-meaning sloppiness of thought',[5] though they may not be in agreement as to its precise nature or as to the extent of its application. The part played by it in continental law is, however, a far more modest one than that which is assigned to equity, in the technical sense, by our law. But its importance cannot be denied because it provides the main foundation on which the judges have based the process by means of which they can escape from a narrow or formalistic interpretation of the letter of the law and can give new life in a different guise to codified rules which have become outworn owing to changes in social conditions.

Bona Fides

In practice this is, perhaps, the most important of the general clauses or overriding principles. It has a familiar ring in English ears, but it must not be assumed that it is equivalent to our concept of 'Good Faith' because, although both are rooted in the same ideal of fair dealing between man and man, the continental view of its nature and characteristics covers a wider field than that assigned to it in our law. Moreover, English law excludes the element of negligence when the presence or absence of good

1 *Op. cit.* vol. I, p. 30; Article 4 of the Swiss civil code provides that, when the law expressly leaves a matter to the discretion of the judge, he must base his decision on principles of justice and equity.
2 *Istituzioni di Diritto Civile*, vol. I, p. 49.
3 David, 'The Doctrine of Unjustified Enrichment', *Cambridge L.J.* vol. v (1934), p. 205.
4 *Baylis* v. *Bishop of London* [1913] 1 Ch. per Hamilton L.J. at p. 140.
5 *Holt* v. *Markham* [1923] 1 K.B. per Scrutton L.J. at p. 513. *Contra*, see the expression of his views by Lord Wright in the *Fibrosa Case* [1943] A.C. at pp. 62 and 63; Winfield, *Province of the Law of Tort*, pp. 128 *et seq.*; *Local Government Board* v. *Arlidge* [1915] A.C. per Lord Shaw at p. 136; *Robinson* v. *Fenner* [1913] 3 K.B. at p. 842.

faith is in issue, whereas continental law treats gross negligence as the equivalent of bad faith. So far as it is possible to translate this concept into terms of English law it appears to connote honest and fair dealing between man and man and to cover the ground which is occupied in our law by 'good faith' together with much of the ground covered by another concept, i.e. that of the standard of conduct envisaged when our law requires that parties to a transaction should act reasonably.

The continental codes do not deal with *bona fides* in a uniform manner. The Swiss civil code which represents the most advanced views as to its functions provides in general terms that 'every person is bound to exercise his rights and to fulfil his obligations in accordance with the principles of good faith', but this code, and the Swiss code of obligations, contain many detailed requirements for the application of the principle in particular instances.[1] In German law the concept assumes the form of *Treu und Glauben*. Article 157 of the German civil code provides, for instance, that agreements must be interpreted in accordance with the requirements of *Treu und Glauben*, having regard to business usages, a provision which is repeated in almost similar terms in the commercial code (Article 346).[2] More important, however, is the requirement laid down by Article 242 of the civil code that performance of a contract must always be such as is required by *Treu und Glauben*, due regard being had to ordinary usages.[3] In French law the concept of *Bonne Foi* appears to have several meanings. In the first place it indicates the state of mind of a person who has acted erroneously but honestly in the belief that his action is in accordance with the law in such circumstances that he ought to be protected by the law.[4] It also connotes the same idea as that which finds expression in Article 242 of the German civil code and calls for the performance of obligations in accordance with current standards of honourable conduct.[5]

Good Morals and Public Order

The circumstances may be such that the enforcement of a rule of positive law might have consequences which would either be shocking to prevalent ideas of morality or would in some way be injurious to the interests of the community. The continental codes have faced this problem, partly, by

---

1 Article 2 and see Williams, *Swiss Civil Code (Sources of Law)*, p. 158.
2 Schuster, *Principles of German Civil Law* (1907), p. 104; Ennecerrus, Kipp and Wolf, *Lehrbuch des Bürgerlichen Rechts*, vol. I, § 53.
3 See the authorities cited in the preceding note; also Von Tuhr, *op. cit.* vol. III, p. 134, note 63.
4 *Vocabulaire Juridique*; see Articles 549 and 201 of the *Code Civil* for illustrations.
5 Cf. Article 1134 of the French civil code.

general clauses instructing the judges to refrain from giving effect to a transaction which is either *contra bonos mores* or would infringe the requirements of public order and, partly, by declaring certain specific transactions to be invalid on one or other of these grounds. Thus Article 6 of the French civil code provides that all agreements which conflict with the principles of *ordre public* and *bonnes mœurs* are to be void, and Articles 1131 and 1133 also deprive a transaction of any legal effect if it is entered into for some *causa* or purpose which is contrary to *bonnes mœurs* or *ordre public*. German law adopts the single criterion of good morals as being inclusive of public order (*Gute Sitten*), and invalidates all transactions which are in conflict with it.

Broadly speaking these two concepts cover the same ground as that which is occupied in English law by the rules relating to immoral transactions and transactions against public policy, but an English lawyer must be on his guard and must not press the analogy too far because the transactions which are invalidated by these overriding clauses are not the same everywhere nor are the grounds on which they are invalidated invariably the same. Thus champerty and maintenance embody ideas which are not found in the continental legal systems, and an unreasonable restraint of trade, which our law regards as contrary to public policy,[1] is treated by French law as immoral.[2] The prohibition of transactions in violation of *Gute Sitten* is a concept which an English lawyer will find somewhat difficult to understand. It appears to include any act which could not be enforced by the courts without giving offence to national sentiment,[3] but the question of the standards to be applied in ascertaining the nature and scope of this national sentiment is left at large, no doubt on the ground that they must necessarily be of a vague character and must fluctuate in accordance with the social, economic and political outlook of the people from time to time. These overriding principles of good morals and public order play a much greater part in continental law[4] than that which is assigned to morality and public policy by our common law. They have not been utilised merely in a disabling or restrictive sense, but have also served a creative purpose in so far as they have furnished means by which the continental judges have been able to break away from established technical principles of interpretation and to mould the law so as to adapt it to current social and economic conditions.[5]

---

1 *Nordenfelt* v. *Maxim Nordenfelt Co.* [1894] A.C. per Lord Macnaghten at p. 565.
2 See Ripert, *La Règle Morale dans les Obligations Civiles* (2nd ed.), at p. 47; Walton and Amos, *op. cit.* p. 167.
3 Schuster, *loc. cit.*
4 A brief but lucid exposition of the comparative aspects of this question will be found in *Rechtsvergleichendes Handwörterbuch* (*Unsittliche Rechtsgeschäfte*), vol. VI, p. 730.
5 Friedmann, *Legal Theory*, p. 259.

The extent and nature of the impact of these and the other general clauses on the development of codified law is a subject which still awaits exhaustive investigation on a comparative basis and calls for a detailed examination of continental case law. But the importance of these over-riding principles is undoubted, as can be seen by reference to the literature which deals with the question. Ripert's famous treatise (*La Règle Morale dans les Obligations Civiles*), for instance, is almost entirely devoted to an examination of the effect of these principles on the development of French law, and it is interesting to observe that the author bases his conclusions almost entirely on the *jurisprudence* or decisions of the courts with a voluminous citation of cases which is reminiscent of the methods of English and American text-book writers. In fact, the use which has been made by continental judges of these general clauses is somewhat astonishing to an English lawyer, who is accustomed to the cautious attitude adopted by our judges whenever the circumstances are such that it may be necessary to invoke the assistance of some general principle in order to prevent possible injustice by the application of a rule of positive law. The doctrine of unjustified enrichment (*enrichissement sans cause*) in French law is the creation of the judges who have utilised the concept *Équité* for this pur-pose. In Germany the problem created by the necessity for the revalorisa-tion of the depreciated mark after the War of 1914–19 was solved by a famous decision of the *Reichsgericht* in 1923 [1] which utilised the *Treu und Glauben* clauses of the civil code for this purpose, though in a manner which can never have been contemplated by the legislator. Article 826 of the German civil code, which declares any act to be unlawful if it results in the infliction of damage on some other person *contra bonos mores*, applies to acts which would otherwise be lawful, and has been employed by the German courts for a variety of purposes, such as·the prevention of unfair competition in business, the suppression of oppressive measures adopted by parties to labour disputes, the invasion of the privacy of individuals, and the checking of the abuse of rights. This is, in fact, the omnibus clause of the German law of tort, though its scope is con-trolled by the limits to be assigned to the concept of *boni mores*.

In conclusion, continental law has placed in the hands of the judges an instrument in the form of these general clauses which gives them powers of the widest description if they are called upon to mitigate the rigidity of a rule of law or to prevent the law from coming into collision with moral dictates or with the paramount interests of the community. On

---

1 *Reichsgerichtsentscheidungen*, vol. CVII, p. 87. This ruling of the German Supreme Court, which was given towards the end of the year 1923, was followed in a number of subsequent decisions.

the whole, the judges have made use of these powers with admirable caution and restraint, but there is always the danger lurking in the background that these overriding clauses may, in unscrupulous or ill-guided hands, provide the means for undermining the rule of law, a peril which is illustrated by the manner in which they have been employed for this purpose in National-Socialist Germany.[1]

---

1 Friedmann, *Legal Theory*, at p. 259, illustrates the supremacy which political principles may acquire over legal principles, in this manner, by reference to the use made by the National Socialists of Article 1333 of the German civil code for the purpose of annulling marriages between aryans and non-aryans.

Chapter VIII

THE COMPARATIVE INTERPRETATION OF STATUTE LAW

THE word 'interpretation' itself is by no means free from ambiguity. It may be used in its widest sense to indicate the creative activities of judges in so far as they may, in the exercise of their functions, extend, restrict or modify the operation of a rule of law which is expressed in statutory form, and when so employed it is usually referred to as 'extensive' interpretation. This is a question which has already been dealt with in connection with the comparative aspects of case law.[1] Our present object is to consider the use of the word in its narrower sense to denote a different process, namely, the explanation by the judges of the meaning of words or phrases contained in a code or a statute.

The technique employed for this purpose is not the same in all jurisdictions, and the matter is, consequently, one of vital importance to a comparative lawyer. It also gives rise to one of the most difficult problems connected with the movement for the unification of private law. Uniformity of law means more than a mere similarity of law, and if unification is not accompanied by an equivalence of interpretation it may well become a pretence and degenerate into a 'hollow shell' which serves no useful purpose.[2]

The first problem with which we are faced is that of endeavouring to form some estimate of the different techniques which are employed in the various legal systems for this purpose. This is no easy task for an English lawyer, because our law is for the most part free from the influence of the theories as to the nature of the interpretative function which are prevalent in the civil-law countries. It is true that English law is much richer than any of the continental systems in canons of construction, but these canons all centre on the duty of the judges to ascertain the intention of the legislator in making use of the particular word or phrase which is to be interpreted. Continental law, on the other hand, is replete with theories of various kinds. Some of these theories have not met with general acceptance, but they have combined in an assault on the

---

1 *Ante* Chapter VII. An illustration of the difficulties which may be encountered in defining the term 'interpretation' can be found in the judgment of Scrutton L.J. in *Guaranty Trust Co. of New York* v. *Hannay* [1918] 2 K.B. p. 670. See also Falconbridge, *Banking and Bills of Exchange* (4th ed.), p. 814.

2 Beutel, 'The Necessity of a New Technique of Interpreting the N.I.L.', *Tulane L.R.* vol. VI, p. 1.

grammatical and logical views of the interpretative function which has had a notable influence on judicial technique.

The extreme position taken up by the 'Free Law'[1] school of thought has, it would seem, been abandoned. According to this theory a judge is invested with the widest powers in dealing with the language of a statute. He may disregard it if it is either incomplete or ambiguous or if he thinks that the wording is calculated to lead to injustice. If he exercises this prerogative he is under a duty to apply the rule which he conceives would have been formulated by the legislator if he had been aware of the consequences. This theory, which represents the swing of the pendulum away from the positive or rigid theories of the interpretative function, had a very brief life and has now been discarded.

More important are the theories which envisage the 'social purpose' of a law as a guide to the intentions of the legislature. In Germany the controversy between the 'positivists' and the 'rationalists' ended in favour of those who hold that, where the meaning of a statute is ambiguous, the judge must adopt the interpretation which accords most closely with the social or economic purpose (*Zweck*) of the statute.[2] A similar concept has found its way into French law in the guise of the doctrine of the *but social*, and has received the powerful support of Gény and other writers.[3] It is not easy to ascertain the extent to which these theories are put into practice by the judges, though it is clear that they are often resorted to when the usual methods of logical interpretation prove to be inconclusive.[4] But the intention of the legislator, which Lord Watson once described as 'a very slippery phrase', is the basis of interpretation in all systems of law, and when the judge in a French or German court embarks on a voyage of discovery of the *but social* or *Zweck* he is, in reality, seeking to ascertain the intention of the legislator. The social or economic purpose of a modern statute must, of necessity, coincide, in most cases, with that intention. It must not be assumed that the legislator has acted capriciously or in an arbitrary manner. The perusal of any modern statute book will show that

1 Eugen Ehrlich, *Freie Rechtsfindung und freie Rechtswissenschaft* (1903); Kantorowicz (Gnaeus Flavius), *Der Kampf um die Rechtswissenschaft* (1906); Gény, *Méthodes d'Interprétation*, vol. II (1919), p. 330. For a concise account of the 'Free Law' movement, see Manigk, 'Formalismus und Freiheitslehre' in Stier-Somlo, *Handwörterbuch der Rechtswissenschaft*, vol. II, p. 474.

2 See, generally, Savigny, *System des Römischen Rechts* (1840); Wach, *Handbuch des Zivilprozeßrechts*; Ihering, *Zweck im Recht* (1877).

3 Gény, *Méthodes d'Interprétation*, supra. See also Planiol, *Traité Élémentaire de Droit Civil* (12th ed.), vol. I (1932), no. 224; Colin-Capitant, *Cours Élémentaire de Droit Civil Français* (6th ed.), vol. I (1930), no. 3. Bonnecase, 'The Problem of Legal Interpretation in France', *Journal of C.L.* (3rd Ser.), vol. XII (1930), p. 79.

4 See the authorities cited in the two preceding footnotes, and Dabin, *La Vie Juridique des Peuples* (Belgique), p. 162.

the overwhelming majority of laws relate to matters of social or economic rather than political importance. A judge on the continent of Europe is entitled, for reasons which will be discussed hereafter, to carry his investigation into the intention of the legislator much further than would be permitted to any of his English colleagues, and it is unlikely that he will travel very far from the path thus marked out for him. It must be conceded, however, that the theory is supple, and it undoubtedly provides judges with loopholes by means of which they can escape from the necessity of giving effect to an interpretation of the normal type which would bring about a result which they regard as contrary to the highest standards of justice, more especially if the statute with which they are dealing is somewhat antiquated or does not cover the ground completely.[1] On the whole the theory finds its chief exponents in university lecture rooms, but it has been adopted authoritatively in certain instances, e.g. in the Swiss civil code, which provides that the judge shall apply its provisions in accordance with the spirit rather than the letter of the text,[2] and in the first Article of the Soviet civil code of 1923 which in terms subordinates the protection of civil rights to cases in which this is required by the economic and social purpose of the law.[3] The truth of the matter appears to be that judges of all jurisdictions display the like reluctance to put themselves in the place of the legislator unless they are obliged to do so for the purpose of avoiding an interpretation which might lead to an obvious miscarriage of justice. Even our English judges, fettered by rigid canons of construction, have, on occasion, shaken off their bonds, as in the case of the equitable interpretation of Section 4 of the Statute of Frauds which established the doctrine of part performance.[4] The continental judges have greater freedom of action where the phraseology of a statute is ambiguous, but this is due to differences in the technique of interpretation rather than to the influence of any theory upon which the interpretative function is founded.

This brings us to the next question, namely, whether there is a common basis on which the process of interpretation rests in all systems of law. This question does not admit of a ready answer. Up to a certain point the

1 See Bonnecase, *loc. cit.* Dr Walton ('Delictual Responsibility in Civil Law', *L.Q.R.* vol. LXIX, p. 92) refers to this as a ground for the greater 'elasticity and power of development' of French law as compared with English law. This may, however, be doubted. English commercial law has, for instance, proved itself to be more flexible than its French counterpart.

2 Swiss civil code, Article 1; *Exposé des Motifs du Code Civil Suisse*, Berne (1902), p. 14; Williams, *Swiss Civil Code (Sources of Law)*, p. 42.

3 Patouillet, *Les Codes de la République Soviétique.*

4 See the opinion of Lord Hardwicke in *Attorney-General v. Day* (1749) 1 Ves. Sen. at p. 217.

English judge and his continental colleague adopt methods which are identical because each of them will take the intention of the legislator into account as the dominant consideration. If the language of the statute is such as to make that intention clear the judge must accept it as it stands, even if the rule does not correspond to his own views of that which would be right and proper in the circumstances. Moreover, each of them must construe the statute as a whole and is entitled to disregard its language if a grammatical interpretation would lead to absurdity or repugnance.[1] But if it is entirely a question of ambiguity of language the English and continental methods of interpretation part company, and we come to the crux of the whole matter.

It is somewhat dangerous to generalise about a complicated question of this kind, but, as we are more immediately concerned with a bird's-eye view of the situation, it may, perhaps, be permissible to attempt a very brief summary of the attitude of the continental systems of law towards the function of judicial interpretation and to outline it in the following way. Statute law, whether in the form of a code or of an amending statute, may give rise to difficulties of interpretation in several ways. It may be imperfect in the sense that it omits to deal, or only deals in part, with the circumstances to which it is applicable *ex facie*. In this event the judge must determine whether the omission is deliberate, or whether it is due to some oversight on the part of the legislator. If it appears that the statute is silent because the legislator intentionally refrained from any expression of his will, the judge must disregard the statute and seek elsewhere for a rule of law to be applied to the matter. If the omission is inadvertent it becomes the duty of the judge to make good the deficiency, but in this case he may be assisted by the possibility of reasoning by analogy to other rules contained in the same code or statute.[2] Problems may also arise owing to the existence of two or more conflicting statutory rules, in which case *lex generalis* must give way to *lex specialis*, and if there is an 'antinomy', i.e. a deadlock, the rules must be regarded as cancelling one another.[3] A statutory rule may become obsolete by reason of some change in social or economic circumstances and so cease to correspond to the *Zweck* or *but social* of the law, or it may be of such a nature that its enforcement would lead to absurdity or injustice. In all these cases the judge must disregard the rule.[4] Finally—and this is the normal case—a

1 See *Becke* v. *Smith* (1836) 2 M. and W. 191; *Grey* v. *Pearson* (1857) 6 H.L.C. 61. Cf. Gény, *op. cit.* at p. 252; Planiol, *op. cit.* vol. I, § 216; Ennecerrus, Kipp and Wolf, *Lehrbuch des Bürgerlichen Rechts*, vol. I, § 51; and Venzi, *Diritto Civile Italiano* (5th ed.), p. 13.
2 Schuster, *The Principles of German Civil Law* (1907), p. 11.
3 Ennecerrus, Kipp and Wolf, *op. cit.* § 51, II (5) and (7).   4 *Ibid.* § 54, I.

difficulty of interpretation may arise because the language of the statute is defective and its meaning is ambiguous. The judge may, in such a case, resort to the historical origins of the rule; he may consult the records of the legislature—including the parliamentary debates which preceded the enactment of the rule—for the purpose of ascertaining the intention of the legislator.

An English judge is in this latter respect not so favourably situated as his continental colleague, owing to the more rigid delimitation of his powers. He must confine himself to what the legislator has said in the statute, and can only take the surrounding circumstances into account so far as they are matters of common knowledge. He must make the best of the text and give effect to any meaning which it bears which is not manifestly unjust or fantastic, even though the result may be to defeat the intentions of the legislator. He may not consult the reports of the debates on the measure in Parliament or any other record of the ministerial or parliamentary deliberations which have led to its enactment.[1] He must ignore the statements made to Parliament by ministers in charge of the draft bill and the reports thereon of parliamentary or governmental committees.[2] The statute simply means what it says in a literal sense and this is all that counts, even though the judge as an individual may be well aware that a reference to the preliminary stages of the parliamentary history of the statute would reveal the actual intention of the legislator beyond doubt.

This rule has been defended on the ground that the worst person to construe a statute is he who is responsible for its drafting because he is disposed to confuse what he intended with the effect of the language which he has employed.[3] This may be so in certain cases, but it seems to be difficult to avoid the conclusion that this deliberate hoodwinking of the judiciary must often result in the distortion of the object of a statute where its meaning is ambiguous. Such devices as those which are adopted, as shown by Professor Beutel,[4] to evade the intention of the framers of the Negotiable Instruments Law might have been checked, for the most part, if the judges had been compelled to take into account the preliminary history of the measure and the deliberative materials which preceded its enactment.

1 *Regina* v. *Hertford College* (1878) 3 Q.B.D. 693.
2 *Davis* v. *Taff Vale Railway Co.* [1895] A.C. 542.
3 See *Hilder* v. *Dexter* (1902) 71 L.J.Ch. 781, 783. This rule has not always been adhered to. See the statement of Lord Nottingham as to the policy of the Statute of Frauds; *Ash* v. *Abdy* (1678) 3 Swans. 664, and the references to the parliamentary procedure in connection with the Uniformity Act in *Hebbert* v. *Purchas* (1871) L.R. 3 P.C. 605. These cases are, however, exceptional.
4 Beutel, *loc. cit.*

The problems arising in connection with the application of the English rules of interpretation to the body of international statute law, which is steadily growing in volume, are illustrated by a recent decision of the House of Lords.[1] Prior to 1925 it was an inflexible rule of maritime law that a seaman's wages terminated *ipso facto* in the event of the wrecking of the vessel on which he was employed.[2] This came to be regarded as a hardship, and it was accordingly provided by an international convention that 'in every case of loss or foundering of any vessel the owner or person with whom the seaman has contracted for service on board the vessel shall pay to each seaman employed thereon an indemnity against unemployment resulting from such loss or foundering'.[3] In accordance with British practice the ratification of the convention took the form of a statute, the Merchant Shipping Act of 1925, which in its preamble recites the fact that it was passed to give effect to the convention. The convention figures as the first schedule to the Act, but the operative words are to be found in the Act itself. The wording of the relevant section of the Act is as follows:

1. (1) Where by reason of the wreck or loss of a ship in which a seaman is employed his service terminates before the date contemplated in the agreement, he shall, notwithstanding anything in section 158 of the Merchant Shipping Act 1894, but subject to the provisions of this section, be entitled, in respect of each day on which he is in fact unemployed during a period of two months from the date of the termination of the service, to receive wages at the rate to which he was entitled at that date.

1. (2) A seaman shall not be entitled to receive wages under this section if the owner shows that the unemployment was not due to the wreck or loss of the ship and shall not be entitled to receive wages under this section in respect of any day if the owner shows that the seaman was able to obtain suitable employment on that day.

In the two cases in which a dispute arose as to the meaning of these words the shipwreck took place within a few days of the date on which the seaman's contract would have terminated in any event, wreck or no wreck. It was, nevertheless, held that the seaman was entitled to wages for the whole of the two months and not merely for an indemnity for the unexpired period of his contract of service, a decision which has the

1 *Ellerman Lines* v. *Murray* [1931] A.C. 126.

2 For the earlier English law on the matter, see Merchant Shipping Act of 1894, s. 158, and the comments thereon in Temperley, *Merchant Shipping Acts* (4th ed.), (1932), p. 104.

3 Convention of Genoa of 1920, Article 2. This Convention was adopted by the International Labour Conference of the League of Nations on 9 July 1920. For the text see Schedule I of the Merchant Shipping Act of 1925.

somewhat curious result of placing the shipwrecked seaman in such a case in a better position than he would have been in if the wreck had never taken place. The argument put forward on behalf of the shipowners was that their obligation to pay was limited to the unexpired period of the contract of service, and they relied for this purpose on the use of the word 'indemnity' in the convention. The majority of the House of Lords held, however, that there was no ambiguity in the statute, and that it was therefore unnecessary to refer to the convention in order to ascertain its meaning.

If the case had been heard by a foreign court the result would have been different, because according to continental practice the text of the convention is not redrafted in statutory form, but derives the force of law from the mere fact of its adoption by the appropriate legislative authority.[1] It is of interest to note that the English judges were prepared to refer to the convention if they had considered that there was any ambiguity in the statute,[2] but that they would have stopped at that point, and they would not have taken into account the *travaux préparatoires* such as the minutes and the report of the Genoa Conference which drafted the convention. They would have been confined to the text of the convention, and if that in turn proved to be ambiguous they could go no further.

The continental method of interpretation in such cases is diametrically opposite. In France consultation of the preliminary proceedings leading up to legislation has long been a 'favourite instrument of judicial interpretation'.[3] The judges will in case of doubt consult not only ministerial statements and reports of parliamentary committees but also the reports of debates in the Chamber and the Senate.[4] The like use is made of these materials by the German courts in cases of doubt where light may be thrown in this way on the intentions of the legislator. Frequent resort is had, in particular, to the preliminary drafts of the German civil code and the reports of the various committees which carried out the work of revision.[5]

---

1 Niboyet, *Manuel de Droit International Privé* (2nd ed.), (1928), no. 31; Stier-Somlo, *Handwörterbuch der Rechtswissenschaft*, vol. v, at p. 662.

2 See *The Croxteth Hall* [1930] P. 197, 201 *et seq.*; *Ellerman Lines* v. *Murray* [1931] A.C. 126, 144 *et seq.* Cf. *The Cairnbahn* [1914] P. 25.

3 Lambert, Pic and Garraud, 'The Sources and Interpretation of Labour Law in France', *International Labour Review*, vol. XIV (1926), p. 24.

4 How wide the field is within which the French judges conduct such researches may be seen by reference to the lengthy list of *travaux préparatoires* contained in Planiol, *op. cit.* no. 218, note (a).

5 See Ennecerrus, Kipp and Wolf, *op. cit.* § 50; Schuster, *The Principles of German Civil Law* (1907), p. 11. The German law reports contain many instances of the employment of this method of interpretation. See *Reichsgerichtsentscheidungen*, vol. XXVII, pp. 3, 27; *ibid.* vol. LI, p. 274.

The attitude of continental judges towards this aspect of the rules of interpretation was brought home vividly to the writer quite recently when he found himself listening to the arguments in a case before the Belgian Court of Appeal. The subject-matter of the dispute concerned the meaning to be placed on a statute which was enacted to deal with certain questions arising between employers and employees as the result of the dislocation of social life by the war of 1914–19. The wording of the statute was admittedly ambiguous, and the main contention advanced by the advocate for the appellant was that he was the only person in court who was qualified to expound the true meaning of the statute, as he had been a member of the government committee which had drafted it. This argument, which would have met with short shrift in an English court, was received without demur.[1]

The practical importance in the international sphere of this divergence between English and continental interpretative technique may also be illustrated by a reference to the Uniform Laws on Bills of Exchange and Cheques which were drawn up by the two League of Nations Conferences held at Geneva in 1930 and 1931 respectively. These measures are likely to result in the standardisation of the continental law of negotiable instruments. Article 33 of the Law on Cheques reads as follows: 'Neither the death of the drawer nor his incapacity taking place after the issue of the cheque shall have any effect as regards the cheque.' The Uniform Law of Bills of Exchange contains no corresponding provision, and it was strongly urged in the course of the deliberations of the conferences that it should also be excluded from the Law on Cheques, because otherwise it might be argued *a contrario* that there was a difference between the Law of Bills of Exchange and the Law of Cheques as regards the effect of the death or incapacity of the drawer. The difficulty was surmounted by leaving both laws as they stood and by inserting in the report of the Conference of 1931 on the Uniform Law of Cheques the following statement: 'It is understood that no argument *a contrario* can be based on this article in favour of the theory that, in the case of bills of exchange, the death of the drawer or his incapacity taking place after the issue of this instrument has any effect as regards the bill.'[2] The continental judge who is permitted to have access to this report will therefore have no difficulty in dealing with the question if it should arise. An English judge would

---

1 Cf. Y.B. 33–5 Ed. I (R.S.) 83, where in an argument as to the interpretation of the Statute of Westminster II, Hengham C.J. clinched the matter by saying to counsel, 'Ne glosez point le statut; nous le savons meinz de vous, quar nous le feimes.'

2 *Records of the Second Session of the International Conference for the Unification of Laws on Bills of Exchange, Promissory Notes and Cheques*, at p. 103 (League of Nations Publications, II, Economic and Financial, 1931, II, B, 22).

have to disregard the report, and it is highly probable that he would be compelled to arrive at a decision which would nullify the intentions of the framers of the Law of Bills of Exchange. In other words, a multilateral convention may operate in a different manner in Great Britain and on the Continent solely by reason of the employment of different methods in the interpretation of the measure. This may lead to untoward results, and it would seem that one of the two divergent methods must give way to the other. Foreign opinion is much against the English conception of interpretation, which is regarded as based on a misapprehension,[1] and unless the English practice is altered it will be necessary for the representatives of Great Britain to exercise the utmost vigilance to see that the object of a convention is not defeated wholly or in part by the application of different methods of interpretation. Many such difficulties could (as in the case of the illustration just given) be overcome by appropriate words or clauses when the text of a convention is transmuted into the form of a British Act of Parliament, but this will not do away with the possibility that ambiguous terms may be construed differently in two jurisdictions, owing to the fact that the continental tribunals have the right to refer for elucidation to a mass of material which is forbidden ground to the English judges.

Before leaving this topic, it may be of interest to refer to a question which has formed the subject-matter of much controversy in continental legal circles. It has been argued that when reference is made to the intention of the legislator the word 'intention' is itself capable of ambiguity. To put it quite shortly, are we to assume that the legislator has in view only the circumstances as they exist when the statute is put into force, or is he to be deemed to intend to lay down a rule for the future which is to be plastic and may thus vary from time to time in accordance with changed circumstances? An example of the difficulty which may arise in this way is furnished by a Scottish case, *Marquis of Linlithgow* v. *North British Railway*,[2] which turned on a dispute as to the meaning of the word 'minerals' in an Act of Parliament. The Act in question, which was passed in 1817, authorised the construction of a canal across land belonging to the vendors, the predecessors in title of the Marquis, and reserved the 'minerals' underlying the surface to the vendors of the land. Below the surface was a valuable deposit of oil shale, which the Marquis desired to

1 See Lévy-Ullman in *Bulletin de la Société de Législation Comparée*, vol. XLVIII (1919), pp. 83 *et seq.*; Lambert, *loc. cit.* at p. 23.
2 (1912) S.C. 1327, reversed on another ground, [1914] A.C. 820. See the discussion of this case in *Law and Language*, an address delivered by Lord Macmillan to the Holdsworth Club of Birmingham University on 15 May 1931, and published by the Holdsworth Club (Birmingham, 1931).

exploit, but he was met by a claim on the part of the railway company, who were the owners of the canal, that the shale underneath the canal belonged to them, because in 1817, when the Act in question was passed, the process of extracting oil from shale was unknown, and consequently shale could not be a mineral within the meaning of the Act. It was contended on behalf of the Marquis that the term 'minerals' must not be regarded as having a meaning fixed once for all in 1817, but as including anything which from time to time would come to be generally regarded as a mineral substance. This argument failed to convince the House of Lords and the Marquis lost his case.

A continental jurist would describe the dispute which arose in this case as a clash between the subjective and objective theories of interpretation. According to the subjective theory it is the duty of the judge to discover the intentions of the lawgiver at the time when the statutory rule of law to be interpreted was first enacted, that is to say, regard must be had solely to the circumstances as they were when the statute was brought into being. The advocates of the objective theory contend, on the other hand, that the rule must be interpreted in accordance with the circumstances as they exist at the time when interpretation takes place. It will be observed that this objective theory involves a progressive or teleological system of interpretation which may give a different aspect to a rule at different epochs, although the text of the law will remain the same.

In point of fact the two theories are drawn closer to one another than might appear at first sight, because it is obvious that the legislator looks not merely at the present but also into the future. He cannot be deemed to intend that a rule which he has formulated is to govern the situation for ever in spite of changing circumstances. A statutory rule must, therefore, not be permitted to control the situation in changed circumstances which can never have been within the contemplation of the legislator. This is the point of view which has prevailed in Germany, but it is not the same as that of the objective school. It merely acts as a check on the enforcement of obsolete or obsolescent statute law, and does not enable the judge to modify statutory rules so as to make them effective in circumstances which have altered entirely since the rules were enacted.[1]

In addition to the difficulties already dealt with a comparative lawyer may also be faced with problems of a linguistic nature. Words and forms of speech when found in a statute must, of necessity, frequently be of a legal technical character. In fact, words and phrases of this description are, in a certain sense, the best vehicle for the law. It is true that they are open to the objection that they are often incompre-

---

1 Manigk, in Stier-Somlo, *Handwörterbuch der Rechtswissenschaft*, vol. 1, at p. 432.

hensible to the layman, but they have this great advantage over so-called 'simple language' that what is lost in lucidity is more than regained in precision. Few measures have caused more litigation than those which purport to be couched in plain language which anyone can understand, and neither is it possible, nor, it is submitted, is it desirable that the draftsman of an international code should refrain from the employment of legal technical terms.

This brings us face to face with another problem of interpretation which is, for the most part, peculiar to international legislation, though it is also encountered in municipal law, e.g. in the case of the Swiss civil code. A multilateral international convention or a uniform law must be drafted in the first instance in one particular language, and the legal terminology of that language must perforce be employed. This may easily lead to discrepancies, because many legal terms are either, in effect, untranslatable, or may receive a distorted meaning at the hands of an unskilful translator.[1] The classic illustration of this problem is, of course, the bilingual Treaty of Versailles, and the skilful use made by the Germans of discrepancies between the English and French versions of the treaty. The Swiss civil code is another case in point. It was originally drafted in German, and was then translated into French and Italian, which at that time were the other official languages of the Confederation. Each of the three texts is authoritative, and a certain amount of difficulty has been experienced from errors in translation. Dr Williams, in her excellent treatise on Swiss law, refers to one case in particular where the same word appears in the plural in the German text and in the singular in the French translation.[2] In Article 28 of the Swiss civil code the German word *unbefugt*, which means 'unauthorised', has been changed into *illicite* in the French text, thus completely altering its meaning.[3] Other instances could be given, if necessary, but these examples will suffice to show that a certain amount of risk is involved if a statute is promulgated in two or more versions of equivalent authority but in different languages. Words which present peculiar difficulty in translation into English are certain French legal terms such as *domicile, force majeure, faute,* and *faillite,* which sometimes appear in multilingual conventions,[4] and the same is true of attempts to translate certain English terms into French, e.g. 'consideration', 'warranty', 'holder in

1 Cf. M. Olivier Jallu, 'Codification of Private International Law', *Canadian Bar Review,* vol. XI (1932), p. 25. It is for this reason that Article 13 of the Convention of 1931 relative to the international Agricultural Mortgage Credit Company provides that the French text is to prevail over the English text in the event of discrepancy.

2 Williams, *Swiss Civil Code (Sources of Law),* at p. 29.

3 Rossel and Mentha, *Droit Civil Suisse* (2nd ed.), vol. I, p. 99.

4 See, for instance, the Geneva Conventions of 1930 and 1931, adopting the Uniform Laws on Bills of Exchange, Promissory Notes and Cheques.

due course', etc. The German term *vorsätzlich* appears to defy translation
into English.[1] A striking instance of the obstacles which may be encountered was the discovery in the course of the discussions at the Geneva
Conference on the Laws on Bills of Exchange, Promissory Notes and
Cheques that it is dangerous to use the word 'good faith' (*bonne foi*)
in a multilingual statute, because it possesses certain 'nuances' in the
French, German and English languages respectively.[2]

The problem is one which has to be faced, and its existence calls for
caution in the drafting of the text of multilingual statutes. On the other
hand, the fact that the text of a statute is drawn up in more than one
language may sometimes prove to be a blessing in disguise. It necessitates
a higher degree of care than is usual in the choice of phraseology, and thus
often facilitates the discovery of looseness of expression or ambiguities
in the first draft. It sometimes happened at Geneva, for instance, that the
English version of a French draft[3] expressed the intention of the assembled
delegates more accurately than the original, or that the process of translation revealed the fact that a term of art employed in the first instance was
inappropriate for the purpose.[4] Dr Williams, when speaking of the multi-
lingual problem in Swiss law, says the very fact that a French translation
of the civil code had to be made led to the altering of the German phraseology to meet the French expressions, so that greater clearness in the German
version was the inevitable result.[5]

A further question of very great importance is that of the possible
influence of national concepts of law on the interpretation of international
statute law. A uniform law owes its existence *ex hypothesi* to a desire to
abolish differences between various systems of national law. It would
therefore seem to be implied that a judge, when construing a statute of

1 The meaning of this term is discussed in Gutteridge, 'The Comparative Law of
Privacy', *L.Q.R.* vol. XLVII (1931), p. 206, note 14. See also Schuster, *op. cit.* at
p. 339; Ennecerrus, Kipp and Wolf, *op. cit.* at p. 547; *Reichsgerichtsentscheidungen*,
vol. LVII, p. 241.

2 See the report on Article 16 of the Uniform Law on Bills of Exchange, *Records
of the First Session of the International Conference for the Unification of Laws on Bills of
Exchange, Promissory Notes and Cheques* (League of Nations Publications, II, Economic
and Financial, 1930, II, 27).

3 Or *vice versa*. For an instance in which the English original of Article 311 of
the Treaty of Versailles was preferred to the French translation, see McNair and
Lauterpacht, *Annual Digest of Public International Law Cases* (1927–8), p. 428.

4 A tribute must be paid to the remarkable efficiency of the translators attached
to the Secretariat of the League of Nations. Their task was one of extraordinary difficulty, which was increased by the fact that they had to work under great pressure, as
no delay was permitted for research into linguistic problems.

5 Williams, *op. cit.* p. 29. Compare an interesting case in which the English
translation of Article 297 of the Treaty of Versailles was resorted to in order to
explain an ambiguity in the French original text. McNair and Lauterpacht, *Annual
Digest of Public International Law Cases* (1925–6), p. 870.

this nature, should examine its language uninfluenced, as far as is possible, by any considerations derived from his own law. This is a principle which is applied in all systems of law to the construction of newly enacted statutes, though it is tempered by the qualification that the pre-existing law may be inquired into for the purpose of clearing up ambiguities.[1]

The application of this principle to international legislation is not altogether free from difficulty.[2] It would appear to be essential that a national judge should in the first instance exclude from his mind any inquiry as to the effect which the international rule may have upon his own law, and that effect should be given to the rule as it stands. But if its provisions are ambiguous, it seems clear that he should be empowered to consult the pre-existing rules, not only of his own law, but of the other systems which have been submitted to the process of amalgamation which is represented by the international code. If this method of investigation into the intentions of the lawmaker is to be banned it is difficult to see how he can become cognisant of the divergences between municipal laws which the international code is designed to abolish and of the policy which was adopted for that purpose.[3] If the national judge reads the words of the code against a background which is wholly constituted by his national law he may very easily misinterpret them in such a way as to defeat the whole object of unification.

It is also conceivable that some disturbance may be caused by the varying value attached to precedents in the different jurisdictions. When an English judge has interpreted a statutory rule his decision is binding on all co-ordinate and subordinate judges, and when the House of Lords has set the seal of its approval on any given interpretation it becomes binding on all the courts of law and can only be set aside or varied by legislation. The situation is somewhat different on the Continent. Theoretically precedents are not binding either on the French[4] or on the German[5] judges. But in practice the decisions of the Court of Cassation in France and of the *Reichsgericht* in Germany, though not absolutely binding, are treated with such respect by the subordinate courts that they are, to all intents and purposes, conclusive. The Court of Cassation may, however, depart from its previous rulings. The *Reichsgericht* may not do so except where this course is decided upon by a plenary session in which the various

1 See *Vagliano* v. *Bank of England* [1891] A.C. 145. Cf. Ennecerrus, Kipp and Wolf, *op. cit.* § 51, 1 (2); Planiol, *op. cit.* § 219.
2 See M. Olivier Jallu, *loc. cit.* at p. 25.
3 The Permanent Court of International Justice found no difficulty in considering evidence as to the negotiations and preliminary drafts leading up to the Treaty of Lausanne. McNair and Lauterpacht, *Annual Digest of Public International Law Cases*, Case 283 (1925–6), p. 371. Cf. Case 284, *ibid.* at p. 373.
4 See *ante*, p. 91.   5 *Ibid.*

divisions of the court sit together.[1] The result is that a continental judge can always, if he chooses to do so, break away from any interpretation of a statutory rule which has been adopted by other judges. He is not likely to do so if a higher court has on several occasions approved of such interpretation (i.e. where there is a *jurisprudence constante*), particularly where such court happens to be the one of the highest rank in the judicial hierarchy.[2] Still there is always the possibility that the English or American judges might be bound by a precedent, whereas on the Continent, in the absence of any *jurisprudence constante*, the judges may be at liberty to place whatever interpretation seems right to them on precisely the same form of words. Thus, in a recent case[3] the majority of the House of Lords construed the word 'wreck' in Section 1 of the Merchant Shipping Act of 1925 as having the same meaning that was given to it by the Court of Appeal in a case decided in 1913,[4] in spite of the fact that the Convention of Genoa, on which the Act is based, uses the words 'loss or foundering'. It is clear that the interpretation adopted by the House of Lords introduces an element which was never contemplated by the framers of the convention. In the absence of any international tribunal to which the matter can be referred for final decision it is always possible that the operation of a unified law might be thrown into confusion in this way. Not only may there be a difference between the interpretation of the law in England and elsewhere, but even within the frontiers of a continental state there may be varying interpretations, so that the rights of a litigant may come to depend on the venue of the trial of his case rather than on any legal principle. In this way we shall get a repetition of the tendency for parties to manœuvre for position which is one of the less pleasant features of present-day private international law. Various suggestions have been made from time to time with a view to overcoming this difficulty, of which the proposal to establish an International Court of Appeal has attracted most attention. There are very strong arguments, however, against this course. It would involve the building of yet another story on to a structure of existing appellate courts which is already top-heavy. It may also be doubted whether a court of this kind would at the present time command that degree of respect which would be indispensable to the satisfactory discharge of its functions.

Some difficulty may also arise from the fact that legal mentality varies

---

1 Ennecerrus, Kipp and Wolf, *op. cit.* § 39, II.
2 Amos, 'The "Code Napoléon" and the Modern World', *Journal of C.L.* (3rd Ser.), vol. x (1928), p. 225; Pound, 'The Theory of Judicial Decision', *Harvard L.R.* vol. xxxvi (1923), pp. 641, 647.
3 *Barras v. Aberdeen Steam Trawling Co.* [1933] A.C. 402.
4 *The Olympic* [1933] P. 92.

from country to country. This particular problem is too complex to be discussed in a general survey of the situation, but a French judge, who has in his mind certain concepts such as that of *abus des droits* or *ordre public*, may well interpret an international rule in a way different from that of his English colleague, who is a stranger to the juridical ideas underlying these concepts. Other instances could be given, such as the different principles governing the fixation of the time or place at which a contract is to be deemed to have been concluded, but the question is too involved and difficult to be discussed here.[1]

It is perhaps desirable to call attention, in conclusion, to a question which has been the subject-matter of some controversy on the Continent of Europe. The French Court of Cassation has ruled that the power of the courts to interpret the terms of an international convention is limited to cases in which private interests are involved. If the provisions of the convention relate to public interests (e.g. a matter of taxation), it has been held that the right of interpretation is vested in the appropriate executive authority and not in the courts of law.[2] It would seem, however, that this view is not generally accepted in France, and the question must be regarded as an open one at present.[3]

Conclusions

It has been the object of this brief survey to deal in outline with the differences between English and continental interpretative technique and with the problems which are peculiar to the interpretation of international statute law. So far as it is possible to arrive at any conclusions with regard to a question which has been but partially explored up to the present, and which has hitherto been dealt with chiefly by writers from a theoretical, as opposed to a practical standpoint, it would seem that the differences which exist do not constitute a fatal bar to the unification of law, although they are, no doubt, of such a nature as to create obstruction and to call for the exercise of caution when international legislation is in contemplation. There is in point of fact quite a considerable volume of international statute law in existence almost entirely in the form of maritime and labour law conventions, but it is of recent origin and no data are yet forthcoming upon which an opinion may be formed of the effect on such

1 Cf. Lauterpacht, 'The So-called Anglo-American and Continental Schools of Thought in International Law', *British Year Book of I.L.* vol. 13 (1932), p. 31, where a different view is taken of this question. It should be noted, however, that other considerations apply to private law conventions from those which are in issue in the case of international treaties.

2 See the decisions reported in *Revue de Droit International Privé*, 1912, p. 343, and Clunet, 1921, p. 970. See also Niboyet, *op. cit.* no. 37.

3 Niboyet, *op. cit.*

legislation of variations in interpretative technique. Two facts, however, appear to stand out. First of all it seems clear that the English and continental judges are in agreement in endeavouring to give effect to the intentions of the legislator. One may be permitted to doubt whether the application of theories of the social purpose of the law to the clearing away of ambiguities of language has in practice any marked influence on the process of interpretation. If a statutory rule is couched in ambiguous phraseology, a judge—whatever the system may be to which he owes allegiance—must find some solution of the difficulty, and it seems clear that he will always try to put himself in the place of the legislator, whether in so doing he claims to be seeking for the social purpose of the rule, or merely confines himself to the declaration of what he believes to have been the intention of the legislator as evidenced by the phraseology of the rule itself and its context. Secondly, if we pass from the question of the basis of interpretation to that of methods, it would seem that the main difference between English and continental interpretative technique is one of very great moment, namely, the fact that the continental judges are empowered to examine into the reports of parliamentary proceedings and other historical material for the purpose of ascertaining the intention of the legislator, whereas this right is almost wholly denied to the English-speaking judges. This is the crucial point, and it is impossible to exaggerate its importance. Professor H. A. Smith has recently argued very powerfully in favour of the continental principle.[1] The English rule, as he points out, has no common-law basis and is of modern origin. It is, moreover, in 'direct conflict with the methods of all rational investigation in the historical or scientific field'. A proposal for its abandonment would be fruitful of controversy, but at least it seems to be desirable to give the matter serious and careful consideration in view of the fact that it constitutes a wide divergence between our practice and that of the Continent which may have very unfortunate repercussions on any attempt for the removal of those legal barriers which constitute an impediment to intercourse between the nations.[2]

1 H. A. Smith, 'Interpretation in English and Continental Law', *Journal of C.L.* (3rd Ser.), vol. IX (1927), p. 153. See also Amos, 'Interpretation of Statutes', *Cambridge L.J.* vol. V (1934), p. 163.
2 This question is very fully discussed in Allen, *Law in the Making* (3rd ed.), Excursus B.

Chapter IX

THE PROBLEM OF LEGAL TERMINOLOGY

TRADITION tells us that confusion of tongues was the first cause of division among mankind. We may dismiss this as a fable, but there is no doubt that differences in the language of the law constitute not the least of the barriers which separate the various legal systems of the world. Other branches of learning possess a common vocabulary. The physician, the theologian, the mathematician, the chemist and the economist employ technical terms which are well understood throughout the scientific world, whilst legal terminology varies to a greater or lesser extent from country to country. Even in the case of laws framed in the same language an expression does not always correspond to the same juridical idea in all the countries concerned, and the same word may, with the lapse of time, even become invested with separate shades of meaning in different systems of law.

This diversity of legal terminology is not merely a source of embarrassment to comparative lawyers. It is also a matter of great practical importance, and it is certain that both the legal and the commercial world would welcome any expedient which can be devised to lessen the resulting inconvenience to intercourse between the nations. But the discussion of possible remedies requires a preliminary examination of the nature of the problem and an estimate of the consequences which result from terminological conflicts in each of the departments of the law in which obstacles are thus created either to scientific study and research or to the functioning of legal rules in practice.

Law, being a science, cannot dispense with the use of technical terms. Even those whose studies are limited to the rules of a single system find that considerable effort is required to master the language of the law, and the mental strain involved becomes much more serious when the comparative method of study and research is employed. Comparative lawyers are only too familiar with the kind of problem which lies concealed behind such words as *causa* and *consideration*. They know only too well the feelings of ineptitude and sometimes even of despair which overtake a person, however deep may be his knowledge of his own system, when he ventures as a novice into the field of comparative law. In fact, it requires a high degree of concentration on the task and very great perseverance if the obstacles presented by differences of language are to be overcome. The greatest strain is naturally experienced by a lawyer who passes from a legal language of the Continent of Europe, founded to a large extent on the phraseology of Roman law, to the curious and for the most part unscientific terminology of Anglo-American law. But the difficulties are mutual. It is true that attempts to find an equivalent in other languages for the *Trust* of Anglo-American law have failed because such renderings as *Fiducia*, *Prêt-Nom* and *Treuhand* must be regarded as unsatisfactory and misleading. Phrases such as *restraint on anticipation* or *special contract* are calculated to puzzle a French or German lawyer. Nor are matters improved by the fondness of English lawyers for Latin phrases and maxims. In fact, the phrase *indebitatus assumpsit* is among the most difficult of English legal expressions to explain to continental lawyers. On the other hand, an Anglo-American lawyer does not find it easy to understand such terms of foreign law as *intérêt négatif* or *positive Vertrags Verletzung*.

Equally confusing but far more dangerous is the situation arising from the employment in several systems of an identical term to denote different legal institutions or ideas. It is almost impossible from the standpoint of comparative studies to exaggerate the perils which lie hidden in terminology. For instance, the word *possession* is one which is used in all western systems of law, but its implications are not always the same. As Sir Maurice Amos and Dr Walton[1] have pointed out the differences between *possession* in French and in English law are 'curious and somewhat intricate' and render it inadmissible to use the word indiscriminately for purposes of comparison. Both English and French law use the word *bail* but in senses which are as far apart as the poles. It would be easy to give other illustrations, but this is not necessary because comparative lawyers are, unfortunately, only too familiar with the problems which flow from divergence in the meaning of technical terms of the law.

Mercantile law has drawn much of its terminology from business language, but the words employed do not always possess an equivalent meaning in all countries. In some instances commercial terms have been clarified and established by legal definition, but in others the courts of law have with great wisdom refrained from definition on the ground that the merchants themselves are not at one on the meaning to be attributed to a particular expression.[2] The vagaries of commercial terminology have led the International Chamber of Commerce to institute an inquiry into the meaning of certain terms in various countries with a view to the formulation of agreed international definitions.[3] This is significant; it

1 *Introduction to French Law*, p. 108, note (1).
2 See, for instance, the observations of Bailhache J. on the phrase 'revolving credit', *Nordskog* v. *National Bank* (1922) 10 Ll.L.Rep. 652.
3 Two manuals have been published by the International Chamber of Commerce, i.e. *Trade Terms* (1929) and *Incoterms* (1936).

would seem to be an answer to the charge so often levelled against lawyers that they are really responsible for difficulties of legal terminology because they desire in their own interests to envelop legal transactions in the camouflage of a jargon which only they themselves can understand. The fact that men of business find themselves in the same predicament is sufficient to dispose of the accusation.

Comparative lawyers suffer to a greater extent from ambiguities of language than the lawyers of the system in which the ambiguities occur, because they cannot always be expected to be aware that a foreign legal term is not well defined. Terminological uncertainty is one of the greatest difficulties which the student of comparative law encounters in his noviabe, and it is not easy to suggest a remedy for this state of affairs. Human speech is, at best, a somewhat imperfect vehicle for the expression of legal ideas, no matter what the language may be which is employed. In any event the removal of such ambiguities of expression is a matter for the attention of the lawyers of the particular system concerned rather than for that of the legal public in general.

The International Importance of Legal Terminology

Public international lawyers of all nations have in the course of time evolved a common terminology which at first sight may seem to be adequate as a basis of intercourse. But a new situation arose after the War of 1914–18, partly owing to the great increase in multi-lingual treaties and partly because the Permanent Court of International Justice was called upon in certain circumstances to apply the general principles of law recognised by civilised nations. This new orientation of the relative positions of public international law and municipal law had important consequences, one of which is that terms employed to denote the rights and duties of private individuals have become operative in the sphere of international relations. Such terms as 'abuse of rights' acquired importance in a wider sphere than that of private law.[1]

Internationally, the importance of differences in legal terminology lies chiefly in their bearing on the operation of international agreements. The drafting of treaties in two or more languages lends itself to misunderstandings which may easily result in contradictions or obscurities.[2] Treaties

1 See *ante*, p. 68, and Lauterpacht, *The Function of Law in the International Community*, Chapter XIV.

2 'No facts are more striking in this respect than the juridical misunderstandings attached to the Treaty of Versailles, the more notorious of which are: the mistake about the powers of President Wilson, the unlucky translation of the Covenant of the League of Nations by the French word *Pacte*, the *nudum pactum* of English law and the ambiguity hanging about the institution of international mandates.' Lévy-Ullmann, 'The Teaching of Comparative Law', *Journal of the S.P.T.L.* (1925), p. 21.

are often framed in the first instance in one of the languages in which they are to be promulgated and are then translated, a process which may, quite unwittingly, distort the real intentions of the treaty makers. The draftsman of the original text has the legal ideas of his own system in mind, and these ideas may be concealed from the translator. Conversely, the translator may be influenced by the concepts of his national law in carrying out his task, and without intending to do so may attribute a meaning to an expression or a phrase which was never contemplated. In *Dies* v. *British and International Mining and Finance Corporation*, Stable J.[1] was called on to construe the words *volonté* and *indemnité forfaitaire*, used in a contract drawn up in the French language. After hearing expert evidence on both sides he made the following observations: 'Where the words used signify, not a concrete object, but a conception of the mind, the process of the translator seems to be to ascertain the conception or thought which the words used in the language to be translated conjure up in his own mind, and then, having got that conception or thought clear, to re-symbolise it in words selected from the language into which it is to be translated. A possible danger, when the document to be translated is one on which legal rights depend, is apparent, inasmuch as the witness who is in theory a mere translator, in practice may construe the document in the original language and then impose on the Court the construction at which he has arrived.'

An instance of the kind of complication which can arise in this way is furnished by Article 296 (2) of the Treaty of Versailles. The original text was drafted by an English lawyer who used the term *suspension of contracts* against a background of the English rule according to which a contract is automatically determined if war breaks out between the countries of which the contracting parties are citizens or subjects. This was not appreciated by the translator, with the result that a conflict of meaning arose as between the English and French texts of the treaty.[2] The expression *equity*, for instance, is often used in international treaties without regard to the fact that *Équité*, *Billigkeit* and *Equity* have different connotations. It is no doubt true that the broad construction which is placed on the language of international treaties may go far towards preventing trouble from this source, but there is always a danger that a term employed in a multi-lingual treaty may be translated in such a way as to give rise to serious difficulties of interpretation, more particularly if each of the versions in different languages is of equal authority.

1 [1939] 1 K.B. at p. 733.
2 See *Binon* v. *The German Reich* (Germano–Belgian Mixed Arbitral Tribunal, 1 June 1922); *Recueil des décisions des tribunaux arbitrales mixtes*, vol. II (1923), p. 217.

The Problems of Multi-lingual Laws and Treaties

Differences of language may give rise to trouble both in municipal and in international law. Laws operating solely within the limits of a particular state may need promulgation in two or more languages owing to racial or other divisions of the population. This is the case, not only in Switzerland, but also in other countries in which there is more than one official language. International conventions concluded under the aegis of the League of Nations were also drawn up in French and English, whether they related to political or to economic questions. A somewhat special case is that of the unified laws of the Scandinavian countries which have been framed in several languages springing from a common origin.

A multi-lingual law or treaty inevitably contains within itself the germs of trouble, although the latent problems do not always come to a head. The difficulty arises, as has already been mentioned, out of the process of translation, because a law or treaty must always be drafted in one of the permitted languages and then be translated into the other language. This process is not always very successful: sometimes the reverse is the case, as in the instance of the English texts of the codes of Louisiana and Quebec. Even in the Swiss codes, which were compiled with meticulous care, difficulties have been created by inaccurate translation. We meet in the Swiss codes with such errors as the substitution of the singular for the plural and mistranslations such as *illicite* for *unbefugt*.[1]

The dangers arising from this source are avoided to a large extent if the multi-lingual texts are drafted in languages derived from a common stock, e.g. in the case of the Franco-Italian draft Code of Obligations and the various unified Scandinavian laws. The problem is most in evidence where the languages concerned differ widely and the subject-matter of the text is of such a nature as to raise the various terminological problems to which reference has already been made. It is obvious that the difficulties encountered in drawing up the two versions of the civil code of Quebec were much more serious than any which can have arisen in framing the Franco-Italian draft Code of Obligations.

Terminology gave rise to certain difficulties at the Geneva Conferences of 1930 and 1931 which resulted in the conclusion of the Conventions relating to Uniform Laws on Bills of Exchange, Promissory Notes, and Cheques. In order to avoid complications on this ground as far as was possible it was agreed that translations into German and Italian of the French and English original texts should be made in joint consultation between the German, Austrian and Swiss delegations and the Swiss and

---

1 For other examples see Williams, *Swiss Civil Code (Sources of Law)*, p. 31.

Italian delegations respectively. This was an example which might well be followed in the future if similar conditions prevail. Incidentally, it is not without interest to note that the translators in this instance were, according to the writer's information, assisted in some degree by the fact that they had an original text in two languages before them. What is not plain in a French text may be made clear in the English version or vice versa.[1]

The problem is nevertheless one which calls for a high degree of caution in the drafting of multi-lingual laws or treaties. In particular, it must be remembered that English judges, unlike their continental colleagues, are not at liberty to resort to _travaux préparatoires_ or other legislative memoranda when they are faced with ambiguities. If a mistranslation creeps into the English text of a multi-lingual law or treaty and the matter has to be adjudicated on by an English court, it may be impossible to avoid the consequences of the blunder.

The Need for Action

The present position in regard to legal terminology is one which seems to call for action. It is not only of great practical importance that some remedy should be found for the existing state of affairs, but something must also be done to relieve the comparative lawyer, as far as is feasible, from the linguistic problems which press upon him. The labour involved in the perusal of advanced legal treatises in a foreign tongue has to be experienced in order to be believed. It may be said without hesitation that difficulties in terminology have operated in the past and still operate to hamper—if not to deter—students and investigators from the employment of the comparative method of study and research. It may not be easy to find a remedy, but that is the next question which calls for consideration.

A Common Language of the Law

It is true, as has already been observed, that the difficulties with which we are dealing are less likely to arise between systems which are based on Roman law than between systems which do not go back to a common origin. This has led to the suggestion that a remedy may, perhaps, be found in a wider use of the phraseology of the Roman jurists.[2]

It is, however, more than doubtful if this expedient would improve matters to any substantial extent. There is a lesson to be learnt in this instance from the history of the law of England. Latin was, at least in theory, the official language of the English courts in the twelfth and

---

1 Cf. Williams, _loc. cit._   2 See _post_, p. 125.

thirteenth centuries, and continued to be used down to the eighteenth century for the purpose of drawing up the official records of legal proceedings.[1] For this and, perhaps, for other reasons, English lawyers, even at the present day, show great fondness for the use of Latin expressions and brocards. The Latin in question is generally of doubtful elegance or purity, owing, no doubt, to its medieval origin. Moreover, it is sometimes employed rather promiscuously. One is reminded of a very illustrious English practitioner of the eighteenth century who delighted in flourishing his Latin in the face of the judges and was rebuked by King George III, who gave him the friendly advice that he should 'stick to his good law and give up his bad Latin'. In any event it cannot be said that the use by English lawyers of expressions borrowed from the *Institutes* of Justinian, the *Digest* or the canon law has done much to lessen the problem presented by divergent terminology.[2] Such expressions are generally used in a sense which is peculiar to English law. It is almost impossible to convey to continental lawyers the exact sense in which an English lawyer uses the terms *in rem* and *in personam*. Even if we take a very widely used expression such as *bona fides*, we shall find that it means one thing in English law and another in the law of the Continent. In fact, it was stated at the Geneva Conference on the Law on Bills of Exchange in 1930 that French and German lawyers do not take the same view as to the precise meaning of *bona fides*.[3]

A good deal of English legal terminology is also of French origin. Down to the end of the seventeenth century the oral proceedings in the English courts were conducted in French. It must be confessed that this so-called *Law French* did not reach a very high standard of purity at any period, and that as time went on it became increasingly debased until it ended ingloriously amid general derision. In spite of this it played a very important part in the building up of the terminology of English law. It was said by Coke, a great English jurist of the seventeenth century, to be *vocabula artis* and to be so woven in the texture of the law as to render it impossible to abolish it.[4] In point of fact, however, the English legal terms which are derived from French or, perhaps more properly, from

1 Holdsworth, *History of English Law*, vol. II, p. 479.
2 See the observations of Lord Wright in *Smith Hogg* v. *Black Sea Insurance Co.* [1940] A.C. 997, at p. 1003: 'Counsel for the appellants has strenuously contended that the master's action, whether or not negligent, was a *novus actus interveniens*, which broke the *nexus* or chain of causation, and reduced the unseaworthiness from a *causa causans* to a *causa sine qua non*. I cannot help deprecating the use of so-called Latin phrases in this way. They only distract the mind from the true problem.'
3 *Records of the First Session of the International Conference for the Unification of Laws on Bills of Exchange, Promissory Notes and Cheques* (League of Nations Publications, II, Economic and Financial, 1930, II, 27).
4 Holdsworth, *loc. cit.* p. 481.

Anglo-Norman sources are precisely those which a continental lawyer finds it most difficult to understand. The sense in which Anglo-American law employs the term *nuisance* will serve as an illustration. The use of languages other than English by the lawyers and judges of England has in any event done little or nothing to lessen the difficulties due to terminological divergences.

It would seem to be clear that a universal language of the law is not merely a dream incapable of realisation but that it is a delusion to think that if it existed it would get rid of the problem with which we are concerned. Indeed a similarity of language often conceals a difference of ideas and so merely serves to create greater confusion. The removal of the curse of the Tower of Babel would fail to solve the problems with which we are concerned.

An International Juridical Dictionary

The proposal for the compilation of a dictionary of legal terms which would embrace the principal systems has many attractions as a possible solution of the terminological problems which present so much difficulty, not only to comparative lawyers, but also to the negotiators of international agreements, to the legal public in general and to the commercial community.

If a lexicon of this kind could be compiled its value would be almost incalculable. It would be a potent instrument in breaking down the barriers of mutual ignorance which at present split the lawyers of the world up into separate units and tend to produce a spirit of national self-sufficiency which does much to hamper the development of the law. We have a great deal to learn from one another in legal as well as other departments of life, and it is a reproach to lawyers that they have hitherto proved incapable of arriving at the free interchange of knowledge and ideas which has been achieved in other branches of learning.

The practical difficulties which the proposal involves are manifest. The task would be one of the first magnitude, giving rise to difficulties of a scientific and administrative character of which it is not possible to foresee the extent. The publication of such a dictionary would not be a profitable speculation from a business point of view, and it is more than doubtful whether a venture of this kind could be undertaken or carried out in an adequate manner by private enterprise.

A proposal for the compilation of an international dictionary or vocabulary of this description has been considered by the Academy of Comparative Law,[1] but no action appears to have been taken for the purpose of

1 See the report presented to the Academy by Professor Altamira, *Acta Academiae Universalis Jurisprudentiae Comparativae*, vol. II, p. 237.

translating the proposal into action. So far as the scheme has taken shape up to the present the suggested vocabulary would fall into two parts. The first of these would deal with terms of the law which are found in more than one system of law, whilst the second would explain terms which are peculiar to a particular system and to that system alone. It is contemplated that it should be drawn up in five languages, i.e. French, German, English, Spanish and Italian. The proposal envisages the establishment, first of all, of a number of committees, each of which would compile a list of the more important terms used in a particular system or group of systems of law and prepare a brief *exposé* of the meaning of such terms. The task of collating and arranging the results of the labour of these committees would devolve on an editorial committee with members drawn from the various systems concerned. The proposal is of a tentative character, and it is recognised that there are serious difficulties to be overcome. It is suggested that some of these could be surmounted by the employment of Latin as the language of the vocabulary.

The crucial question seems to be whether it is feasible to compile anything in the nature of such a dictionary or vocabulary. There are certain terms in every system of law which cannot be translated into another language *simpliciter* but must be explained at some length. If this should prove to be necessary to any considerable extent the result might be to deprive a work of this nature of much of its value because it would then cease to be a dictionary and become merely an epitome of foreign law. Prudence would, therefore, appear to dictate preliminary spade work of an experimental character. It would be possible, for instance, to select a particular topic such as the law of negotiable instruments and banking and to restrict the number of languages to be employed. If the subject selected is not too wide the number of languages could be increased, or if the languages are restricted in number then the nature of the subject-matter could be extended. But it is essential that the experimental stage should not be spread over an area which would be so wide as to prevent the completion of the task within a reasonable time and without undue labour and expense. If the experiment were to end in success not only would the results obtained be of value in themselves but much useful experience would have been gained as to the possible scope of the undertaking as a whole and of the problems arising in connection with its editorial and administrative aspects.

It is, however, essential that some international body of a representative character should make itself responsible for the undertaking, and this duty is one which would appear to fall within the scope of the Social and Economic Council of the new world organisation which has replaced the League of

Nations. This would help to secure the enterprise against the danger of the predominance of any particular school of legal thought which so often proves to be a peril to international legal collaboration, and would also avoid any difficulties that might otherwise be encountered in the provision of the necessary funds for the enterprise and the impartial selection of an adequate and competent editorial staff. The obstacles to be surmounted are without doubt formidable, but there is no reason to think that they are such as could not be overcome if the world can be persuaded of the importance and value of the work.

Many years must, however, elapse before the proposed international legal lexicon can even begin to take shape in any final form. In the meantime, when a serious obstacle to comparative study is presented by terminological problems, the wisest course would seem to be to resort to an expedient which is usually referred to as 'team work'. If this method is adopted the research is undertaken by two or more investigators, representing the various systems of law which are involved, thus giving an opportunity for consultation and collaboration which should go far to surmount any difficulties created by terminology. Even if complete success cannot be attained in this way, the pitfalls which lie in the way of the unwary will be discovered and the research will be preserved from the danger that its results may prove to be either erroneous or misleading owing to any misunderstanding of the language of the law.

Chapter X

COMPARATIVE LAW & LEGAL EDUCATION

As we have seen,[1] the recognition of comparative law as a factor in legal education can be traced back, so far as England is concerned, to the year 1869, when Maine became the first holder of the Chair of Historical and Comparative Jurisprudence at Oxford. But, in spite of the efforts which have been made, since that date, to establish comparative legal studies on a firm basis, little or no progress has been made, and the position, at the present time, cannot be described as satisfactory. It has, in fact, been described as 'shocking' when contrasted with the position on the Continent of Europe,[2] and, although this may appear to be a strong term to use in the circumstances, it is not without justification.

The failure of comparative law to secure wider recognition in the educational sphere is due to a variety of causes, most of which have no relation to its merits as an element in the training of students or to the possibilities which it offers in connection with legal research. The main obstacle to its development lies in the fact that the curricula of our University faculties and professional law schools are so tightly packed with subjects for examination that a late-comer such as comparative law must almost inevitably be excluded. The burden placed on the back of the student is quite as much as he can bear, and the tendency seems to be in the direction of the narrowing rather than the widening of curricula. 'Law' is a vast field of study with many aspects, some of which are what is known as 'cultural' whilst the others are 'vocational'. The Universities and the professional law schools have not, as yet, been able to come to terms with regard to the parcelling out of the territory between them. They are competitors, and the result has been that the Law Faculties seek to escape from the accusation that their teaching is purely theoretical whilst the Professional Bodies strive to avoid the charge that they only produce technicians, not scholars. For this reason a legal curriculum in England tends to develop into a jumble of cultural and vocational subjects often combined with a

1 *Ante*, p. 17. As regards the position in Scotland, see Lord Macmillan, 'Scots Law as a Subject of Comparative Study', *Acta Academiae Universalis Jurisprudentiae Comparativae*, vol. II, p. 9; Gardner, 'Study of Comparative Law in Great Britain', *Journal of C.L.* (3rd Ser.), vol. XIV (1932), p. 201. See also the Report of the Committee of the American Bar Association (Section of International and Comparative Law), 1940, *American Bar Association Journal*, vol. XXVI, p. 115, and *Journal of C.L.* (3rd Ser.), vol. XXIII (1941), at p. 62.

2 Lee, *Journal of the S.P.T.L.* (1936), p. 1.

system of 'options' which may lead to such strange results as the possibility that a student may submit himself for examination in Equity without knowing the Law of Property and vice versa. It goes without saying that cultural subjects, unless they are compulsory, are apt to be evaded by the average student, sometimes because he finds them difficult, but usually because he is doubtful of their value to him in his subsequent career as a practitioner. It is not a matter for surprise, therefore, that comparative law has so far been unable to gain more than a very modest footing for itself. An unfortunate consequence of this situation is that it has proved to be impossible to test the value of comparative instruction except to a very limited extent; its potentialities are thus, in a large measure, still uncertain.

For present purposes the question at issue must be examined in the light of the requirements of each of the three departments into which the study of the law is conventionally divided, namely, (*a*) undergraduate instruction, (*b*) post-graduate study, and (*c*) research. It is clear that different considerations must apply to each of these departments of study, because the circumstances in which the student carries out his task vary very widely in each instance. There are, however, certain problems which are common to all, and it may be profitable to examine these in the first instance before proceeding to discuss the matter as it arises in each individual case.

The Language Problem

How far is a knowledge of languages essential to a course of comparative study? The linguistic problem is the most obvious of the many difficulties which must be overcome, and there is no doubt that it often acts as a deterrent to comparative study. It is, usually, the first question to be raised by a would-be comparative student, and it is one which does not admit of a ready answer. Its importance is often exaggerated because a great deal of valuable comparative work can be done by a person who is in no sense of the word a linguist. It is, of course, true that certain types of comparative study can only be undertaken by those who have the gift of tongues. There are, for instance, aspects of comparative commercial law which cannot be pursued with profit without a knowledge of the principal European languages. On the other hand, it is possible to make a comparative study of the laws of England and those of other countries, such as Scotland, the Dominions, India[1] and the United States, without any linguistic trouble other than that resulting from possible differences

---

[1] There are gratifying signs of increased interest in comparative studies so far as the Indian law schools are concerned.

in legal terminology. Quite apart from this it is feasible to reduce the problem almost to vanishing point by confining the comparison to two systems of law as in the case of English and Roman law or English law and the French civil code. In other words, although the impediment of language may in certain circumstances prove to be a very serious obstacle, it cannot, standing alone, be regarded as a bar to comparative work.

The language problem is most in evidence in the domain of post-graduate study and research. In the case of the more simple or elementary forms of comparative study it assumes relatively slight proportions. So far as research is concerned, the remedy for the language difficulty, if one be needed, would seem to lie in the direction of 'team work'; but this is a matter which will be discussed later.

The Materials for Comparative Study

The most serious handicap imposed on comparative study in England lies in the paucity of suitable books and in the difficulty sometimes experienced in obtaining access to such of them as are available. This obstacle, combined with the language problem, has done much to discourage the use of the comparative method, but there is no reason to think that it constitutes an impediment which cannot be removed.

There are already a few introductory books which will help the beginner. Amos and Walton's *Introduction to French Law*, Lee's *Introduction to Roman-Dutch Law* and Buckland and McNair's *Roman Law and Common Law* fall into this category, though the last-mentioned work presupposes an intimate knowledge of both systems which is not possessed by everyone. Schuster's *Principles of German Civil Law* and Williams's *Swiss Civil Code* are hardly suited to novices, and are, moreover, to some extent obsolete. Burge's famous treatise on *Colonial and Foreign Law* in its modern garb [1] is incomplete and largely out of date. Certain other very useful works, such as Walton's *Egyptian Law of Obligations*, are intended for specialists rather than the general reader. The beginner is, in fact, ill-provided with text-books, and unless he is a linguist of some ability is often left to struggle along as best he can with the aid of such snippets of information as can be extracted from the foreign codes and other sources.

As regards Scots law, the excellent institutional works which exist give great scope for comparative study to this particular subject, and there is, of course, no language barrier to be surmounted. Scots law in many respects furnishes the most valuable training ground in comparative methods for the English law student, but it is doubtful whether the contrast between its rules and those of the common law is sufficiently marked

1 New Edition (1907–28).

to stimulate the interest of the student. The Restatements published by the American Law Institute[1] have opened the way to a quickening of knowledge of American Law on this side of the Atlantic and to a closer appreciation of the divergences between our law and that of the United States. As in the case of the laws of the British Empire the similarity of principle and of language between English and American law enables comparative studies to be pursued without the aid of introductory manuals provided that the other materials are available. The problem of text-books for the beginner is, however, a real one in the case of most foreign systems of law and one can only hope that it may be overcome eventually by the publication of more introductory manuals. Treatises of this kind could be most suitably produced by team work between an English comparative lawyer and a foreign colleague since it is only possible in this way to steer clear of the danger, on the one hand, that the foreign law may be misunderstood and, on the other hand, that the subject may be presented to an English student in a way which is unattractive or perhaps even unintelligible to him. In a work of this kind it is essential that the legal mentalities of the two systems should be focused on the point at which they impinge on one another and this is a task which calls for collaboration.

If we pass from the requirements of the novice to those of persons engaged in post-graduate study or in comparative research the situation is somewhat discouraging owing to the difficulty of securing the necessary materials. This means that unless the student has the means and the time to travel in search of them he will, at the very least, be seriously hindered in his work and may even be compelled to abandon it. A distinction must be drawn in this respect between research into the law of the British Empire or the United States and the study of rules of the civil-law countries. In the case of the first-mentioned systems the obstacles are not so grave though they are sufficiently disconcerting to invite the attention of the authorities responsible for the upkeep of the English law libraries. There is not only a dearth of books on Imperial and American law but much of the material which is available is out of date. There is room in this direction for the benevolence of those who have at heart the promotion of closer cultural relationships between the English-speaking nations. The meagre endowment of legal research in England is mainly responsible for this state of affairs, as the resources of most of our libraries are, in the financial sense, almost entirely absorbed by the purchase of the necessary

---

1 The restatements of main interest to English lawyers are those which deal with the law of Contract, Agency, Torts, Conflict of Laws, Property, Trusts and Restitution.

English law books. It is no doubt true that a diligent search in the libraries of the Dominion and Colonial Offices and the Inns of Court might bring to light the greater part of the Statute Law and the law reports of the British Overseas Possessions, but there is a scarcity of text-books and legal periodicals which makes it extremely difficult for an English lawyer to keep in touch with developments in the rest of the Empire. Mr Justice Greenshields, of the Quebec Bench, in his address to the Conference of the Universities of the Empire held at Cambridge in 1932, called attention to this matter and to the difficulty which it might place in the way of the argument of appeals to the Privy Council. In any event the position is one which does not reflect credit on this country, more especially when regard is had to the fact that all this material is available in the principal law libraries of the United States.

In the case of American law books the situation is also unsatisfactory. There is a complete run of the Federal and the State Reports in the library of the Middle Temple which has been placed there by the generous action of American lawyers who have always regarded this as the one of the Inns of Court with which they have the closest ties. Some of the American law reviews, but not all, are available, whilst the leading American text-books are very poorly represented on the shelves of our libraries.

When we turn to foreign law, in the wider sense of the term, the position is even less encouraging, though it furnishes no ground for thinking that research is rendered impossible. The main repositories of these books are the Library of the Foreign Office, the Squire Law Library at Cambridge and the Schuster Library of Comparative Law at the London School of Economics.[1] If the researcher has the time to explore the contents of these libraries he will find that he can in one place or the other procure access to the principal French, German and Italian text-books, and collections of statutes and law reports. Whether he is likely to discover anything beyond this is a matter for speculation.

The most up-to-date of these collections is, probably, that in the Squire Law Library at Cambridge, which houses some 2000 foreign law books, the great majority of which have been purchased recently. There are still some serious gaps in this collection, but according to the testimony of foreign lawyers, by whom it has been inspected, it may be described as containing a reasonable minimum of the materials required by comparative students. It is strongest in books on the law of obligations and private

1 At the moment of writing the Bodleian Library at Oxford is poorly provided with foreign law books, but there are grounds for the belief that steps will shortly be taken to remedy this state of affairs. A search in the Library of the British Museum sometimes brings foreign law books to light. See Pollock's note, *Journal of C.L.* (N.S.), vol. v (1903), p. 85.

international law to which particular attention has been directed, and contains items such as the Swiss law reports and certain foreign legal periodicals which are not obtainable elsewhere in England at present. Next to it ranks the library bequeathed to the Society of Comparative Legislation by the late Dr Schuster and transferred to the London School of Economics.

The general result is that if one looks long enough and hard enough it is possible to obtain the more important books of the principal law systems, but the question which leaps to one's mind is why a person engaged in research should be compelled to indulge in this waste of time and effort? In any event it is clear that the facilities available in England are far inferior to those to be found, for example, in the Harvard Law Library. Moreover, the distribution of existing books over a wide area in England without any attempt being made to indicate their location and the absence of any real systematic effort to keep some of the collections up to date is a reproach to English legal scholarship. It is well that this issue should be faced squarely because it is more than doubtful whether any very marked progress can be made in comparative studies in this country until some steps are taken to remedy this unfortunate situation.

Much can be done by putting existing resources to the best use. In the first place effect could be given to the strong recommendation of the Atkin Committee on Legal Education that a special committee should be formed to co-ordinate the activities of the English law libraries and to secure 'the pooling of their resources and the repair of deficiencies'.[1] This report deals, in particular, with two important matters. First of all, attention is directed to the fact that 'without recourse to each library it is difficult to ascertain where a book, absent from the one in which the student is working, is to be found. Printed catalogues in some cases exist, but they are not up to date. It is unfortunate that the wealth of material should not be made more easily available to students and practitioners alike. We consider that one of the first steps in promoting legal research should be the formation of a central catalogue of the contents of the London Law Libraries.'

A central catalogue of this kind is such an obvious solution of one of the great obstacles to legal research that it is somewhat surprising that nothing has yet been done in the matter, for the labour and expense would not be excessive, even if the central catalogue should—as is eminently desirable—be extended to the law libraries at Oxford and Cambridge. But further than this the Legal Education Committee also recommended that steps should be taken to secure 'co-operation between the libraries

---

1 *Report of the Legal Education Committee* (1934), Cmd. 4663.

and the pooling of their resources'. The Committee pointed out that this applies chiefly to Dominion and Colonial text-books and reports and important series connected with foreign law, but extends also 'to all the material necessary for adequate research in comparative law, the most fruitful of all forms of legal research'. To maintain a complete series of even all the colonial reports taxes the resources and the space of any law library. The states and provinces from which reports issue are very numerous, and it is probable that while one set should be reasonably available, it is not necessary for every library to have a complete series. Nor in fact do they, but there is no co-ordination, and duplicate sets from one colony might be found in some libraries, while reports from others are wholly lacking from all. 'It would', say the Committee, 'obviously be of advantage if some measure of agreement could be attained by which the provision of the text-books, statutes and reports of specific colonies could be undertaken by specific libraries, and if the same method could be applied to material for the study of foreign law.' The Committee urged that the various library authorities should be called together to carry these suggestions into effect, but, up to the present, the matter still rests where it was. It is possible that this state of suspense may be due to the fact that public attention has become concentrated on the main recommendation of the Committee for the establishment of an Institute of Legal Research in London, but it is to be regretted that no steps have been taken to give effect to a suggestion which could be carried out without in any way prejudicing other issues.

The creation of an Institute of Legal Research would, no doubt, involve the building up of a library of comparative law as an annexe to the Institute, and the question therefore presents itself of the policy which should be pursued in carrying out a scheme for the establishment of a collection of foreign law books in an English environment. To begin with, we may stress the undesirability of piling up a vast and indiscriminate assortment of books purchased at random from booksellers' catalogues. No library can afford to give unlimited space to foreign law books, and a process of selection, therefore, becomes inevitable. This process will, broadly speaking, be governed by the following considerations: first of all, what is the geographical area to be covered? Is an attempt to be made to cover the law of all countries or only that of certain selected countries? Secondly, is the collection to be of a general character and to cover every aspect of law or is it to be confined to certain topics? Lastly, is any restriction to be imposed on the type of law book to be admitted to the shelves? These are, in outline, the questions to be decided.

Theoretically, a collection of foreign law books should, no doubt, cover the whole field of law, but, in practice, the wisdom of such a policy is open to question. Quite apart from the difficulties of a financial or administrative order which it would create, it would result in an accumulation of a mass of obsolete or obsolescent law unless an almost superhuman degree of vigilance is exercised. An attempt might be made to maintain a complete collection of codified law and to keep it up to date, but this policy can be criticised on the ground that rules of law are apt to mislead unless they can be read against a background of their interpretation by the national judges and the criticism of legal authors. There appears to be little doubt that some selection is imperative and, in this connection, it should be remembered that the importance of a system of law to a comparative lawyer may have little to do with the political or economic importance of the country to which the system belongs. Swiss law is, for instance, in many ways the most instructive and interesting of the modern systems. It may be added that no useful purpose seems to be served, as a rule, by the acquisition of books in languages which no one using the library is likely to understand.

The second question, namely, whether a library of comparative law should be confined to certain legal topics, is an aspect of a major problem, i.e. of the extent to which comparative study and research can be pursued with profit. It will be sufficient to say that the library policy must be adjusted to the general policy which is followed by the institution of which the library forms part.

The last question, namely, the choice of books within the predetermined categories is, probably, the one which, in practice, tends to give rise to the most serious difficulty. The volume of legal literature published annually in foreign countries is such as to beggar all description. One example will suffice: in the United States alone over 62,000 statutes were passed during the five years preceding the War of 1914–18, and during the same period over 65,000 decisions were included in the printed volumes of American reports.[1] In 1933 the American law reviews alone numbered more than 600 volumes[2] whilst from every quarter in Europe statutes, law reports, legal periodicals, text-books, theses and monographs come pouring from the press in a never-ceasing stream. It is quite impossible for an English comparative lawyer to find his way amid this impenetrable jungle of paper and ink, and he must rely on such expert advice as he can obtain from abroad and on book reviews. The very greatest care is neces-

---

1 *Ex relatione* Elihu Root in presenting the report which led to the foundation of the American Law Institute ('The American Law Institute', by Hessel E. Yntema in *Legal Essays in tribute to Orrin Kip McMurray*, at pp. 664–5).

2 This figure is taken from the Introduction to *Selected Readings in the Law of Contract*, published by the Association of American Law Schools.

sary, therefore, in the purchase of treatises or other books on foreign law, and it is well to act on the presumption that any particular book, which is not obviously important, is not needed. This is more especially the case as regards the doctorate theses which are published on the Continent in vast numbers in order to comply with University regulations. Some of these dissertations are valuable, and no work should be rejected solely because it happens to fall within this category, but the great bulk of this material can be disregarded. Legal periodicals published abroad also furnish a serious problem because, although they are, generally speaking, of great value to the researcher, they are apt to be looked at askance by the librarian who sees in them an ever-increasing demand on available shelf room, a constant drain on income owing to the renewal of subscriptions and a *damnosa haereditas* in the shape of the necessity of constantly recurring expense for binding. But it is desirable to include as many of these periodicals in a collection as is reasonably possible because they furnish one of the best means available of keeping in touch with developments abroad. Here again, the question of the languages in which they are published is an important element to be taken into account.

The difficulties and problems with which we have been dealing are of a formidable character. So far as they are financial or administrative in character they must be solved by the authorities of the learned bodies charged with the promotion of legal research in England, and much might be done in certain directions if effect were given to the recommendations of the Legal Education Committee.[1] The matter of providing access to information on current changes in the law is, however, one which has an international aspect and is of great importance to all the countries concerned. Valuable work in disseminating information is done by certain learned societies,[2] but they are handicapped, as a rule, by the fact that they are in much the same position as the individual student or researcher, and have to obtain their material indirectly instead of being in a position to demand it as of right from the governments concerned. There is thus

[1] The establishment of the proposed Institute of Legal Research would be of great value in this connection. The Institute would be able to get into touch with similar bodies abroad and to act to some extent as a clearing-house of information as to changes in the law. It would, in a measure, be able to discharge the functions of the French Government Bureau of Foreign Legislation. But, immediately, the most important need is for some degree of co-ordination of the existing library facilities in England.

[2] The Society of Comparative Legislation publishes an annual survey of the legislation of the British Empire and the United States. Other useful publications are the *Annuaire de Législation* of the Société de Législation Comparée, the *Annuario di Diritto Comparato* issued by the Istituto di Studi Legislativi under the editorship of Professor Galgano, the *Revue de Droit Maritime* and the *Bulletin of the International Juridical Institute*.

in some cases very considerable 'time lag' in making the information available. A question which will undoubtedly arise in the future is whether the governments of the world should not be asked to give the same assistance to legal as they already do to medical research, and one of the services which they might very appropriately render would be the establishment of an international centre for the collection and distribution of information as to current changes in the law of all countries.[1] It is only in this way that comparative study and research can be freed from its greatest bugbear at present, namely, the difficulty in discovering the exact state of the law of a country at any given moment.

Comparative Law as an Undergraduate Subject

It is generally assumed that comparative law is an unsuitable subject for students in the earlier stage of their apprenticeship to the law, and there are many cogent arguments in favour of this view. The difficulties involved are manifold and obvious; some of them are educational, others are connected with the administrative machinery of law schools. All are, however, of a serious character, and if comparative law can be introduced at all into elementary legal education, it seems clear that this can only be done in a very tentative form and to a limited extent. A scrutiny of the syllabus of any one of the elementary examinations in law is sufficient to afford convincing evidence of the very serious practical difficulties which attend any attempt to widen the scope of the teaching and examination to which the syllabus is related.

Nevertheless, it does not appear that the use of the comparative method in elementary legal instruction is either inherently impracticable or undesirable. There is no need to elevate comparative law to the dignity of a separate subject, with its own lectures, teachers and examination papers. It should be perfectly feasible to dovetail comparative instruction into one of the courses devoted either to the usual English law subjects, or, perhaps, to one of the cultural subjects, such as jurisprudence or conflict of laws. A compact topic within the subject could be selected and treated comparatively and the comparison could be limited to English law and one other system of law, preferably Scots law, Roman law, or the French

---

1 Action of this nature was foreshadowed in the third recommendation of the Final Act of the International Conference on Bills of Exchange held at Geneva in 1930: 'The Conference further recommends that the Parties to the Convention providing Uniform Law for Bills of Exchange and Promissory Notes should communicate to one another the text of the most important judgments given in their respective territories coming under the application of the said Convention.' *Records of the First Session of the International Conference for the Unification of Laws on Bills of Exchange, Promissory Notes and Cheques* (League of Nations Publications, II, Economic and Financial, 1930, II, 27).

civil code.¹ 'Offer and acceptance' could, for instance, be dealt with in this way within the four walls of a course on the English law of contract without imposing any undue strain on the teacher or his pupils. In the hands of a competent instructor two—or, at the most, three—lectures along these lines would arouse the interest of the student and stir him up to think for himself. Law teachers are only too familiar with the type of student who accepts a rule of law as axiomatic and is content to memorise it without stopping to consider why the rule was brought into existence, what it was designed to achieve, and whether it is the only just and reasonable solution of the problem in human affairs to which it relates. Maine observed that 'the student who has completed his professional studies is not unnaturally apt to believe in the necessity, and even in the sacredness, of all the technical rules which he has enabled himself to command',² and this is as true of our students to-day as it was of those contemplated by Maine more than sixty years ago.

There is another argument frequently advanced against the use of the comparative method in legal instruction. It is said that it becomes superfluous because the element of comparison is already provided for by the inclusion of Roman law as well as English law in courses leading to a first degree. This is an argument which would carry very considerable weight if it were not for the fact that Roman law is not always a compulsory subject and that, in any event, the average student is not likely to indulge in comparison unless he is encouraged to do so by his teachers or examiners.

The suggestion is sometimes made that comparison may have the effect of creating confusion in a student's mind. This is an objection which does not appear to rest on solid grounds. In the first place, if there is any substance in the suggestion, it should operate equally—and perhaps even with greater force—to exclude the teaching of Roman law. Secondly, provided that the topic for comparison is selected with due care, its effect, far from creating confusion, should be to impress the relevant rules of English law more clearly on the student's mind. He will see them projected against a background of another system of law and therefore in stronger relief than is the case when they are presented to him in an axiomatic form. Foreign travel is usually regarded as possessing high cultural value, and it is difficult to see why an occasional and reasonably limited excursion by teachers and pupils into the territory of foreign law should not prove to be of equal benefit to both.

There are grounds for the belief that experiments made with elementary

---

1 An experiment of this kind seems to have been made in the paper on the Digest in the Honour School of Jurisprudence at Oxford. See Lee, in *Journal of the S.P.T.L.* (1936), at p. 7.   2 Maine, *Village Communities*, p. 6.

comparative teaching, on the lines indicated, have met with some success.[1] The language problem is not likely to arise because, if the comparison is limited to English and either Roman law, Scots law or the French civil code, such elementary teaching need not call for a greater knowledge of languages than that possessed by the average law student. Roman law undoubtedly lends itself well to comparison with certain aspects of English law, but there is much to be said in favour of extending the comparison to modern civil law. University students are apt to look on Roman law as 'dead' law, and feel that they have had as much of it as they can stomach by the time they are required to turn to the study of English law. Their interest in Roman law might, in fact, revive if they were shown how a modern civil-law system seeks to adapt the Roman principles and rules to the requirements of present-day society.

It would be idle to attempt to disguise the existence of certain practical difficulties which lie in the way of the adoption of the proposals which have been outlined. The text-book problem arises, but such works as Buckland and McNair's *Roman Law and Common Law* and Walton and Amos's *Introduction to French Law* will go far towards meeting the difficulty, and it is to be hoped that other works of this kind will make their appearance when the need for them is recognised. A more serious matter is the relative scarcity of teachers who would be competent or willing to give some of their instruction on comparative lines. It is not to be expected that law teachers will, in existing conditions, be prepared to equip themselves in large numbers as comparative lawyers; the subject does not at present offer much opportunity of a livelihood or of academic or professional distinction. But this problem should not be treated as insoluble, especially as there are now in this country many scholars from foreign lands whose services could be utilised in this direction. Moreover, if post-graduate study and research should develop, as appears probable, along comparative lines, the teaching strength available for this particular purpose would be materially increased.

The Post-graduate Study of Comparative Law

The term 'post-graduate' is commonly used to indicate that type of legal study which is undertaken by students who have already obtained either a professional qualification or a first degree in law. Many of them desire to widen their knowledge but are unable or unwilling to embark

---

1 *Ex relatione*, Professor Goodhart, Mr F. H. Lawson and Dr Wortley. See *Report on Comparative Law*, and *Journal of C.L.* (3rd Ser.), vol. XXII (1934), p. 74. The regulations for the optional paper in Scots Law of Contract and Reparation in Part II of the Law Tripos at Cambridge make definite provision for the comparison of the relevant rules of English and Scots law.

upon a course of research either because they have not the necessary leisure or because they do not feel themselves competent to undertake a task of such difficulty.

This particular sphere of legal education seems to be well adapted to the employment of comparative methods of study. The students concerned may be presumed to be mature and to have acquired a sound knowledge of the principles of their own law and a certain acquaintance with some of its more detailed aspects. The administrative difficulties which arise in the case of undergraduate or elementary study are mostly absent or assume a less acute form. There is much less difficulty in regard to lecture time-tables or to the provision of the necessary instruction. At least two Universities, Cambridge and London, have definitely adopted the policy of making comparative law one of the subjects for their post-graduate degrees. In the case of the Cambridge LL.B. degree all students, with certain exceptions of a special and limited character, must pass in a paper on the comparative aspects of a selected subject in English and Roman law.[1] Candidates for the London LL.M. degree who take Conflict of Laws must study the subject comparatively. There are good grounds for thinking that in both these cases the new venture has justified itself.

A restricted knowledge of languages and the scarcity of suitable books may create difficulty. These problems are, in effect, closely connected, because, although the text-books are there, most of them are in foreign languages. This obstacle, however, is not insuperable, since a fair knowledge of Latin and French is all that is necessary in most cases. The language difficulty also disappears if the comparison is made between the English law and the law of Scotland or the British Dominions and the United States, though, oddly enough, the necessary text-books may in this event be even more difficult to procure in this country than French or German law books. It would seem, at first sight, as if the future of comparative legal instruction lies almost entirely within the sphere of study for a post-graduate degree, but the number of students who are prepared to enter upon a course of this kind is relatively small, and many of them are foreigners anxious to obtain an English law degree. If comparative instruction is to become an important element in legal education one may, perhaps, be permitted to doubt if much will be achieved until such instruction is able to find its way not only into the post-graduate but also into the undergraduate spheres of study, even if only in a tentative and restricted form.

The case of the foreign law student is of a somewhat special character. He cannot, as a rule, afford the time to obtain a first degree in English

1 See Mr Hanbury's observations on this paper in *Journal of S.P.T.L.* (1931), p. 22.

law in the ordinary way. Most of these students can only spare one or, in rare cases, two years to the study of English law. The existing post-graduate courses of study are hardly suitable to them. The average foreign student can, of course, be examined over again in subjects which he has already studied abroad, but he cannot be regarded as having a knowledge of English law which will fit him for a post-graduate course. For this reason the University of Cambridge has instituted a Diploma in Comparative Legal Studies, which enables a student, with the approval of the Law Faculty, to select a subject for comparative study. He engages in a year's work under supervision and is required to submit a dissertation on his subject. This need not display originality, but must afford evidence of the fact that the candidate has made a serious study of that part of the law of England which bears on his subject. The outbreak of war has, for the time being, frustrated the development of this scheme, and it is, therefore, not possible to say more than this—that it has proved to be an attraction to foreign students and has led to good work being done. The weekly Seminar in Comparative Law held at Cambridge has done much to encourage the study of foreign law, and some published work of modest, though not negligible, character stands to its credit.

Research

The problem of comparative research is closely bound up with the question of legal research in general. In certain authoritative quarters doubt has been expressed as to the value of legal research, except in the domain of legal history, jurisprudence, and public and private international law. This attitude towards research is based on a belief that the fundamental notions of law have assumed a definite form and that legal research tends consequently to degenerate into an over-elaboration of minor legal problems, which are in some instances purely of academic interest and in others of no particular value either in promoting legal knowledge or in leading to the development or reform of the law. It is unwise to generalise on any question of this nature, but it would certainly seem that in the case of English law there is very little room for academic research unless it is historical or is connected with legal philosophy or international problems. The fields of the common law and equity have been ploughed up to such an extent that the area left for further cultivation is of a very limited description.[1] There are, it is true, certain departments of English law, such as commercial law, in which much research remains to be done, but the person described by Maine 'as a learner who has just

1 Cf. Cohn, 'The Task and Organisation of Comparative Jurisprudence', *Juridical Review* (1939), p. 134.

mastered his subject' is not, as a rule, qualified or equipped to undertake a task of this kind, which requires considerable experience of the working of the law and a certain familiarity with business practice. The result has been to create a condition of stagnation which is revealed by the very small number of Doctorates in Law which are being conferred, at present, by the English Universities.

What is the remedy for this state of affairs? The answer seems to be obvious. So far as research students are concerned, comparative law offers opportunities for creative work which can hardly be equalled. The territory which it covers is largely virgin soil, and the researcher, as a rule, runs very little risk that his discoveries may have been anticipated. The subjects for investigation are so numerous and varied that he will find little difficulty in selecting one which will enable him to engage in work which suits the bent of his mind and coincides with whatever plans he may have made for the future. Jurisprudentialists, Roman lawyers, legal historians, international lawyers, students of the common law and equity and legal specialists of all kinds find that the employment of the comparative method opens up new avenues of research along which an escape can be found from stagnation. Comparative research also affords great opportunities for 'team work', and may thus render possible the carrying out of investigations in circumstances of difficulty which would be a deterrent to individual research.

But comparative research, together with all other forms of legal research, suffers severely from the reluctance of graduates in law to enter on the task. The majority of English University law students are satisfied to obtain a first degree and the necessary qualification to practise in the branch of the legal profession which they have chosen. It is only rarely that they are prepared to extend their University career beyond the period of three years which normally suffices for the acquisition of a degree in law. They are, moreover, actively discouraged from undertaking research by the attitude of the legal profession; they are told that 'the law'—by which is meant the practice of the law—'is a jealous mistress', and that they must never allow themselves to be diverted from their purely professional preoccupations by activities which do not operate directly to bring grist to the professional mill. Thus it comes about that the younger generation of our lawyers, particularly if they are members of the Bar, are made to feel that their careers may be jeopardised if they should be so unfortunate as to become known as theoretical rather than practical lawyers. The writing of a book which does not take the form of a practitioner's manual, severely practical in character and devoid of all literary flavour, is a highly dangerous adventure for the young barrister or solicitor.

This impediment, however, is not peculiar to comparative research; it is created by the lack of co-ordination and collaboration which, unfortunately, still exists in England between the profession and the Universities. The causes which underlie this phenomenon and the steps which could be taken to find a remedy are outside the scope of our present inquiry. Nor are we concerned with questions of University organisation or administration, because, apart from the vital matter of library facilities, there is no reason to believe that any permanent obstacles to comparative research exist in this connection. The language problem, though it undoubtedly restricts the potential area of research, cannot, for reasons which have already been stated, be regarded as an insurmountable barrier. One of the most serious impediments lies in the scarcity of the materials obtainable in this country for comparative work in general, though this is a question which is mainly of a financial nature, as the difficulty could be overcome by a relatively modest expenditure of money, which can only be regarded as prohibitive to the extent to which it might result in funds being diverted from other and more pressing needs of education and research. Further, the difficulties created by the shortage of materials could, in most cases, be overcome either wholly or in part by permitting and encouraging the researcher to travel in search of his materials and to study on the spot and with the help of experts the foreign aspects of the subject which he has chosen for investigation.

It is, however, undeniable that comparative research, unless it is merely of a descriptive nature, requires a very high degree of care, patience and industry. The difficulties which must be surmounted and the toil which is involved may be such as to daunt even the most able and best equipped investigator. This has resulted in the adoption of 'team work' for the carrying out of a great deal of recent comparative research. Team work is still in the experimental stages and has not yet been tried out to the full extent, but enough has been done to make it fairly clear that it will ultimately solve many of the problems which arise. It assumes several forms. An individual investigator may select his own collaborators; or machinery for collective research may be created by the establishment of 'Institutes of Comparative Law', such as those which have become very popular in the civil-law countries. Some of these Institutes are either official or semi-official in character, such as the Rome Institute for the Unification of Private Law, the Italian Institute of Legislative Studies, and the Berlin Institute for Foreign Law and Private International Law. Others are attached to Universities, such as the Institutes of Comparative Law in Paris and Lyons. In certain cases the work of an Institute may be carried on by a more or less permanent staff, but the University Institutes build up their teams from the general body of research students. In fact, the University Institute is often merely the outward symbol of the existence within the walls of the University of facilities for comparative research. The special type of Institute which enjoys official sanction and support is, as a rule, the more efficient body; it can command the services of trained and skilled personnel and is financially and materially better equipped. It is also more likely to be in a position to establish contacts with non-legal elements which may have to be consulted in order to secure the best results from comparative research of certain types, e.g. government departments or professional or commercial bodies. On the other hand, it may be subject to certain disabilities, due to the fact that it comes more or less under State control. Excellent work has been done by the University Institutes, but their output is somewhat uneven in quality owing, no doubt, to the fact that their personnel is of a fluctuating character and to the occasional necessity of giving an innings to the weaker members of the team. The system of collaboration between individual researchers has certain advantages over the other forms of collective research. It appears on the whole to be more flexible; the person whom we may describe as the principal investigator can choose his colleagues at large and select those best fitted to give him the assistance which he requires. He is also free from any restrictions which may, in certain circumstances, be imposed by governmental or academic policy. On the other hand, he is often handicapped by financial and other obstacles, which are less likely to arise if an Institute makes itself responsible for the carrying through of a piece of research work. Where it is a question of large-scale research, such as that embarked on by the League of Nations in the case of the civil status of women, there can be little doubt but that the Institutes are best fitted to deal with the situation.

The problem of adequate teaching strength does not loom so large in the case of research as in other spheres of legal education. It is, however, desirable, if not essential, that the research student should be able to resort to someone of greater knowledge and experience than himself for advice in connection with the choice of his subject, the method he is to pursue and the materials which are available. This is a matter which arises in connection with research of all kinds, whether legal or otherwise it presents no special features in the case of comparative law, though it raises the question, incidentally, of the necessity for the inclusion in the teaching staff of Universities of the necessary personnel for the purpose.

The only conclusion at which it is possible to arrive at present is that comparative research has not yet entered on the final stage of its development. Individual research, team work by individuals and the organisation of research by bodies especially created for the purpose—all these expedients are called on to play their part in the development of comparative legal studies. Much will, of course, depend upon the nature of the research which is being undertaken and on the capabilities of the researchers, but the situation is such as to call for the employment of every agency which may help to keep comparative research in being and to promote its development. The appreciation of the relative merits of the results achieved in each case must be left to the judgment of posterity.

Chapter XI

THE MOVEMENT FOR THE UNIFICATION OF PRIVATE LAW[1]

A WORK which purported to indicate the nature and aims of comparative law without giving some account of the movement for unified law would be incomplete, because not the least important, and, certainly, the best known, of the purposes for which the process of comparison can be utilised is its employment in connection with the unification of private law. Moreover, a certain confusion of thought prevails as to the purpose of unification, and as to the circumstances in which it can be regarded as an effective instrument for the removal of barriers to international intercourse and co-operation, created by the existence of conflicting rules of law. No apology would, therefore, seem to be required for a brief examination of the movement for 'unified law' and of the aims which have inspired it.

The Origin and Development of the Movement for Unification

The movement is essentially modern in its origin. It is true that the first impulse towards unification appears about the beginning of the seventeenth century and coincides with the emergence of conflicts of law due, in part, to the growth of centralised government and, in part, to the breaking down of barriers which formed an obstacle to trade and to travel. The gradual disappearance of provincial autonomy in western Europe was followed by a movement for the internal unification of local customs and ordinances, but how far this process took the form of the reception of Roman law, and how far it consisted in the blending of existing rules of local law, is a matter beyond the scope of this work.[2] It is interesting to recall that King James I was probably the first of the unificationists. He contemplated the unification of the laws of England and Scotland but was dissuaded from proceeding with it by Lord Bacon.[3]

[1] Much has been written on the various separate attempts which have been made to unify specific rules of law, but the literature on the question as a whole is not voluminous. Reference may be made to Giannini, 'Le mouvement pour l'unification du droit privé en Europe', *Nouvelle Revue de Droit International Privé*, vol. I (1934), p. 21; Kennedy, 'The Unification of Law', *Journal of C.L.* (Ser. 2), vol. X (1909), p. 214; Balogh, *Acta Academiae Jurisprudentiae Universalis*, vol. I, p. 894 *passim*; Nolde, 'La Codification du Droit International Privé', *Recueil des Cours de l'Académie de D.I.* (1936).

[2] See Hazeltine, 'The Renaissance and the Laws of Europe' (*Cambridge Legal Essays*), pp. 163 *et seq.*

[3] 'A Preparation for the Union of Laws', see *ante*, p. 15.

The first proposals for unification of law on a world-wide scale seem to have been those submitted by Professor Leone Levi[1] to the Prince Consort in connection with the Exhibition of 1851. They took the form of a suggested draft International Code of Commercial Law, but Leone Levi was much in advance of the times, and the scheme came to nothing, though it affords evidence of the fact that at this date men's minds were beginning to consider the desirability of unified law.[2] The first definite steps towards unification coincided with the revival of interest in comparative studies, but were at first limited to the field of maritime and commercial law. In 1863 a resolution in favour of the unification of the Laws of Bills of Exchange was passed at a Congress of the Union for the Advancement of the Social Sciences held at Ghent,[3] and in 1865 an International Congress was held at Sheffield to consider the possibility of unifying certain branches of maritime law.[4] The latter part of the nineteenth century was also characterised by a growth in the impulse towards international collaboration in legal matters, though of a somewhat different nature, and in this connection mention may be made of the Berne Convention of 1890 on the Carriage of Goods by Rail, the General Postal Convention of 1874, the Berne Convention of 1886 on Copyright, and the unification in 1881 of the laws of the Nordic countries relating to negotiable instruments. The year 1877 witnessed one of the most important successes achieved in the field of unification, namely, the York-Antwerp rules on general average which were framed under the auspices of the International Law Association.

On the whole the period before 1900 was one of exploration rather than of achievement, though much useful spade work was done which was subsequently to yield a harvest. This was more particularly the case as regards maritime law and certain aspects of commercial law, notably the Law of Negotiable Instruments. Unification of law is a slow and arduous process which is apt to be impeded and sometimes frustrated by developments in the international sphere which have no connection with the law but spring from political or economic or social sources. The serious nature of the many obstacles which had to be overcome was as yet imperfectly realised, and the years between 1900 and 1914, although marked by a

1 Leone Levi published the results of his comparative studies in two volumes entitled *Commercial Law, its Principles and Administration*, with the sub-title 'The Mercantile Law of Great Britain as compared with Roman Law and the Codes and Laws of 59 other countries' (1850-2). The second edition of this work was published in 1863 and bore the title *International Commercial Law*.

2 Balogh, *op. cit.*, refers to another early proposal of a similar nature, i.e. De Parieu, *D'un Projet de Code de Commerce International*.

3 See League of Nations Publications, C. 487, M. 203, 1923, III, E. 106.

4 *Pro rata* freight; shipowners liens, etc. See the *Report of the 30th Conference of the International Law Association* (1921), p. xi.

wave of enthusiasm for unified law, were destined to raise many hopes which were doomed to disappointment. Certain topics, such as the Law of Collisions at Sea and the Law of Negotiable Instruments, were ripe for the unifying process, and the greatest success was achieved in this direction. The work commenced by the Comité Maritime International in 1902 in unifying the Law of Collisions at Sea passed into the hands of a diplomatic conference summoned under Belgian auspices, and in 1910 a convention was signed which in the case of Great Britain has been carried into effect by the Maritime Conventions Act of 1911. The draft Hague Conventions of 1910 and 1912 on the Law of Negotiable Instruments were also adopted by a certain number of countries and were destined to become the groundwork of the Geneva Conventions of 1930 and 1931, which unified the laws of the continental countries and constitute one of the most successful achievements up to the present in the field of unified law. But the attempt to secure uniformity of the rules of private international law relating to such matters as the Law of Marriage, Divorce, Succession, the Guardianship of Minors and certain aspects of legal procedure, though it resulted in the adoption by the Hague Conferences on private international law, in the years between 1902 and 1928, of a number of conventions, was doomed to failure. This want of success can be explained on several grounds. The effort to secure unification was, perhaps, premature. The many problems which lay concealed under an apparent similarity of rule were not clearly recognised and emerged many years afterwards to play their part in undoing the work of many years of debate and drafting.[1] The principal cause of the failure of the conventions was, however, the abrupt termination of international intercourse following on the outbreak of war in 1914 which destroyed any prospect there might have been of extending the sphere within which these conventions would be effective. The English-speaking countries have been censured for standing aloof from the Hague Private International Law Conventions, but experience would seem to suggest that their attitude was not a vital factor in the situation. The solution of the problems at issue would in no way have been facilitated by the introduction of the elements of English and American law into the matter. The unification of the law of the Continent, standing alone, presented problems of a very serious character for which no solution has yet been found.

The end of the First World War gave birth to another wave of enthusiasm

---

1 An illustration of this is to be found in the repudiation by Sweden, Switzerland and Germany of the Convention of 12 July 1902, on conflicts of jurisdiction in matters of divorce and separation. This was due to the fact that the Convention operated in certain cases to deprive married women who were separated from their husbands and thereafter restored to their premarital nationality the right to be divorced by their national courts (see Gutteridge, *British Year Book of I.L.* vol. 19 (1938), p. 19).

for unified law. The period between 1919 and 1939 presents certain analogies to the movement in the earlier years of the century. We find the same belief that unification is feasible and an equal desire to bring it about as speedily as possible. These factors were reinforced by faith in the future of international collaboration in the interests of justice, and by the creation of a new meeting-place and new machinery for international negotiation in the shape of the Economic and Legal Sections of the League of Nations and the International Labour Office. The 'Geneva' atmosphere was regarded as being of special importance, since it was hoped that it might lead to the active co-operation of the English-speaking countries in future efforts to secure uniformity of law. These aspirations, animated by a great and noble ideal, might well have been realised if the course of history had been different. There can be no doubt that the League provided a much-needed co-ordinating authority to deal with plans for unification which often tended to overlap one another and to lead to a useless expenditure of time and effort. Its policy, however, was to interfere as little as possible with any projects for unification which were sponsored by other bodies and were still in being. No attempt was made, for instance, to supersede the activities of the Hague Conferences on private international law or of the body known as CITEJA which was dealing with the liability of carriers by air. The question of an international code of rules relating to C.I.F. contracts was left to be dealt with by the International Law Association. In one case, namely, that of the unification of the Law of Negotiable Instruments, the venue of international discussion was changed from the Hague to Geneva, but this was due to the hope that it might result in the adoption by the English-speaking members of the League of a less intransigent attitude towards the question. Other projects for unification, sponsored by the League, were proposals for uniform rules relating to arbitration agreements and the enforcement of arbitration awards, which resulted in the adoption of the Protocol on Arbitration Clauses of 1923 and the Convention of 1927 on the Enforcement of Arbitral Awards, also in draft conventions for the unification of the Law of Sale of Goods, the Law of Arbitration, the Law relating to Innkeepers, the law concerning the civil liability of the owners of automobiles, and the vexed question of the enforcement of maintenance orders in foreign countries. The only one of these projects which had proceeded beyond the preliminary stages before the outbreak of war in 1939, namely, the proposed unification of the Law of Negotiable Instruments, met with a high degree of success. The two international conferences which were held at Geneva in 1930 and 1931 resulted in the adoption of two conventions dealing respectively with bills of exchange and promissory notes and with cheques. The conventions were ratified by practically all the civil-law countries, thus reducing the number of separate systems of the Law of Negotiable Instruments from a very large number to two, namely, the Geneva and the Anglo-American systems.[1] This is no mean achievement, but it has fallen short of complete success owing to the abstention of the United States and the British Commonwealth, an attitude which was not prompted by hostility towards the idea of unification, but was inevitable because the acceptance of the Geneva system would have necessitated radical changes in the banking practice of the English-speaking world and would, further, have disturbed the high degree of uniformity which had resulted from the very close relationship between the British Bills of Exchange Act 1882 and the American Negotiable Instruments Law. It is significant as illustrating the difficulty of securing uniformity of law that the Geneva codes were the outcome of nearly seventy years of preliminary discussion and attempts to bring about unification.

Some success has been achieved in unifying certain aspects of maritime law, but here again the process has worked with difficulty and considerable delay in spite of the fact that this branch of law would seem, together with the law of the air, to offer the most promising field for unified law. A number of conventions have been entered into dealing with the law of safety at sea, the rules of the road at sea and the law of collisions, the limitation of the liability of shipowners in collision actions, maritime salvage, maritime liens and mortgages, the immunity of State ships, and the responsibility of shipowners for the safe carriage of cargo.[2] Unfortunately, these conventions still await embodiment in the law of some of the maritime nations, and the result can only be described as disappointing. In the case of the law of the air the situation would appear to be more promising because it is possible, in this instance, to anticipate the difficulties which would arise if a number of conflicting systems of law were permitted to come into existence. But even so the results of attempts to secure uniformity of law cannot be described as satisfactory. As early as 1919 the Convention of Paris was concluded and forms the foundation of much of what may be called the public law of the air. Certain important States, however, stood outside this convention, e.g.

---

1 See Gutteridge, 'The Unification of the Law of Bills of Exchange', *British Year Book of I.L.* vol. 12 (1931), p. 13.

2 See Cleminson, 'The International Unification of Maritime Law', *Journal of C.L.* (3rd Ser.), vol. XXIII (1941), p. 163; Gutteridge, 'The Unification of the Law of the Sea', *Journal of C.L.* (3rd Ser.), vol. XVI (1934), p. 246; Colombos, 'The Unification of Maritime Law in time of Peace', *British Year Book of I.L.* vol. 21 (1945), p. 96.

Germany, the U.S.S.R., the U.S.A., Brazil and China. The American countries have, in fact, preferred a system of their own based on the Havana Convention of 1928. On the other hand, the Warsaw Convention of 1929 dealing with carriage by air has found almost universal acceptance. The Rome Convention of 1933, which regulates the liability of the owners of aircraft for damage to persons or property, has only been adopted by a few states.[1] The question of further measures for the unification of this branch of the law would appear to be urgent and ripe for consideration by the Economic and Social Council under the provisions of the Charter of the United Nations.

Perhaps the greatest activity in the field of unification has been displayed by the International Labour Office, and this has resulted in the adoption of a large number of conventions dealing with such matters as the conditions of employment in general, the employment of women and children, industrial health, safety and welfare, social insurance and the protection of emigrants.[2]

In the case of private international law the attempts made at different times to secure some degree of uniformity have met with very little success. Allusion has already been made to the failure of the International Conferences held at the Hague to achieve any results of real or lasting value, but some success has marked the efforts to obtain regional unification in the case of the Latin-American Republics. The Bustamante code drafted by the Pan-American Congress at Havana in 1928 has been adopted by fifteen of the republics. Of the remainder, five have preferred an earlier code which was adopted in 1889 by the Congress of Montevideo. Partial unification of the rules of conflict relating to negotiable instruments was reached at Geneva in 1930 and 1931, but the abstention of the United States and Great Britain has very much limited the scope of the relevant conventions. The failure, or relative failure, of the various attempts to secure uniformity in a sphere of law in which the need for it is urgent was, however, not entirely due to difficulties of a legal nature.[3]

There are certain international agreements which cannot, perhaps, be regarded as unifying measures, but have the effect of removing or minimising existing legal barriers. Examples of such measures are the Copyright Union constituted by the Berne Convention of 1886, as amended

---

1 For details of the various conventions, of the efforts which have been made, and are being made, to secure uniformity of the law of the air, see Shawcross and Beaumont, *Air Law*, Chapter I.

2 For a complete list of these conventions see *The International Labour Code*, 1939, published by the International Labour Office, Montreal, 1941.

3 See Gutteridge, 'The Unification of the Rules of Conflict relating to Negotiable Instruments', *Journal of C.L.* (3rd Ser.), vol. XVI (1934), p. 53.

by the Act of Paris, 1896, and revised at Berlin in 1908, and at Rome in 1928, and the International Convention for the Protection of Industrial Property which deals with patents, trade marks and designs which was last revised at London in 1934. Bilateral conventions have also been entered into which deal with such matters as the enforcement of foreign judgments and the service abroad of legal process. The most interesting attempt to secure bilateral unification was the Draft Franco-Italian Code of Obligations which was the work of a strong committee of eminent French and Italian lawyers, but came to nothing owing to political friction between the two countries.

So far we have been concerned with unification in the international sense, but there is another form of the unifying process which stands apart from the movement which has just been described because it is limited in its scope to the laws of a particular country. The phrase 'internal unification' has been applied to it in order to denote that its operation is limited to attempts to secure uniformity of law in a territory, subject to a single sovereign, in which several systems of law are to be found.[1] It differs in many respects from unification of the international type, but is of great interest from the comparative standpoint because it points the way to possible unification on a larger scale, and has extended into fields of law which have either not been affected by the movement for international uniformity or have only been dealt with very tentatively.

Unification, in this secondary or restricted sense, has been widespread. A silent, but none the less effective, process has, for example, been in operation in the British Commonwealth of Nations, which has resulted in the adoption by its constituent members of a very considerable body of English law, thus producing a substantial degree of uniformity, principally, though not entirely, in the field of commercial law. The establishment in the United States of the Conference of Commissioners for Uniform State Laws has led to the enactment of a number of measures with the object of unifying certain of the laws of the different states, and, here again, the greatest degree of success has been attained in the domain of commercial law. The work of the Commissioners has raised problems of importance and interest which will be discussed hereafter.[2]

On the Continent of Europe the leading example of internal unification is, perhaps, to be found in the case of the Swiss codes,[3] which have resulted in the fusion of the laws of twenty-five different cantons. The process

---

1 See *post*, p. 154.   2 See *post*, p. 167.
3 The Civil Code and the Code of Obligations. See Williams, *Swiss Civil Code* (*Sources of Law*), pp. 24, *et seq.* The criminal laws of the different cantons have also undergone a process of unification ('Swiss Criminal Law', *Canadian Bar Review* for November and December 1944).

of unification called, in this instance, for a selection between the laws of the cantons which based their system on French law and the laws of other cantons which had come under the influence of Austrian or German law. In many respects Swiss law represents modern continental law in its most highly developed form, and a striking tribute was paid to it by the action of the Turkish Republic in adopting it, almost in its entirety, in place of the Ottoman laws which had ceased to correspond to modern requirements.

At the close of the War of 1914–18 the government of the newly constituted Republic of Poland was faced with the difficult task of dealing with five different systems of law which were in force within its territory, namely, Austrian, Russian, German, French and, to a lesser degree, Hungarian law. This task, entered upon and carried out with exemplary vigour and skill, resulted in the creation of a considerable body of unified law which was not merely inspired by the pre-existing law but also by the comparative study of other laws, notably the Swiss codes.[1] A similar problem was encountered in the case of the Czecho-Slovak Republic, though, in this instance, the task of selection was of a less complicated nature, since the greater part of the territory of the republic was under the régime of the Austrian codes, and it was only in certain districts that Hungarian law had to be taken into account.[2] How far the systems of law, which were thus built up in Poland and Czecho-Slovakia, will survive the catastrophic conditions created by the Second World War is at present a matter of conjecture, but they will, in any event, have a claim to be numbered among the most interesting experiments which have been made in the field of internal unification.

In many respects the most interesting example of successful unification is to be found in the steps taken by the Nordic or Scandinavian countries to secure uniformity of law in directions in which it is most needed. In form, this is an instance of international or external unification, but, in essence, it is internal in character, because the similarity of language, religion, and modes of life, as well as of law and legal institutions, between these countries, has engendered an atmosphere of goodwill and mutual confidence which must be regarded as exceptional.

The movement for the unification of the law of the Nordic nations[3]

---

1 Nagorski, 'Codification of Civil Law in Poland', in *Studies in Polish and Comparative Law*.

2 Srb, 'Preliminary steps towards a New Civil Code for the Czecho-Slovak Republic', *Journal of C.L.* (3rd Ser.), vol. IX (1927), p. 197; see also, Szegö, 'Evolution of the Private Law of Czecho-Slovakia', *ibid.* p. 228.

3 Norway, Denmark and Sweden. Iceland and Finland also participated in the movement at subsequent dates.

came into being towards the end of the nineteenth century, and was, at first, limited to maritime and commercial law. But it has now spread to other branches of the law, and uniformity has been reached, for instance, on such questions as the principles of the Law of Contract, the Law of Agency and the Law of Sale of Goods. Even in the case of family law and the law of succession it has proved possible to attain a considerable degree of uniformity. In particular, the vexed question of jurisdiction in divorce has been solved by the Stockholm Convention of 1931 in a manner which merits serious consideration by those who are seeking to find a remedy for a world-wide problem which is a reproach to civilisation.[1]

1 See Gutteridge, 'Conflicts of Jurisdiction in Matrimonial Suits', *British Year Book of I.L.* vol. 19 (1938), p. 19.

Chapter XII

THE NATURE & CHARACTERISTICS OF UNIFIED LAW

'UNIFICATION' is a term employed to denote the process by which conflicting rules of two or more systems of law are replaced by a single rule. It is also used to indicate the expedient of framing international rules in advance for the purpose of anticipating conflicts which might arise if several states were to legislate independently in order to meet a situation of a novel and unprecedented character.[1]

The process of unification may take several forms: it may consist in the selection of a rule from one or another of the competing systems and its adoption by the rest, or, it may result in the abandonment of the existing rules and the formulation of entirely new rules. It may be *complete* or *incomplete*, according to the extent to which it has been found possible to unify all the conflicting rules or, as the case may be, to secure the adoption of the unified rules by all of the countries concerned. It may also be *bilateral* or *multilateral*. Bilateral unification is confined to the laws of two countries, whilst multilateral unification embraces the laws of several countries. Where the process is confined to the rules of certain neighbouring countries it is sometimes referred to as *regional* unification. There are many other aspects of unification. It may, for instance, be *internal* or *external*; in the first case its object is to do away with conflicts of law existing within the territorial area of a single state; in the second case it is designed to secure uniformity of rule between the laws of several states. Examples of internal unification are to be found in the Uniform Laws of the United States and in the Swiss codes, and of external unification in the Brussels Conventions on Maritime Law and the Geneva Uniform Laws on Negotiable Instruments. Unification may also be *entire* or *partial*. If it is entire, the various systems concerned abandon their national rules and adopt the unified rules for all purposes. If it is partial, each system retains its own rules for the purpose of adjudication in disputes of a domestic character, and confines the application of the unified rules to disputes containing some foreign element, such as the residence of the parties in different jurisdictions or the situation of the subject-matter of the dispute in a foreign country. The Geneva Uniform

1 E.g. the conventions for the regulation of international aerial traffic. See *ante*, p. 149.

Laws on Negotiable Instruments illustrate 'entire' unification, whilst the Warsaw Convention of 1929 on the Carriage of Goods by Air affords an example of 'partial' unification.[1]

The Objects of Unification

The causes which have provoked the desire for the uniformity of law are largely, but not entirely, economic in character.[2] It is, of course, obvious that diversity of law must be a disturbing factor in international commerce. Traders are not concerned with the niceties of legal technicalities. Their main endeavour is to guard themselves against risk, whether of the loss of their goods, or of the dishonesty or insolvency of their debtors, or of any other impediment which may be placed in the way of the enforcement of the engagements into which the parties to a commercial contract have entered. They are, for instance, not so much concerned in the question of the moment at which property in the goods is transferred from the seller to the buyer under a contract of sale, as in that of the time at which the risk in the goods falls upon the buyer. Among the risks with which they have to contend is that of uncertainty as to the effect of foreign rules of law on the transactions which they undertake. Foreign trade is ambulatory, and a commercial or maritime contract may fall under the regime of several systems of law before it is performed. The position is well illustrated by the famous case of *Lloyd* v. *Guibert*,[3] in which a ship flying the French flag was chartered at a Danish West Indian port to proceed to Hayti and there load a cargo to be carried to England or France at the charterer's option. The ship was damaged on the voyage and put into a Portuguese port of refuge where the master borrowed money on a bottomry bond in order to enable him to complete the voyage. The ship ultimately arrived at Liverpool, and the plaintiff was compelled to pay off the bond in order to gain possession of the cargo. He sought to recover the amount so paid from the shipowner, and the following systems of law were potentially applicable to the transaction. Danish law was the *lex loci contractus* of the charter party; French law was the law of the flag; Haytian law was the law of the port of loading; English law was the law of the port of destination; and Portuguese law was the law of the place in which the bottomry bond was executed. This is, of course, an extreme case, but it is by no means exceptional when the subject-matter of a dispute is a through contract of

1 The Convention only applies to 'international carriage' as defined by Article 1 (2) (a).
2 Cf. Bryce, *Studies in History and Jurisprudence*, vol. I, p. 144.
3 (1865) L.R. 1 Q.B. 115.

carriage or a negotiable instrument. Chalmers mentions the case of a bill of exchange drawn in Bolivia on London, which was circulated in Jerusalem and other eastern localities, and was accepted after fourteen months of wandering.[1]

Diversity of law may, however, lead to insecurity and hardship in other directions besides those which spring from economic causes. Increased facilities of travel and communications have led to a notable increase of foreign residents in certain countries, and intermarriage between persons of a different domicile or nationality is now more frequent than in the past. Conflicts of law are, therefore, much more likely to arise than heretofore, so that the resulting problems are of extreme difficulty and of the type which has been responsible for the aphorism that 'hard cases make bad law'. Thus a woman may be a wife in one country and her husband's mistress in another. Her children may be legitimate according to one system of law and yet be bastardised by the rules of another system. Rights of succession to movable property have become involved in a tangle of conflicting rules, and the confusion has been increased by doubts as to the nature and effect of the doctrine of *renvoi*. But unification may also be desirable for reasons other than those of the encouragement of international trade and the protection of individuals from hardship. It may, for instance, be an indispensable element in any movement for the improvement of the conditions of labour. A country adopting a policy in this connection, in advance of the law in other countries, may find itself handicapped in its foreign trade, because its products cannot be sold in competition with those of the other countries which have a lower standard as regards wages, hours of work, the employment of child and female labour and the like. Unification has also been found to be necessary for the protection of such forms of property as patents, trade marks and copyright. In fact, the area of possible unification is extremely wide, and may even extend to certain aspects of public law such as the extradition of criminals and preventive measures against particular forms of crime such as coinage offences.

It is, however, unnecessary to stress the arguments for unification in appropriate circumstances. If any proof of its value is needed it can be found in the prolonged and sustained efforts which have been made over a long period of years to secure uniformity in many branches of the law. No one would wish to see the legal systems of the world reduced to the same dead level; all civilised nations have derived a precious heritage from the past in their legal traditions, and the common fund of human

---

1 *Report to the League of Nations on the Unification of Laws relating to Bills of Exchange and Promissory Notes*, League of Nations Publications, C. 487, M. 203, 1923, III, E. 106.

wisdom and experience has been enriched from the individuality of experiment which is a characteristic of the existence of several competing systems of law. But such considerations ought not to act as a bar to the removal of differences of rule which are obstacles to free and cordial intercourse between the nations or may impose unnecessary hardships on individuals.

The Problems of Unification

When it is remembered that attempts to unify the law extend over a period of something like eighty years the results are disappointing. They illustrate the extreme difficulty experienced in carrying through even the most modest schemes for unification, and the conclusion to be drawn is that much remains to be done before unification of law can be regarded as an effective force in the promotion of a better understanding between the nations and the removal of sources of international friction and commercial insecurity. How far this unsatisfactory situation is due to the inherent difficulty of the process, and how far it has been created by faulty methods of carrying it into effect, is the next question which demands consideration.

It would seem that much of the blame for the failure to achieve more definite and permanent results must be attributed to an excess of zeal fostered by an exaggerated belief in the need for unification and over-confidence in its feasibility. It is, perhaps, difficult for an enthusiast—and most 'unificationists' fall within that category—to realise that he is engaged in promoting a cause which is unpopular among lawyers and makes little appeal to the general public. One cannot, for instance, conceive of a situation in which there would be popular demonstrations in favour of the uniformity of the Law of Negotiable Instruments, or even for the assimilation of the Laws of Marriage and Divorce. Unification can only be achieved by lengthy and patient efforts which will ultimately convince those in all countries, who are in a position to sponsor and carry through changes in the law, that it is a matter of urgent necessity to take steps in order to remove sources of inconvenience and friction in the international sphere. Unification cannot be achieved by a stroke of the pen, nor can it be carried out within the four walls of law libraries, practitioner's offices or professorial studies. The ground must be very carefully surveyed, and the interests concerned must be won over before any action is undertaken. It is necessary, for our present purpose, to underline the fact that many of the woes from which the movement for unification suffers are undoubtedly due to premature and ill-advised attempts to draft schemes for unified law which have little or no prospect of acceptance. Apart from these errors of judgment which are largely responsible for the setbacks hitherto experienced, it is beyond doubt that unification is, in any circumstances, confronted by other obstacles of a psychological character. National pride makes itself felt in the realm of the law as well as in other spheres. The abandonment of national rules of law seems to imply that there is something amiss with the rules which are to be displaced, and national *amour propre* suffers accordingly. The citizens of many countries are deeply attached to their national law: at one extreme we have, for instance, the Frenchman who carries in his pocket the *Code Civil* or the *Code de Commerce*, the dog-eared leaves of which bear witness to the frequency with which these volumes are consulted, and, at the other end of the line, we find the Englishman who never looks at a law book but is nevertheless convinced that his common law is the quintessence of human wisdom and justice. It must not be forgotten that to invite the citizen to give up a rule of law to which he has become accustomed may be to demand almost as great a sacrifice as the abandonment of his national speech or religion.[1] Moreover, lawyers of all nationalities are apt to be hostile to unification, very largely because they may not have the leisure or the inclination to investigate the reasons by which it is prompted. Judges and practitioners have a distinct and not altogether unreasonable suspicion of proposals for the reform of law which have an international flavour. Their views carry great weight with the man in the street, particularly in England, where the legal profession, in spite of the many jibes of which it is the victim, probably stands higher in public esteem than elsewhere. It may be easy to pour scorn on this attitude of the professional elements of the community in regard to changes in the law, but respect for the law is an element in securing the stability of society both in the national and the international spheres, the importance of which is manifest and cannot be disregarded.

The danger that national sentiment may prevent or delay the acceptance of proposals for uniform law is recognised by some unificationists, and an attempt has been made to surmount it by a form of the process which we have described as 'partial unification'. It will be remembered that unification of this type does not displace national rules of law; they still continue to apply to domestic transactions, and the unified rules are only operative in the case of legal relationships containing a foreign element. The argument advanced in favour of this expedient is that it is more likely to meet with acceptance than 'entire' unification because it does not involve interference with the law applicable to transactions in which the bulk of the community is concerned, and does not lead to the abandonment of any of the fundamental conceptions on which a national

[1] '*Patrius Mos* is dear to all men and men are bred and nourished up in the love of it', Bacon, *Certain Articles or Considerations touching the union of England and Scotland.*

system of law is based. It is urged, in particular, that it would facilitate assimilation in the case of the common-law and the civil-law systems, separated as they are by a wide gulf of differing traditions and concepts. Theoretically, there is much to be said in favour of partial unification, but the practical difficulties to which it gives birth appear to counterbalance its apparent utility. If unification is to be successful it must offer a better solution of conflicts of law than that furnished by private international law, and this object is not attained by partial unification. Under it a state of complexity and uncertainty would arise which is, at least, as serious and troublesome as the situation which it is the object of unification to avoid. At the very outset, a problem of the greatest difficulty arises, namely, the division of the area of possible litigation into the spheres to be governed, respectively, by national rules and the rules of unified law. What is to be the criterion for the assignment of a dispute to either sphere? If it is to be the domicile, residence, or nationality of the parties, the further question will arise whether we mean the domicile, residence, or nationality of the plaintiff or that of the defendant. On the other hand, if we adopt some test such as that of the place of conclusion of the contract or the place of its performance, we are back again in the welter of controversy which is the bane of private international law. Moreover, even if this form of unification should succeed in disarming a certain volume of opposition it would probably intensify it in other quarters. The existence of a dual system of rules would double the labour and responsibility of judges and practitioners by compelling them to keep pace with developments in both. It is also very doubtful whether the commercial community would be favourably disposed to proposals creating one law for the trader who confines his dealings to the home market and another law for the merchant who seeks his fortune abroad. There would also be difficulties of a practical nature where so-called 'string contracts' are concerned. Contracts of this type are entered into on exchanges by brokers in circumstances which make the identity of the ultimate buyer of the goods a matter of uncertainty, and the 'string' will often include a number of sellers and buyers of different nationalities or different domiciles. Under a system of partial unification an intermediate seller or buyer would often—if not invariably—be in doubt as to the law which will ultimately govern his rights and liabilities, and his position might well be more insecure than it is at present.[1] The advocates of 'partial' unification are, however, in no way deterred by these objections to their proposals but endeavour to overcome them by the argument that, in course of time,

---

1 The definition of transactions which are to be regarded as 'international' for the purpose of the application of the unified law may also give rise to difficulties. See *Grein* v. *Imperial Airways Ltd.* [1937] 1 K.B. 50 and *Philippson* v. *Imperial Airways Ltd.* [1939] A.C. 332.

the superiority of the unified rules would become manifest and the national rules will tend to disappear. In other words, the real object of partial unification would seem to be to prove the way for unification in the domestic as well as in the international sphere. Few attempts have been made, as yet, to employ the process of partial unification, with the exception of the Warsaw Convention of 1929 on Carriage by Air, and certain proposals for the unification of the Law of Arbitration, and the Law of the Sale of Goods, which have not, so far, passed beyond the preliminary stages of discussion.

The Sphere of Unification

There are many factors which combine to narrow down the field within which attempts to secure uniformity of law can be made with any prospects of success. It is, of course, obvious that the process cannot be applied indiscriminately; there are certain branches of the law which must be regarded as lying wholly outside its operational sphere. It would, for instance, be ridiculous to invite countries whose prosperity is dependent on their export trade in wine to join in framing a uniform prohibition law, or to expect countries which have no outlet to the sea to participate in the unification of maritime law. Experience has also proved the need for the reconciliation of conflicting interests and neglect to observe this precaution is, probably, responsible for many of the abortive attempts to secure unification. A rule which can be accepted by a majority of the countries concerned may be inadmissible from the standpoint of the minority, because it cannot be brought into line with the general structure of their institutions or may involve such far-reaching changes in their business practices as to put it beyond the limits within which concessions can be made in the cause of international co-operation. There is, moreover, an ever-present danger that certain interests may seek to utilise the process of unification in order to secure advantages for themselves. *Blocs* of states may be formed for the purpose of forcing their proposals through international assemblies summoned to consider the drafting of uniform laws. Exporting countries may press for a rule which would be to their benefit but would prove injurious to the interests of importers; in fact, a point is often reached when the only escape from failure is to be found in a compromise which deprives the process of unification of any real value. There are also technical difficulties caused by the diversity of languages in which the uniform laws may have to be drafted and by the unsatisfactory nature of the agencies which are employed in the preparatory stages leading up to the submission of definite proposals for unification.

There are, in addition, branches of private law which do not lend themselves to unification. Rules of law which solely concern domestic interests, such, for instance, as those applicable to relations between husband and wife or parent and child, must vary in accordance with differences in racial temperament and outlook, or religious sentiment. Other branches of the law could, no doubt, be unified, though it is difficult to see what benefit would accrue from the process. It would, for example, be idle to unify the rules governing property in immovables, because there is general agreement that this question must in the last resort be governed by the law of the site. Certain aspects of the law could only be unified with the greatest difficulty; the law of tort, or delict, furnishes a good illustration of an obstacle of this nature, owing to the widely divergent views which are held as to the nature and extent of liability for civil wrongs. Further, it would often be futile to strive for uniformity in rules, such as those to which allusion has been made, because any uniform laws would be highly vulnerable to the overriding effects of national rules of public policy or *ordre public*, and any uniformity which could be achieved would, for the most part, be a mere pretence. On the other hand, there are certain departments of the law which offer a wide scope for the employment of the unifying process. Maritime and commercial law and the law of the air are not hemmed in by national frontiers in the same way as other branches of the law, and experience has shown that successful unification is possible in this instance provided that care is taken to avoid violence to any of the fundamental principles of any of the systems which are submitted to the process. Private international law also is in urgent need of unification in many directions. The law of labour is another field which offers abundant opportunities for the employment of the process.

In certain respects 'bilateral' unification possesses many advantages over other forms of the process. It is a more flexible instrument than unification on the grand scale, because it escapes many of the complications which have to be faced whenever an attempt is made to reconcile the divergent rules of several systems of law. The various international conventions for the mutual enforcement of judgments illustrate the possibility of securing bilateral unification in circumstances in which an attempt to bring about uniformity on a larger scale would have had small hope of success. Regional and internal unification may also succeed in spite of serious obstacles where—as in the case of the Scandinavian countries and Switzerland or Poland—uniformity of law is an urgent national necessity.

The position, in general, appears to be that the process of unification must, at present, be regarded as passing through an experimental stage. Success or failure in its employment depends on a variety of considerations, some of which are not of juridical order. On the other hand, little as it may have achieved so far, 'it can scarcely be denied that it shows a much better way towards a satisfactory solution of one of the world's most urgent legal problems than does private international law',[1] and it may, in the future, prove to be one of the most effective instruments of international collaboration in the domain of the law.

Great Britain and the Movement for Unification

It is sometimes said that Great Britain has obstructed the realisation of unified law from selfish motives, and that there are forces at work on this side of the Channel which are determined to oppose any attempt to assimilate the rules of the common and the civil laws. These accusations are, however, not borne out by the facts, and, if the peculiar position of the common-law countries is taken into account, it is plain that Great Britain has done all that can reasonably be expected from her in support of the unifying movement.

It must be admitted there were certain factors in the situation which may, in the past, have led observers in other countries to draw the conclusion that Great Britain was inclined to stand aloof from any proposals for unification, and to regard them as no concern of hers. An unfavourable impression was created by the decision of Great Britain to abstain from taking any part in the Hague Conferences for the Unification of Private International Law and the Conferences of 1910 and 1912 held to discuss a proposed Uniform Law of Negotiable Instruments. This impression was strengthened by the fact that, when this policy was reversed after the War of 1914–18, some of the British delegates attending international conferences tended to adopt an attitude which, in substance, was an echo of the famous cry *Nolumus leges Angliae mutari*. At all events, there was a feeling in the continental countries that Great Britain could not be relied upon to support any proposals for unification unless these were in some way or another beneficial to her interests.

The fact remains, however, that with the exception of the attempts to unify private international law, which have, for the most part, proved to be unsuccessful, and the Geneva Uniform Laws of Negotiable Instruments of 1930 and 1931, the movement for unification owes much to British initiative and collaboration. It is only necessary to refer to such unifying measures as the York-Antwerp Rules of General Average, the various Brussels Conventions on Maritime Law, the Hague Rules of 1921 on the Liability of Shipowners and the Foreign Judgments (Reciprocal Enforcement) Act of 1933 in support of this contention. Even in the case of the Geneva Uniform Laws of Negotiable Instruments the British Government, whilst declaring its inability to become a signatory to the

---

[1] Cohn, 'The Task and Organisation of Comparative Jurisprudence', *Juridical Review* (June 1939), p. 136.

main conventions, instructed its delegate and his technical adviser on banking practice to give every aid in their power to the negotiation of the conventions as between the other nations. Great Britain has also adhered to the Warsaw Convention of 1929 on the Law of Carriage by Air, and to many of the conventions concluded under the auspices of the International Labour Office.

Even if British collaboration in the movement has been marked by a certain attitude of reserve, as is undoubtedly the case, it is clear that her policy during the last twenty years has not been one of abstention based on egotistic considerations, and that the charge of obstruction rests on no solid foundation. The difficulties involved in the participation of the common-law countries in schemes for unification are not fully realised in the civil-law countries. It is unnecessary to dwell at any length on the fundamental differences between the Anglo-American and continental systems which make unification a most formidable task; they have been stated so often and are so obvious that repetition is needless.[1] In any event the record of the unifying movement shows that even as between countries whose law is derived from a common stock, whose legal institutions are of the same type, the unifying process is apt to break down or to culminate by way of compromise in conventions which have no value except on paper. The signature of a convention for the introduction of unified law is often accompanied by reservations on the part of the signatories, which go a long way to deprive the so-called unification of its claim to be regarded as more than a pious fiction. In such circumstances the cautious approach of the British government to proposals for uniformity of law cannot, in all fairness, be regarded as evidence of any desire to be obstructive.

The attitude of Great Britain towards unification rests on considerations of a very different nature from those which flow from divergences between the common and the civil law. The English-speaking countries have arrived at a high degree of uniformity of law as between themselves. Not only are their fundamental principles of law and their legal institutions the same, for the most part, but their modern amending legislation largely follows the same lines. The British Overseas Dominions,[2] the Colonies and Protectorates have shown a marked tendency to adapt their law to changes which are made in the Mother Country, and this is also true at least in commercial matters of British India. The Negotiable Instruments Law and the Law of Sale of the United States are to a certain

---

1 E.g. Gray, *Nature and Sources of Law*, p. 199 *passim*; Kuhn, *Commentaries on Private International Law*, pp. 57–9.

2 The Union of South Africa which is under the regime of Roman Dutch Law must *ex necessitate rei* adopt a somewhat different attitude to that of the other Dominions.

extent textual reproductions of the corresponding English statutes. On the other hand, changes in the law of the Dominions and the United States have had their repercussions in English law.[1] In this way a system of unified law has come into existence which rules the destinies of no inconsiderable proportion of the human race, and represents an achievement of such magnitude that it should not be impaired without good reason. It is, indeed, unthinkable that Great Britain should be called upon to undertake any independent action not supported by the other English-speaking communities. Any isolated move on her part would not only be of doubtful value but might even in the long run jeopardise the prospects of general unification. So that, although her attitude towards unification may, at first sight, appear to be unduly rigid, if not egotistical, it is in fact inspired by motives which have nothing to do with insularity of thought and policy, or with any considerations of national *amour propre* which are not equally in evidence in other countries.

It may, however, be urged that English lawyers should show themselves to be more sympathetic towards the movement than has been the case in the past. As Lord Justice Kennedy pointed out, it is unreasonable to cling 'obstinately to theoretical symmetry or to look askance at a reasonable compromise'[2] where this is possible. *Nolumus leges Angliae mutari* may prove to be a policy which is both unwise and dangerous, if its consequences are to drive other nations to settle their differences without regard to the contribution which English law is able to give to the common cause. As Lord Justice Kennedy also observed, 'Where a number of equal and independent units have fused their differences in an agreement, it is justly difficult for a unit which has chosen to stand aloof from the discussion which produced the agreement afterwards to persuade them to reopen the matter.'[3] These words were written many years ago, but they apply with greater force at present, when increased collaboration between the nations in economic and other spheres has developed into one of the most urgent needs of humanity.

Unification within the British Empire

The position as regards unification of law within the British Commonwealth of Nations is one of some delicacy. Even prior to the enactment of the Statute of Westminster it was always a matter of difficulty to carry through the Imperial Parliament any measures which were designed to

1 The change of attitude of the law of England towards certain questions, such as that of unjustified enrichment, has undoubtedly been due in large degree to the influence of American law as set out in the Restatement on Restitution.
2 'Lord Justice Kennedy', *Journal of C.L.* (N.S.), vol. x (1909), at p. 212.
3 *Ibid.* at p. 216.

have effect outside the British Isles.[1] It was necessary, in the first place, before introducing the measure, to obtain the assent of all the self-governing units of the Empire, and this was sometimes a protracted and laborious undertaking. Secondly, when this had been done, Parliament had to be induced to adopt the outcome of the negotiations without any amendments of substance. The Commonwealth of Australia Constitution Act, 1900, was nearly wrecked for this reason, but a better illustration of the difficulties involved is, perhaps, to be found in the fate of the efforts to unify the laws of copyright in the Empire. The Imperial Act of 1911 was originally drafted as a unifying law in reliance on the resolutions of the Colonial Conference of 1910. The Conference accepted the principle of uniformity, though its assent was qualified by a proviso that any international conventions with foreign countries should not be binding on any self-governing unit of the Empire without its consent.[2] The result was that the Copyright Act of 1911 ceased to be a unifying measure and dwindled down into a 'model law', which the self-governing units of the Empire could modify or reject at their pleasure. Newfoundland alone adopted the measure in its entirety; the other Dominions either modified it or enacted legislation of an independent character. The difficulty in inducing a number of autonomous communities to unify their law is certainly no less since the Statute of Westminster came into force, but experience has proved that a well-thought-out and carefully drafted measure on a matter of common interest will often be adopted by the British Dominions and possessions. The lead given by the Bills of Exchange Act, 1882, and the Sale of Goods Act, 1893, has been followed, either in its entirety, or with slight modifications, by practically all the British Dominions and possessions.[3] Imperial Statutes have also been enacted to give effect to agreements made with the Dominions, and possessions for reciprocity in such matters as the grant of administration,[4] the proof of public documents,[5] and the enforcement of judgments.[6]

Law reform in England has its repercussions in the Dominions and possessions. The work of the Law Revision Committee has been followed

1 Ilbert, 'Unification of Commercial Law', *Journal of C.L.* (3rd Ser.), vol. II (1920), at p. 77.
2 *Report of the Colonial Conference*, 1910 (Cmd. 5272), cf. Sections 25-7 of the Copyright Act, 1911.
3 See the list of adoptions of the 'Bills of Exchange Act' in Falconbridge, *Banking and Bills of Exchange* (5th ed.), at p. 488; as to the Sale of Goods Act, see Chalmers, *Sale of Goods Act*, 1893 (11th ed.), at p. 167.
4 Colonial Probates Act, 1892; Colonial Probates (Protected States and Mandated Territories Act, 1927).
5 Evidence (Foreign, Dominion and Colonial Documents) Act, 1933.
6 Administration of Justice Act, 1920, Part II; Foreign Judgments (Reciprocal Enforcement) Act, 1933.

with deep interest throughout the Empire, and its reports have inspired legislation on the same lines as that of the United Kingdom.[1] On the other hand, the legislative activities of the Dominions have had their influence on changes in the law of England. The passing of the Inheritance (Family Provision) Act, 1938, was largely inspired by the example set by New Zealand, and the *Eighth Report of the Law Revision Committee* on the doctrine of contributory negligence makes certain recommendations which in substance embody the existing legislation of certain of the Canadian Provinces.[2]

It must always be remembered that the process of unification within the Empire can only be set in motion with the willing assent of the self-governing units, and rests on a realisation of the mutual advantages which flow from uniformity in appropriate circumstances. Any attempt to force the pace is, therefore, to be deprecated; the degree of uniformity which already exists is very substantial, though it is tempered by requirements imposed by differences of race and religion and by economic conditions. It represents a great achievement and a contribution of the very highest order to the cause of unification. To imperil it in any way by premature or injudicious action would be disastrous.

In conclusion, it should be noted that the Dominion of Canada has played an important part in the movement for internal unification. The independent action of the different provincial legislatures has naturally resulted in diversity of legislation quite apart from the existence in the Dominion of two separate systems of law, the one based on the common law of England and the other deriving its principles from the law of France. There may also be a need for common action in cases which are not covered either by the common or the civil law. These considerations have created a demand, especially in commercial circles, 'that legislation should be made uniform throughout the provinces to the fullest extent possible'.[3] In 1918 the first Conference of Commissioners and Representatives of the Provinces was summoned to Montreal for the purpose of promoting uniformity of legislation in the Dominion. Since that date the Commissioners have met annually, and down to 1943 twenty-five uniform laws were drafted of which thirteen have been adopted by five or more provinces. These laws include measures dealing with insurance, the assignment of book debts, bulk sales, *commorientes*, contributory negligence,

1 In New Zealand, for instance, 'full advantage has been taken of the work of this committee' in framing the Law Reform Act, 1936; McElroy and Gresson, *The Law Reform Act*, 1936, p. 2.

2 *Law Revision Committee, Eighth Report (Contributory Negligence)*, 1939 (Cmd. 6032), at p. 17.

3 *Proceedings of the Canadian Bar Association*, vol. X (1943), p. 235.

intestate succession, legitimation, reciprocal enforcement and warehouse liens. It would appear, however, that the movement has, more or less, come to a standstill owing to the fact that wholly non-controversial material for unification has come to an end, and that at present the Conference is engaged in the preparation of minor measures, aimed at the revision of the law dealing with such questions as the registration of liens on automobiles and the rights of the owners of chattels which have been affixed to the land.[1]

The American Uniform Laws

In the United States of America a demand for unified law has made itself felt owing to the existence of no less than forty-eight separate jurisdictions, each with its own system of private law and 'with hundreds of courts, many of which are farther apart than London is distant from Quebec, Petrograd or Constantinople'.[2] The need for uniformity is more pronounced, in this instance, than in the case of the Dominion of Canada, not merely because of the multiplicity of jurisdictions in the United States, but because the western provinces of the Dominion have adopted the statute law of England to an extent which makes the problems created by diversity of law less urgent than in the United States.[3]

The situation in the United States would, indeed, be impossible were it not that the law, with a few exceptions, rests in all the States on the basis of the common law of England. But, even so, expense and inconvenience and even injustice have been experienced.[4] The result has been a movement for the unification, in certain directions, of the laws of the different States—a movement which is unfortunately little known to English lawyers, and imperfectly understood by them, owing to the fact that American law operates in an ambient which is, in many respects, very different from the circumstances in which the law of England is called on to function.

The task of securing uniformity which, in this instance, is one of unusual difficulty, was confided in 1892 to the National Conference of Commissioners on Uniform State Laws. The Commissioners meet annually and have drafted a number of uniform laws on various legal topics. The procedure adopted by the Commissioners has been described by one of them in the following words: 'The business of the Commissioners is first,

---

1 See Lawson, 'Uniformity of Laws: A Suggestion', *Journal of C.L.* (3rd Ser.), vol. XXVI (1944), p. 23; Willis, *University of Toronto L.J.* (1944), p. 365; *Minutes of the Canadian Bar Association* (1944), p. 278.
2 Barratt, 'The Tendency to Unification of Law in the United States', *Journal of C.L.* (3rd Ser.), vol. V (1923), at p. 227.
3 Lawson, *loc. cit.*   4 Williston, *Life and Law*, p. 217.

to determine the subjects in which there is most serious need for uniformity and a possibility of meeting the need. When this preliminary decision has been made, a draftsman is appointed to prepare a Statute. Sometimes the draftsman is one of the Commissioners; often he is not. When the Statute has been drawn and submitted to the Conference of Commissioners, it is carefully discussed, usually amended in some particulars, and when satisfactory, recommended for adoption by the several states.'[1] It may be added that the draftsmen are in the habit of consulting not only the American Bar Association but also any commercial interests concerned in the matter. For instance, the American Warehousemen's Association co-operated with Professor Williston in the drafting of the Uniform Warehouse Receipts Act, which was recommended by the Commissioners for adoption in 1906.[2] Down to about 1937 the Commissioners had recommended the adoption of sixty-eight uniform laws, and there were 704 adoptions, 341 of which related to eleven of the uniform laws. Only one of the uniform laws, i.e. the Negotiable Instruments Law, has been adopted by all the States, but the Uniform Sales Law has been accepted by the majority of them. A more limited acceptance has taken place in the case of the uniform laws relating to Bills of Lading, Partnership and Stock Transfers.[3] In one instance, i.e. that of the Uniform Written Obligations Law, only two States (Pennsylvania and Utah) have adopted this law.

How far the results of half a century's toil are to be regarded as an adequate return for the efforts which have been made is a question on which it would be impertinent for an English writer to express any views, especially if regard is had to the division of opinion which exists in the United States. It would appear that the process of unification is faced with certain difficulties, some of which are connected with the special features of American law taken as a whole. To begin with, unification is in competition with a movement for the extension of federal powers either through direct legislation or by constitutional amendment or by indirect legislation such as the federal laws which regulate inter-State commerce.[4] Secondly, the task of securing uniformity in the laws of forty-eight different States is one of almost incredible difficulty. How formidable it can be is shown by the fact that in the early days of the movement it was necessary, in the period from 1918 to 1923, to resort

1 Williston, *Life and Law*, p. 218.
2 *Ibid.* p. 222. See also Gutteridge, 'The Law of England and America Relating to Warehouse Receipts', *Journal of C.L.* (3rd Ser.), vol. III (1921), p. 5.
3 Lawson, *op. cit.* at p. 22.
4 Barratt, *op. cit.* p. 227. An illustration of a law of this character is the Federal Bills of Lading Act which concerns the carriage of goods beyond the boundaries of a single state. Williston, *op. cit.* p. 223.

to the legislatures of the various States on no fewer than 343 occasions in order to give effect to thirty drafts prepared by the Commissioners.[1] Further, it is urged that it is idle to speak of unification when a draft uniform law is only adopted by a minority of the States, though, as Professor Williston points out, this is not, standing by itself, any argument against the value of attempts to arrive at uniformity.[2] The strongest objection advanced against the movement seems to be one which is not limited to the problem of internal unification in the United States but is common to unification in all its various forms, namely, the possibility that a uniform law which is of universal application may be interpreted in a different way in each of the several jurisdictions adopting the law.[3] The remedy for this state of affairs is, no doubt, to provide for a central tribunal of appeal which could undertake the task of ensuring uniformity of interpretation, but there is no such tribunal in existence. It would seem that this objection, coupled with the difficulty of securing complete uniformity, has been the chief factor in producing a considerable volume of active or latent hostility towards the movement for unification. But, as Professor Williston points out,[4] with commercial laws, at all events, 'every approach to uniformity is a gain'. Moreover, there is no reason to hold that difficulties created by conflicts of interpretation or incomplete unification have destroyed, though they may, perhaps, have impaired, the utility of such measures as those, for instance, which have been based on the Brussels Conventions on Maritime Law.

To us in England the importance of the uniform laws of the United States lies, first of all, in their value in providing an indication of certain directions in which our law is susceptible to improvement. The American Uniform Warehouse Receipts Act, for example, points the way to a much-needed revision and simplification of the difficult and obscure part of English commercial law which relates to dealings with documents of title to goods.[5] The American Uniform Sales Act, which is largely based on our Sale of Goods Act, 1893, is also, in certain respects, an improvement on its prototype,[6] and there is much to be said in favour of

---

1 MacChesney, 'Progress in Passage and Formulation of Uniform State Laws', *Journal of the American Bar Association* for October 1923.   2 *Op. cit.* at p. 219.

3 Pound, 'What may we expect from Comparative Law?', *Journal of the American Bar Association* (1936), p. 58; Beutel, 'The Necessity of a New Technique of Interpreting the N.I.L.', *Tulane L.R.* vol. VIII, p. 1. It should be noted that most of the uniform laws contain a provision that interpretation shall be such as to 'effectuate' the purpose of securing uniformity but it seems doubtful whether this expedient can be regarded as a solution of the difficulty.

4 *Op. cit.* p. 219.   5 See Gutteridge, *op. cit.*

6 Lawson, *loc. cit.*, refers to an opinion said to have been expressed by Mr Arthur Cohen to that effect. See Gutteridge, 'An International Code of the Law of Sale', *British Yearbook of I.L.* vol. 14 (1933), at p. 79.

a revision of the English Act which would bring the two measures nearer to one another.[1]

It has also been suggested that the American uniform laws might provide a basis for some degree, at all events, of unification of the commercial laws of the United States and the British Commonwealth.[2] This, however, is a question which calls for more detailed examination than is possible in this brief summary of the situation. The difficulties which lie in the path of any such enterprise are obvious. To begin with the process of unification of the commercial laws of the several states of the American Federation is incomplete, and the same is true, though to a lesser extent, of the laws of the British Commonwealth. The problem presented by the possibility of divergent interpretations of any unified law which might be agreed upon also looms heavily on the horizon. But if certain branches of commercial law, e.g. the Law of Sale of Goods and of Negotiable Instruments, should, at some future date, become approximately uniform in each of the two spheres concerned, the proposal would at once enter the sphere of practical politics. In the meantime, it is of interest to note that a movement is taking place in the United States for the compilation of a Federal commercial code, and that work has already begun on the law relating to sale of goods. The American Law Institute is seeking the co-operation of the Conference of Commissioners on uniform State laws in the preparation of the code, and the hope has been expressed that this may be an important step towards the ultimate adoption of an international commercial code.[3]

1 See Gutteridge, *loc. cit.* and McCurdy, 'Some Differences between the English and the American Law of Sale of Goods', *Journal of C.L.* (3rd Ser.), vol. IX (1927), p. 15.
2 Lawson, *op. cit.*
3 W. Draper Lewis, 'The American Law Institute', *Journal of C.L.* (3rd Ser.), vol. XXV (1943), p. 25.

Chapter XIII

THE MECHANISM OF UNIFICATION

THERE is no standard process for the unification of divergent rules of law. The methods employed must necessarily vary, according to the type of unification which is contemplated, and the subject-matter of the rules which are to be unified. Thus procedure which is well adapted to meet the case of bilateral unification might be inappropriate if the rules to be unified are drawn from several systems of law. Then again, 'lawyer's law', such as the rules of private international law, can be dealt with by methods which would be out of place when the interests of commerce and industry are at stake. But, in practice, the great majority of the attempts to secure unification have been made by international assemblies of various descriptions, and the methods adopted in such cases have, in substance, become more or less stereotyped. The procedure which is followed is in brief as follows.[1] The assembly in question is convened to consider proposals for unified law which emanate either from one of the governments concerned or from some private organisation which is interested in the matter. If the assembly has diplomatic powers the proposals are usually, though not invariably, submitted in the form of a draft uniform law which can be annexed to an international convention. If, on the other hand, the assembly is a meeting convened by a private organisation, the proposals are framed as 'Rules', which are intended either to provide a basis for future diplomatic action, or to be adopted voluntarily by the members of the organisation.[2] The proposals are discussed in first, second and third readings, and, when agreement is reached, are referred to a drafting committee (*comité de rédaction*) which prepares the final resolutions to be submitted to the assembly.

It rarely happens that the proposals are accepted as they stand. Usually they undergo very considerable amendment and are, moreover, in many

1 Except in the case of bilateral unification which is usually a matter for negotiation between the foreign offices of the governments concerned. The procedure in such event follows the usual diplomatic course. For an example of such procedure, see the *Report of the Foreign Judgments Committee*, 1932 (Cmd. 4213).

2 For an example of a draft convention with a uniform law annexed see the Geneva Convention of 1930 providing a Uniform Law for Bills of Exchange and Promissory Notes, *Records of the First Session of the International Conference for the Unification of Laws on Bills of Exchange, Promissory Notes and Cheques* (League of Nations Publications, II, Economic and Financial, 1930, II, 27). The York-Antwerp Rules, 1924, on the Law of General Average, afford an illustration of unification of a voluntary character. The minutes of the Hague Conferences on Private International Law and of the meetings of the Institute of International Law and the International Law Association should be consulted by those who are interested in the details of the procedure usually adopted.

cases only adopted subject to 'reservations' (*réserves*). These reservations constitute a definite stumbling block to effective unification, because they may be so far-reaching as to reduce uniformity to vanishing point. In such conditions unification becomes a pretence,[1] and in some circles the view is held that reservations should never be permitted. Another expedient which may deprive agreements to adopt unified law of much of their value is the device of a 'model' law (*loi modèle*). This means that no government is bound to accept the law as it stands, but only undertakes to give effect to its purport, thus creating many loopholes for escape from the consequences of unification. The drawbacks to this expedient are, however, so apparent that it has found little favour.

Where a uniform law is scheduled to an international convention it is usual to provide that it shall be ratified by a certain number of States before a certain date, and that if this is not done the obligations of signatory States under the convention shall not arise. Other clauses, which are 'common form', provide for denunciation of the convention by signatories after the expiry of a stated period, and for the revision of its terms on application being made for that purpose by a fixed number of signatories. If a State with colonial possessions is a party to the convention it is also necessary to include in the convention such provisions as may be required in order to enable a signatory State to extend the convention to any of its colonies or protected or mandated territories.

So far no mention has been made of a feature of the normal process of unification which is of particular interest to comparative lawyers, namely, the 'Report' (*Rapport*). When provisional agreement has been reached as to the terms of a uniform law or uniform rules, a memorandum known as the 'Report' is prepared either by a member of the assembly designated for that purpose (*Rapporteur*), or by a small committee. The 'Report' usually takes the form of a running commentary on the law or, as the case may be, on the rules, article by article. Its object is to explain the reasons which have led to the framing of a uniform law or of uniform rules and to clear up any ambiguities which might be thought to arise from their phraseology. Continental lawyers are strongly opposed to the insertion of 'definition' clauses in statutes or treaties, and if there has been a difference of opinion in the preliminary stages as to the meaning of certain words which are employed it is usual to dispose of the matter by dealing with it in the 'Report'. One very often hears it said at international conferences that time need not be wasted on debating the effect of the employment of particular phraseology because any difficulties can be cleared up in the 'Report'. In this connection it must be remembered

---

1 Resolutions of this kind have been picturesquely described as *unification de façade*.

that the 'Report' forms part of the *travaux préparatoires* or preliminary matter which can be referred to by a continental judge in order to aid him in the interpretation of a written rule of law. On the other hand, an English judge must, in like circumstances, disregard the 'Report', and this difference in practice may have far-reaching consequences.[1] Linguistic troubles may also arise because uniform laws are sometimes drafted in more than one language.[2] In fact, the problems which occur in the course of the unifying process are manifold, but they appear, for the most part, to be inseparable from any attempt to arrive at international agreement.

The above outline of the procedure which is generally followed in carrying through proposals for unification does not pretend to be more than an imperfect summary of the position; its object is to pave the way for a consideration of the methods employed, and a discussion of the measures which could conceivably be adopted for their improvement. It is hoped, however, that enough has been said to provide the necessary background for a discussion of unification in its more technical aspects, and, in particular, to emphasise the fact that the process is one of complexity calling for the intervention of agencies of a widely differing character.

Unification is, at best, a protracted and laborious enterprise; it must of necessity pass through several stages, and the difficulties encountered cannot be appreciated unless each of these stages is considered apart from the others. The first, which may be described as the 'preliminary' or 'exploratory' stage, consists in the employment of the comparative method in order to ascertain whether unification is possible and, if so, along what lines. The second or 'formulatory' stage involves the formulation of proposals for unified law, which will furnish the necessary groundwork for discussion and negotiation between the countries, or between the private interests which are concerned in the matter. The nature of such proposals is indicated by the term which is sometimes applied to them, i.e. *bases de discussion*. The third stage, which may be referred to as the 'operative' stage, consists in the drafting of uniform laws or rules which can be submitted to the governments or private interests for formal ratification. The mere fact that proposals are adopted by an international assembly does not mean that unification has been achieved. A final stage is necessary in which the resolutions of the assembly are ratified by the governments or other interests concerned, and are, if necessary, put into effect, either by legislation, or, in the case of private interests, by the incorporation of the draft rules in printed forms of contract, or in some other way.

---

1 *Ante*, p. 108. For an interesting exception to this rule see Lauterpacht, 'Interpretation of Treaties', *Harvard L.R.* vol. XLVIII (1935), p. 567.

2 *Ante*, p. 111.

The Preliminary Stage

A comparison of the divergent rules is an indispensable preliminary to any proposals for the unification of private law. Such comparison must be more than a pedestrian compilation of similarities and differences. The laws must be examined in the light of their political, social or economic purpose, and regard must be paid to their dynamic rather than to their static or doctrinal aspects. This is usually a complicated task and may involve protracted investigations which would be beyond the powers of an individual investigator. It is, consequently, entrusted, as a rule, either to a committee of experts appointed *ad hoc*, or to one of the scientific institutes which are engaged in comparative research. These scientific institutes are few in number, and only one of them, namely, the International Institute for the Unification of Private Law at Rome, was created solely for the purpose of unification.[1] The Institute of Intellectual Co-operation, which resembled the Rome Institute in so far as it was a subsidiary organ of the League of Nations, also engages in the work of unification within its allotted sphere, e.g. copyright law, etc. The Rome Institute is still in being, but, at the time of writing, the fate of the Berlin Institute of Foreign Private Law and Private International Law is not known. Certain continental universities have established Institutes of Comparative Law, notably in France, where much comparative research of value has been carried out in the institutes attached to the Universities of Paris, Lyon, Strasbourg, and Toulouse. No organisation of this kind exists in Great Britain, though the Institute of Advanced Legal Studies suggested by the report of Lord Macmillan's Committee would, if it comes into being, be equipped to carry out comparative work bearing on problems of unification. In the United States the preliminary stage of unification is carried out by draftsmen appointed by the Commissioners on Uniform State Laws assisted by expert advisers.[2] Up to the present the scientific institutes have not, with the exception of the Rome and Berlin Institutes and the American Law Institute, played a very prominent part in the movement for unity of law, and the spade work which must precede the actual process of unification has, for the most part, been carried out by committees of the bodies which engage in the unifying process. It is only fair to add that both the scientific institutes and the committees of experts draw the greater part of their materials from sources which have been created by the efforts of individual investigators. These sources are scattered; they are often in many languages, and it is the function of the

1 For an account of the activities of this Institute see *British Year Book of I.L.* vol. 17 (1936), p. 190.   2 See *ante*, p. 167.

comparative lawyer to reduce the material obtained from them to such form as will allow of its use in pointing the way to unification. The work in this preliminary stage of the unifying process is, generally speaking, carried out very competently. In addition to supplying the unificationists with the information they need it has also resulted in contributions of great value to knowledge of the law.[1]

The Formulatory Stage

It is at this point that the difficulties connected with unification begin to appear. Concrete proposals must be framed for the consideration of an international assembly, and this gives rise to a series of problems. It must be ascertained how far the interests which may be affected would welcome unification, and how far and in what way the obstacles created by certain difficulties, which are inherent in all proposals to unify law, can be overcome. In particular, care must be exercised to interfere as little as is possible with the procedural rules of the systems of law concerned, and vigilance is necessary to avoid any invasion of the extremely debatable territory occupied by the bogey of all unificationists and private international lawyers, namely, the national rules of public policy. In general, it is essential to ascertain in advance how far the interests concerned are prepared to abandon their national rules and to accept uniformity of law. A method which is often employed for this purpose is to issue a questionnaire addressed either to government departments or associations of lawyers, chambers of commerce and similar bodies. The value of this expedient is doubtful, because experience suggests that a questionnaire seldom produces the information which is desired. It is extremely difficult, without undue prolixity, to frame a questionnaire in such a way that it will produce the replies which are needed. Moreover, government departments and private organisations are reluctant to commit themselves in advance and, however carefully the questionnaire may be framed, the replies will often be either incomplete or evasive.

The formulation of proposals to be laid before an international assembly may, in certain circumstances, prove to be a lengthy process. The preparation of a draft International Law of Sale by the Rome Institute, on behalf of the League of Nations, extended over a period of no less than ten years. The work of drafting is entrusted, as a rule, to a committee of experts representing, so far as is possible, the various systems of law which may

---

1 Notable instances are Dr Rabel's magisterial treatise on the Comparative Law of Sale (*Der Warenverkauf*) of which only one volume has, so far, been issued, and Professor David's report to the Rome Institute on the Comparative Law of Arbitration (*Rapport sur l'Arbitrage*).

be affected. This feature of the process causes much delay; it involves getting together a committee composed of persons, some of whom reside at a great distance, or are only available at certain times of the year. In order to minimise inconvenience from this source it is usual to group the systems which are of a kindred nature such as those of the Latin countries and to appoint a member to represent each group. In some cases a member who is unable to attend is empowered to nominate a substitute; every effort is, in fact, made to avoid delay though not always with success. The members of these committees are usually lawyers, but, more especially when the rules of commercial law are to be unified, they are assisted by advisers who possess the necessary knowledge of the business technicalities involved.

Drafts prepared by committees of experts are, as a rule, accompanied by a 'Report' which sets out the arguments in favour of the draft and also places on record any differences of opinion there may have been as between the experts.

The Operative Stage of Unification

The next step is to submit the proposals to the scrutiny of an international assembly. Assemblies convened for this purpose are, broadly speaking, of two kinds. The membership of an assembly may consist, on the one hand, of delegates duly appointed by their governments and invested with authority to sign any convention which may be the outcome of the deliberations. A body of this kind is styled a 'Diplomatic Conference'. On the other hand, the assembly may be devoid of any official character, having been called into being by one of the private organisations which has made itself responsible for framing proposals for unification. These organisations, which will be referred to hereafter as 'the Societies', have, up to the present, been the most active and influential element in the unifying movement. Some of them are professedly legal in character; others are associations of men of business. Both have this in common, that they seek to bring together persons interested in international affairs either from a legal or an economic standpoint. The division between legal and other problems, arising internationally, is not always observed, and questions which are primarily of legal importance may come up for discussion at the meetings of a commercial organisation and vice versa. In Europe the most important of the legal societies are the Institute of International Law, the International Law Association, and the Congress of Comparative Law, and in the United States the Special Section of the American Bar Association on Comparative and International Law, and the American Foreign Law Association. The most important of the commercial societies are the International Maritime Committee, composed partly of lawyers and partly of persons engaged in the shipping industry, and the International Chamber of Commerce. Both these bodies have taken an active part in the movement for the unification of maritime and commercial law.

A society which occupies a special position is the Institute of International Law (*Institut de Droit International*). Its personnel, which is limited in numbers, is constituted on a co-optative basis, being recruited from the ranks of recognised experts in public and private international law. Membership of the Institute is regarded as a distinction, and its deliberations and decisions command a high degree of respect. So far as unification is concerned its activities are confined to the domain of private international law.

The assemblies of the 'Societies' are usually held annually or biennially, and, on each occasion, in different countries, though in certain instances, such as that of the Congress of Comparative Law at the Hague, the place of meeting may be of a permanent character. The attendances at these assemblies are sometimes very large, and an assembly is often divided into sections which meet separately. Each section passes its own resolutions and drafts its own report, but these are submitted to the assembly as a whole for adoption or rejection. The proceedings are, for the most part, conducted in the French language, but some of the Societies allow considerable liberty in this respect—a concession which often slows down the rate of progress as it may involve the use of interpreters. It is a common practice to have a shorthand note taken of the proceedings, and this, together with the reports and resolutions which have been adopted, are embodied in minutes which are printed and circulated to the members. These records are often of very considerable value to students of comparative law. The resolutions adopted by the Societies have only a persuasive value, and this may result in the same subject-matter being placed on the agenda in successive years, the proposals for unification being in that event redrafted in the light of the experience gained at assemblies of earlier date.

It should be observed that, although the methods adopted by Diplomatic Conferences and the assemblies of the Societies are, in substance, the same, they differ essentially in one respect. The resolutions of a Diplomatic Conference in favour of unification are passed for the definite purpose of subsequent legislative action, and this has certain consequences. In the first place, they are drafted in a form which will enable them to be enforced without passing through the hands of a parliamentary draftsman. The reason for this is that in certain of the civil-law countries the terms of an international convention may become effective as soon as the convention is approved by the legislature, and it is not necessary, as in the common-law countries, to embody them in a statute. On the other hand, it is not contemplated that the resolutions of the Societies shall be binding on anyone, and so they are frequently nothing more than an expression of the belief that unification might be possible along the lines indicated in the resolution. Secondly, the fact that the resolutions of a Diplomatic Conference carry with them at least a *prima facie* obligation to give effect to a convention may result in a great many reservations or in conditional signatures. This consideration does not apply to resolutions of the Societies, so that although these may be adopted without dissent it does not follow that they have met with general acceptance. It is therefore necessary in many instances to discount the face value of such resolutions.

It is unnecessary to dwell on the operation of the mechanism of unification in its preliminary stage, for, as we have already seen, no serious fault can be found with the methods employed in ascertaining the position from a purely comparative point of view. On the other hand, there appear to be certain objections to the present practice in its later stages, namely, those of the formulation of proposals for unified law and their subsequent discussion. In the first place, owing to the number of agencies employed there is sometimes a regrettable absence of co-ordination in the efforts made to arrive at unification. It is by no means rare to find more than one organisation engaged on the same task, and the result may be considerable overlapping of effort and confusion. It may even happen that the meeting of an international assembly is selected as the arena for a conflict between rival schemes for unified law presented by two or more organisations. How far it may be possible to remedy this situation by the centralisation of the process of unification is a matter to be discussed hereafter.

The second objection to the present system is that proposals for unification are often submitted to international assemblies without adequate consideration of the difficulties which are involved. Insufficient precautions are taken to ensure that all the interests involved are consulted; there may have been no real effort to obtain such advice and assistance as may be available for carrying out the delicate task of reconciling rival points of view and overcoming obstacles of a technical nature. There is, moreover, a regrettable tendency to assume that unified law has a virtue which is quite its own, and that its merits only require exposition in order to secure its immediate acceptance. This is unfortunately not the case. Unified law is called upon to function in many varied environments, and it may well be that a rule which might operate successfully in the case of certain countries cannot be dovetailed into the legal and economic systems of other countries.

The inadequacy of the steps taken by framers of proposals to discover any extrinsic problems which may have to be faced or to ascertain the views of the governments, the legal profession and commercial circles in the countries affected is, however, not always a matter for which they can be blamed. Government departments are not always easy of approach. Legal practitioners and judges are for the most part apathetic in matters of law reform, even if they are not hostile. The co-operation of men of business is more easily secured because they are more closely affected by conflicts of laws, though, as matters now stand, it is not always easy for those responsible for the process of unification to establish the kind of contact with business circles which is desirable. Changes in the law do not always operate evenly throughout a particular trade; the impact of a proposed new rule on the interests of importers and exporters may not be the same. 'Big business' tends to predominate in the commercial societies, and 'big business' is apt to have its own solutions of the questions at issue, in the shape of the rules embodied in standard forms of contract, and to be less interested in the problem than those who trade on a more modest scale. It must be said, however, that the commercial societies, and, in particular, the International Chamber of Commerce, have always shown the greatest readiness to afford any assistance in their power, and that any shortcomings which there may be in the present method of testing the effect of proposed changes on the business situation cannot fairly be laid at their door.

It is sometimes suggested that committees and other bodies engaged in the process of unification should always contain an element of business men, but this is an expedient which is rarely successful. Lawyers and merchants do not always understand one another: law has its own jargon and so has commerce. It is too much to expect a busy man of affairs to spend his time listening to a discussion of legal technicalities which mean nothing to him. The problem of co-operation is, in fact, one of very great difficulty, though its solution is a matter of urgent necessity.

Thirdly, the present method of drafting proposals for unification in the form of a statute or rules may have unfortunate consequences. Proposals of this kind must often be accepted or rejected as they stand, and this may have the effect of destroying the prospect of agreement along different lines. It may happen that the proposals are misconceived, but that there are alternative solutions which would have a good chance of success. In existing circumstances the debate must centre round the draft convention or rules as presented for discussion, and the door is apt to be closed to the consideration of possible alternatives. Attention may also be diverted, in this way, from the problems awaiting solution, and be concentrated on points of detail and the minutiae of draftsmanship. The argument that it is very difficult to secure an adequate discussion unless proposals take the form of draft rules of law is one which carries weight, but situations may often arise in which proposals of a general character would obtain sympathetic consideration although strenuous opposition would be aroused by solutions crystallised in the rigid form of a set of rules.

It is submitted that the main defect in the procedure adopted at present is that the 'Report' which is annexed to proposals for discussion is pushed into the background by the draft unifying rules. This is an inversion of the method which would be most likely to produce good results. The draft rules could with advantage be treated, not as the definite proposals, but as representing the kind of form that unified law would assume if the proposed unification were put into legislative shape. The result would be that the nature of the changes to be carried out in existing laws would be clearly indicated, and that the premature discussion of points of drafting would be avoided.

The fourth and, perhaps, the most important criticism of the present procedure is that which concerns the scrutiny of proposals for unification by the various bodies which are charged with this task. Diplomatic conferences are not open to this criticism in the same degree as the miscellaneous assemblies convened by the private organisations. The delegates attending Diplomatic Conferences are selected with care, and it may be presumed that they are competent to arrive at conclusions which are of a serious character. This is also the case with the deliberations of such bodies as the Institute of International Law and the International Maritime Committee. But the same cannot, unfortunately, be said of all the Societies. It is difficult to resist the conclusion that many of the ills which have overtaken the unifying movement are due to what may, for the sake of convenience, be termed the 'Congress' method. The meetings of certain Societies are attended by large numbers—an assembly of some three or four hundred people being by no means unusual. The members drift from one section of the assembly to another as the fancy takes them, and if they happen to be present when a resolution is moved they may vote on it whether they have listened to the previous discussion or not, regardless of the fact that the matter at issue may be one of which they have only a superficial knowledge or no knowledge at all.[1] The value to be

---

[1] Rabel very truly remarks that even where a Society limits its membership to persons with expert knowledge the result of discussions may well be to emphasise rather than to minimise differences of opinion: 'Kongresse pflegen den wissenschaftlichen Meinungsstreit zu bereichen, aber nicht zu schlichten...' ('Die Fachgebiete des Kaiser-Wilhelm Instituts für ausländisches und internationales Privatrecht', in *25 Jahre Kaiser-Wilhelm Gesellschaft zur Förderung der Wissenschaften*, vol. III, at p. 78).

attached to resolutions of this nature is, consequently, almost negligible, but, unfortunately, this is not always appreciated by the outside world, and these resolutions may pass muster as authoritative expressions of opinion, and be quoted by text-book writers and even by international tribunals. Where unification is in question this unsatisfactory feature of the proceedings of these Societies very much diminishes the importance to be attached to proposals emanating from them. But quite apart from this, the 'Congress' method is open to other objections. It is often a source of mortification to the executive officials of a large international assembly if it breaks up without passing some sort of a resolution. The tendency is, therefore, to endeavour to steer the proceedings in the direction which is most likely to secure the votes of the majority of those who are in the assembly room at the crucial moment. If the assembly shows any signs of reluctance the members present are exhorted to lay aside their individual convictions and to vote for the resolution in the interests of the sacred cause of international unity. Pressure is also brought to bear on recalcitrant members in the lobbies of the assembly room and in the lounges and smoking rooms of hotels. If all else fails concessions may be made which destroy the practical effect of any resolution which is passed, or the delegates of some of the interests concerned may be permitted to attach reservations to their votes, with a like result. National blocks of members may also endeavour to force a decision which is favourable to the interests of their countries.

There are other aspects of the 'Congress' method which detract to a certain extent from its usefulness. The rules of procedure of these Societies are often treated with scant respect, and resolutions may be moved on the spur of the moment and carried in a snap division. Much may depend on the venue of the meeting of a peripatetic society, because it is inevitable that the majority of those attending an assembly should come from the country in which the meetings are held or from countries within easy reach. A feature of these congresses which must be referred to, though only with reluctance, is that their work may be hampered by the introduction of an element of 'joy riding' into the proceedings. An elaborate programme of hospitality is drawn up and banquets, receptions, excursions and social activities of various kinds may occupy a disproportionate amount of the time and energy of the assembly. The business in hand may consequently be conducted at high pressure, and resolutions may be pushed through by masterful chairmen in order to allow time for attendance at some function or other. Anyone who has experience of international conferences will be aware of occasions on which matters of importance have been under discussion, but the exigences of debate have had to yield place to the demands of luncheons, banquets or trips by charabanc or on a river steamboat. Social intercourse is, of course, an element of great value in securing international agreement, and it is not intended to suggest that entertainments should be banned, but a plea is submitted for a policy which would confine them within such limits as may be required to avoid conflict with the measured and unhurried deliberations of international assemblies.

Finally, since effective unification of law involves legislation by all the countries concerned, it does not seem to be out of place to refer to certain difficulties which have to be faced if the participation of Great Britain in unification is to be ensured. These centre, for the most part, round the methods of embodying the relevant proposals in the form of draft codified rules to which allusion has already been made. The assemblies engaged in promoting unification are, generally speaking, multi-lingual, and their resolutions are sometimes drafted in English, more often in French and rarely in some other language. The result is that the draftsman, who inevitably has at the back of his mind the drafting technique of his own law and its legal principles and terminology, tends to impress on his product the features of a particular system. He may, for instance, use terms which are not capable of translation into another language without giving rise either to a false meaning or to some expression which is bereft of any meaning. He may base his draft on some legal concept which is not common to every system of law or on a rule of law which is peculiar to his own system. In any of these events the rules which he formulates may give rise to difficulties in the international sphere.

Further, the technique of legal draftsmanship is not the same everywhere. In the Latin countries the draftsman aims at a concise, well-phrased and logical expression of a rule; in England the preference is for a more pragmatical statement, which has no claims to literary or legal elegance, but is designed to meet the practical situations which the draftsman has in mind. The English practice of inserting definition clauses in Acts of Parliament is viewed with disfavour on the Continent, whilst cross-references to other sections of the same statute, which are anathema to English lawyers, are common practice on the Continent. Differences in legal terminology are sometimes a stumbling block, and at other times a source of danger. These difficulties are, perhaps, inevitable, but they emphasise the necessity for the exercise of the greatest care and the avoidance of undue haste in presenting proposals for unification.

The Future of the Unifying Process

The situation which now exists in the field of the unification of private law is one which readily lends itself to criticism, but it is not so easy to suggest appropriate remedies. So far as faulty technique may be to blame for the meagre results of the movement for unification, the main question, which calls for careful consideration and discussion, is whether the present practice of submitting draft uniform laws to international assemblies is the best method that could be devised. We have already given reasons for thinking that it would be preferable to confine the proceedings at assemblies of this nature to the discussion of any differences that there may be between the various systems of law, and to the passing of resolutions of a general character as to the manner of removing the points of conflict. In this event the duty of drafting the appropriate uniform laws could be confided to skilled hands, and be discharged without undue haste, free from exposure to the vagaries which, at present, only too often characterise what we have described as the 'Congress' method.[1] A further question, which arises in this connection, concerns the principle of 'One nation one vote' which prevails at present, and is apt to be a serious impediment to unification if important commercial or other interests are involved. 'It is not satisfactory', said Sir Montague Chalmers with reference to the attempts to unify the law of negotiable instruments, 'that the combined vote of England and the United States should be neutralised by the votes of Hayti and Montenegro.'[2] It is, however, difficult to suggest a solution of this problem, as alternative methods of counting votes on the basis of population would confer an undue advantage on certain countries. The best and most rapid road to uniformity of law may, perhaps, be to confine the process of unification, in the first instance, to the laws of the countries most deeply concerned, and, if agreement is reached, to invite the other countries to come into line.

The most urgent problem of all, however, is that of the waste of effort and confusion that has, at times, been caused by the existence of competing agencies engaged in the work of unification. The remedy for this state of affairs would seem to lie in the establishment of a rallying ground for unificatory activities—a kind of international clearing house—which would co-ordinate and supervise activities of this nature and also facilitate the

---

1 Chalmers illustrates the unsatisfactory character of the present practice by reference to the proceedings at the Hague Conference on the Law of Bills of Exchange. He observes that 'some questions were debated at considerable length, while others, and not always the least important ones, were sometimes perfunctorily and inadequately discussed'. *Journal of C.L.* (N.S.), vol. XI (1910), at p. 279.
2 *Ibid.*

collection of any information that might be required, either from governmental or other sources. It is not necessary that an authority of this kind should itself undertake the work of drafting the uniform laws. This could, as was done in the past by the League of Nations, be delegated by it to the appropriate bodies. But it would be possible, in this way, to avoid the overlapping of attempts to achieve uniformity, and to discourage the ill-timed, or over-ambitious, projects which are largely responsible for the paucity of success which has hitherto characterised the movement for the unification of law.

The exercise of these co-ordinating and supervisory functions would appear to be a task falling within the province of the Economic and Social Council established under the provisions of the Charter of the United Nations. It is, in any event, certain that the solution of most of the problems which, at present, render the unification of law in the international sphere a matter of such great difficulty can only be reached by the provision of some means by which the movement may be guided into the proper channels, so that the law may be unified in the directions in which uniformity is both necessary and practicable.

Appendix[1]

LIST OF FOREIGN LAW REPORTS & LAW REVIEWS

[Note.] This list does not claim to be complete, especially as regards the period after 1939. Its principal aim is to present an exhaustive compilation of Law Reports and Law Reviews in matters of private law. Consequently, Law Reports and Law Reviews specialising in one of the following subjects, i.e. Administrative Law, Constitutional Law, Criminal Law and Criminology, International Law, Legal History, Public Insurance and Tax Law, have been omitted, though not invariably.

The survey of the Reports and Reviews of each country is divided into two parts. Part I deals with official or general Reports. Part II deals with other Reports and with Law Reviews. The usual abbreviations are indicated on the left side of each page.

AUSTRIA

See Bibliografia Giuridica Internazionale, vol. I, 1 (1932), p. 71; vol. IV, 1 (1935), p. 135; Zeitschrift für ausländisches und internationales Privatrecht, vol. II (1928), p. 181.

I. Official and general collections of decisions

G.U.	Glaser und Unger. Sammlung von civilrechtlichen Entscheidungen des K.K. Obersten Gerichtshofes.
G.U. (N.F.) or P.S.	Glaser und Unger. Neue Folge, ed. Pfaff und Schey.
S.Z.	Entscheidungen des österreichischen Obersten Gerichtshofes in Zivil- und Justizverwaltungssachen.
	Entscheidungen des österreichischen Obersten Gerichtshofes in Strafsachen und Disziplinarangelegenheiten.

II. Other collections of decisions and Law Reviews

Adler-Clemens.	Sammlung von Entscheidungen zum Handelsgesetzbuch.
Czel.	Czelechowsky. Sammlung wechselrechtlicher Entscheidungen des Obersten Gerichtshofes.
G.H.	Gerichtshalle. Zeitschrift für Rechtspflege und Volkswirtschaft.
G.Z.	Gerichts-Zeitung.
I.A.Bl.	Internationales Anwaltsblatt.

1 Compiled by K. Lipstein, Ph.D., Research Assistant in the Faculty of Law of Cambridge University. Law Reports and Law Reviews published in the U.S.A. and the British Empire are not included.

J.Bl.	Juristische Blätter.
N.Z.	Notariatszeitung.
O.A.Z.	Österreichische Anwalts-Zeitung.
O.V.Bl.	Österreichisches Verwaltungsblatt.
R.Z.	Österreichische Richterzeitung.
Rtspr.	Die Rechtsprechung (ed. by Austrian Banks and Bankers).
V.A.	Versicherungs-Archiv.
Z.Bl.	Zentralblatt für die juristische Praxis.

Bartsch, Pollak, Warhanek. Jahrbuch höchstrichterlicher Entscheidungen.

BALTIC COUNTRIES

Danzig

See Bibliografia Giuridica Internazionale, vol. I, 1 (1932), p. 98; vol. IV, 1 (1935), p. 131.

Danz. Jur. Mon. Schr. (or)	Danziger Juristische Monatsschrift.
Danz. J.M.	
Danz. Jur. Z.	Danziger Juristen-Zeitung.

Esthonia

See Bibliografia Giuridica Internazionale, vol. I, 1 (1932), p. 101; vol. IV, 4 (1935), p. 401; vol. V, 2/3 (1936), p. 365. Annuario di diritto comparato, vol. IV/V, 1 (1930), p. 503; vol. II/III (1929), p. 952.

| Riigikohtu otsused. | (Decisions of the Supreme Tribunal.) |
| Valge, J. | Riigikohtu administratiiv-osakonnas. (Decisions of the administrative section of the Supreme Tribunal.) |

Periodicals

| Õigus. | (The Law.) |
| Politsei | Eesti Politseileht. (Journal of the Esthonian Police.) |

Latvia

See Bibliografia Giuridica Internazionale, vol. IV, 2 (1935), p. 149; Zeitschrift für ausländisches und internationales Privatrecht, vol. II (1928), p. 957.

I.   Official or general collections of decisions

Latvijas Senāta Civilkasācijas departamenta spriedumi. (Decisions of the Department of Civil Cassation of the Senate.)

Latvijas Senāta Kriminālkasācijas departamenta spriedumi. (Decisions of the Department of Criminal Cassation of the Senate.)

| Konradi and Walter (or) | Izvilkumi no Latvijas Senāta Civilkasācijas departa- |
| Izv. | menta spriedumiem. (Extracts from decisions of the Department of Civil Cassation of the Latvian Senate.) |

Kamradziuss, F.	Latvijas Senāta Kriminālā kasācijas departamenta spriedmu tezu pilnīgs kopojums. (Complete collections of the principles contained in the decisions of the Department of Criminal Cassation of the Latvian Senate.)

II. Other collections of decisions and Law Reviews

Jur.	Jurists (The Lawyer).
R.Z.R.W.	Rigasche Zeitschrift für Rechtswissenschaft.
T.M.V.	Tieslietu Ministrijas Vēstnesis. (Journal of the Ministry of Justice.)
Z.i.S.	Zakon i Sud. (The Law and the Court.) (In Russian.)

LITHUANIA

See Bibliografia Giuridica Internazionale, vol. IV, 2 (1935), p. 181; vol. v, 2/3 (1936), p. 355.

Toliušis ir Požela	Vyriausiojo Tribunolo...metų civilnių kasacinių bylų sprendimų rinkinys. (Collection of the decisions of the Supreme Tribunal in matters of civil cassation.)

Vyriausiojo Tribunolo visuotinų susirinkimų nutarimai baudžiamųjų ir civilnių kasacinių bylų sprendimai. (Decisions of the Supreme Tribunal in full session, its judgments in matters of criminal and civil cassation.)

Vyriausiojo Tribunolo baudžiamųjų ir civilnių kasacinių bylų sprendimai. (Decisions of the Supreme Tribunal in matters of criminal and civil cassation.)

Vyriausiolojo Tribunolo baudžiamųjų kasacinių bylų sprendimai. (Decisions of the Supreme Tribunal in matters of criminal law.)

Periodicals

Pl.	Policija. (The Police.)
Ts.	Teisé. (The Law.)

BELGIUM

See Bibliografia Giuridica Internazionale, vol. I, 1 (1932), p. 81; vol. IV, 1 (1935) p. 107; Annuario di diritto comparato, vol. IV and v, 1 (1930), p. 471.

I. Official or general collections of decisions

B.J.	La Belgique Judiciaire, Gazette des Tribunaux belges et étrangères.
J.T.	Journal des Tribunaux.
P.P.	Pandectes Périodiques.
Pas.	Pasicrisie Belge, Recueil général et mensuel de la jurisprudence des cours et tribunaux de Belgique.
R. Tijd.	Rechtskundig Tijdschrift.
R. Week.	Rechtskundig Weekblad.

II. Other collections of decisions and Law Reviews

An. Not.	Annales du notariat et de l'enregistrement.
Bul. Ass.	Bulletin des assurances.
Bul. D. Cpr.	Bulletin de l'Institut belge de droit comparé.
Bul. Jur. I.	Bulletin des juridictions indigènes (Elisabethville).
J. Paix.	Journal des juges de paix.
Jur. A.	Jurisprudence du Port d'Anvers.
Jur. B.	Jurisprudence commerciale de Bruxelles.
Jur. Div.	Jurisprudence du divorce et de la séparation de corps.
Jur. Fl.	Jurisprudence commerciale des Flandres.
Jur. L.	Jurisprudence de la Cour d'Appel de Liège.
Jur. Ouv.	Jurisprudence du louage d'ouvrage. (Revue des Conseils de prud'hommes.)
Jur. V.	Jurisprudence commerciale de Verviers.
	Recueil de la jurisprudence de la propriété et du bâtiment.
	Recueil des Sommaires. (Suppl. aux Pandectes Périodiques.)
Res. Im.	Res et Jura Immobilia.
Rev. Acc.	Revue des accidents du travail et des questions de droit industriel.
Rev. Ass. resp.	Revue générale des assurances et des responsabilités.
Rev. Col.	Revue de doctrine et de jurisprudence coloniales.
Rev. Cong.	Revue juridique du Congo Belge.
Rev. D. Adm.	Revue de l'administration et de droit administratif.
Rev. D. Bel.	Revue de droit belge.
R.D.I.L.C.	Revue de droit international et du législation comparée.
Rev. D. Min.	Revue de droit minier.
Rev. D. Pénal.	Revue de droit pénal et de criminologie.
Rev. P. Not.	Revue pratique du notariat.
Rev. P. Soc.	Revue pratique des sociétés civiles et commerciales.

BULGARIA

See Bibliografia Giuridica Internazionale, vol. IV, 2 (1935), p. 145; Annuario di diritto comparato, vol. IV/V, 1 (1930), p. 489.

Periodicals and Law Reviews

Adv. Pr.	Advokatski Pregled. (Journal of the Advocates.)
God.	Godišnik na Iuridičeska Fakultet pri Sofijskia Universitet. (Yearbook of the Faculty of Law of the University of Sofia.)
Pr. M.	Pravna Missăl. (Legal Thought.)
Săd. V.	Sădijski Vestnik. (Journal of the Judges.)

Yur. Ar.   Yuridiceski Archiv. (Juridical Magazine.)
                          Zakonodatelen Pregled. (Review of Legislation.)

                          Collection of Decisions

Igounatoff.   Decisions of the High Court of Cassation. Sofia, 1927.
                          (In Bulgarian.)

CZECHOSLOVAKIA

See Bibliografia Giuridica Internazionale, vol. IV, 4 (1935), p. 447; Zeitschrift für ausländisches und internationales Privatrecht, vol. III (1929), p. 377; vol. VIII (1934), p. 482; vol. X (1936), p. 606.

I. Official or general collections of decisions

Váz.   Vážný. Sbírka rozhodnutí nejvyššiho soudu. (Col-
                          lection of the Decisions of the Czechoslovak
                          Supreme Court of Justice.)

For collections of decisions of the Supreme Court in matters relating to Slovakia and Carpatho-Russia see Z. für ausl. int. Priv. R. vol. X (1936), p. 607; *infra* Jur. Z.T.R. (Suppl.).

II. Other collections of decisions and Law Reviews

Adm. vest.   Administratívny vestník. (Journal of Administration.)
                          Bratislava.
Bull. dr. tch.   Bulletin de droit tchécoslovaque.
                          Časopis pravné a statné vedu. (Review for juridical
                          and political science.)
Č.P.   České právo. (Czech Law.)
                          Česká advocacie. (Czech Advocates.)
                          Deutsches Anwaltsblatt für das Gebiet der Tschecho-
                          slowakischen Republik.
Jur. Z.T.R.   Juristenzeitung für das Gebiet der Tschechoslo-
                          wakischen Republik (with Suppl.: Entscheidungen
                          des Obersten Gerichtes in Brünn=Decisions of the
                          Supreme Court, Brno).
N.Z.   Notariatzeitung. Plzen.
Poj.   Pojistny obzor. (Collection of Insurance.)
Pr.   Právník. (The Lawyer.)
Pracovní pr.   Pracovní právo. (Labour Law.)
Pr. Arch.   Prager Archiv für Gesetzgebung und Rechtsprechung.
Pr. Jur. Z.   Prager juristische Zeitschrift.
Právo čsl.   Právo československé. (Czechoslovak Law.)
Pr. Obz.   Právny obzor. (Collection of Law.) Bratislava.
                          (Slovak.)
                          Richterzeitung. Eger.

Schaff.	Schaffen und Wettbewerb = Soutěž a tvorba. (Production and Competition.)
S.L.	Soudcovské listy. (Judicial Gazette, Journal of the Association of Czech judges.)
	Všehrd. (Journal of the Czechoslovak Lawyers.)

EGYPT

See Bibliografia Giuridica Internazionale, vol. IV, 2 (1935), p. 176.

Periodicals, Law Reviews

Ég. Cont.	Égypte Contemporaine.
Moh.	al-Muḥāma.
Gazette.	Gazette des Tribunaux mixtes.
Ég. Jud.	Égypte Judiciaire.
al-Quānūn	al-Quānūn wal Iqtiṣād. (Law and Economics.)
	Bulletin de Législation et de Jurisprudence Égyptiennes.

Collection of Cases

| 'Abd al-Ḥamīd 'Umar. | Qaṣd as-sabīl ilā qawā 'id al-qānūn allatī qarraratha maḥkamat an-naqḍ wal-ibrām fil-mawād al-madaniyya. (Collection of the maxims in matters of private law laid down by the Court of Cassation.) Cairo, 1935. |

FRANCE

See Bibliografia Giuridica Internazionale, vol. I, 2 (1932), p. 197; vol. IV, 4 (1935), p. 475.

I. Official or general collections of decisions

D. (or) D.P.	Dalloz. Recueil périodique et critique de Jurisprudence, de Législation et de Doctrine.
D.H.	Dalloz. Hebdomadaire de Jurisprudence.
Gaz. Pal.	Gazette du Palais.
Rec. Gaz. Pal.	Recueil de la Gazette du Palais.
Rev. trim. dr. civ.	Revue trimestrielle du droit civil.
Sem. Jur.	Semaine juridique.
S.	Recueil général des Lois et des Arrêts fondé par J.-B. Sirey.

II. Other collections of decisions and Law Reviews

Ann. de dr. comm.	Annales de droit commercial.
Bull. Soc. Législ. Comp.	Bulletin de la Société de Législation comparée.
Dr. aér.	Droit aérien.
Dr. ouvr.	Le droit ouvrier.
Gaz. Trib.	Gazette des Tribunaux.

Journ. des Soc.	Journal des sociétés civiles et commerciales.
Journ. dr. int. (or) Clunet	Journal de droit international.
Journ. Jug. Paix.	Journal des Juges de Paix.
	La propriété industrielle.
Nouv. Rev. dr. int. pr.	Nouvelle Revue de droit international privé.
Rec. Jur. Doctr. et Lég. col.	Recueil général de jurisprudence, de doctrine et de législation coloniales et maritimes.
Rec. Jur. Soc.	Recueil juridiques des Sociétés.
Rec. Lég. Doctr. Jur. col.	Recueil de législation, de doctrine et de jurisprudence coloniales.
Rec. pér. des ass.	Recueil périodique des assurances.
Rev. aér. int.	Revue aéronautique internationale.
Rev. alg. tun. et mar.	Revue algérienne, tunisienne et marocaine de législation et de jurisprudence.
Rev. critique.	Revue critique de droit international.
Rev. crit. de lég. et jur.	Revue critique de législation et de jurisprudence.
Rev. gén. ass. terr.	Revue générale des assurances terrestres.
Rev. gén. des ass. et des resp.	Revue générale des assurances et des responsabilités.
Rev. gén. dr. aér.	Revue générale de droit aérien.
Rev. gén. du droit.	Revue générale du droit, de la législation et de la jurisprudence en France et à l'étranger.
Rev. gén. dr. int. publ.	Revue générale de droit international public.
Rev. dr. fr. comm. mar. et fisc.	Revue de droit français commercial, maritime et fiscal.
Rev. dr. int.	Revue de droit international (De Lapradelle).
Rev. dr. int. privé.	Revue de droit international privé (Darras). *Now:* Revue critique de droit international *and* Nouvelle Revue de droit international privé.
Rev. dr. mar. comparé (Dor.).	Revue de droit maritime comparé.
Rev. dr. public.	Revue de droit public.
Rev. jur. d'Als. et L.	Revue juridique d'Alsace et Lorraine.
	Revue nord-africaine de législation et de jurisprudence commerciale et maritime:
Rev. Sc. et Lég. fin.	Revue de science et de législation financières.

GERMANY

See Bibliografia Giuridica Internazionale, vol. I, 1 (1932), p. 104; vol. IV, 2 (1935), p. 195; vol. V, 2/3 (1936), p. 146.

I. Official or general collections of decisions

R.G.Z. (or) RGZ.	Entscheidungen des Reichsgerichts in Zivilsachen.
R.G.St. (or) RGSt.	Entscheidungen des Reichsgerichts in Strafsachen.
R.A.G. (or) RAG.	Entscheidungen des Reichsarbeitsgerichts.
R.Fin.H. (or) RFH.	Entscheidungen des Reichsfinanzhofs.
J.W. (or) JW.	Juristische Wochenschrift. *Now:* Deutsches Recht
D.R.	vereinigt mit Juristische Wochenschrift (since 1939).

II. Other collections of decisions and Law Reviews

Anw. Bl.	Anwaltsblatt.
	Archiv für Eisenbahnwesen.
Arch. Funk.	Archiv für Funkrecht.
Arch. öff. R.	Archiv des öffentlichen Rechts.
Archiv. civ. Pr. (or) AcP.	Archiv für die civilistische Praxis.
A.W.R.	Archiv für Wettbewerbsrecht.
Bank A.	Bank Archiv.
Bensh. Samml. Arb. R.	Bensheimer. Sammlung arbeitsrechtlicher Entscheidungen. *Now*: Arbeitsrecht, Sammlung der Entscheidungen des Reichsarbeitsgerichts....
Bl. Int. Pr.	Blätter für Internationales Privatrecht (Suppl. to Leipziger Zeitschrift für Deutsches Recht).
D. Arb. R.	Deutsches Arbeitsrecht.
D.J.Z.	Deutsche Juristenzeitung.
D. Justiz.	Deutsche Justiz.
D.R.	Deutsches Recht.
D.R.Z.	Deutsche Richterzeitung.
Eger.	Eisenbahn- und verkehrsrechtliche Entscheidungen und Abhandlungen.
Goltd. Arch. Gruchot.	Archiv für Strafrecht und Strafprozess. *Now*: Deutsches Strafrecht. Beiträge zur Erläuterung des deutschen Rechts.
GRUR.	Gewerblicher Rechtsschutz und Urheberrecht.
Hans. R.Z.	Hanseatische Rechtszeitschrift.
Hans. R. Ger. Z.	Hanseatische Rechts- und Gerichtszeitung.
J. Rdsch.	Juristische Rundschau. *Now*: Deutsches Gemein- und Wirtschaftrecht.
Jurist. Rundschau f. d. Privatversicherg.	Juristische Rundschau für die Privatversicherung.
	Judicium.
	Kartell-Rundschau.
	Konkurs und Treuhandwesen.
L.Z.	Leipziger Zeitschrift für deutsches Recht.
M.u.W.	Markenschutz und Wettbewerb.
Meckl. Z.	Mecklenburgische Zeitschrift für Rechtspflege und Rechtswissenschaft.
Niemeyers Z.	Niemeyers Zeitschrift für internationales Recht.
N.Z.f.A.	Neue Zeitschrift für Arbeitsrecht.
Z. Ostr.	Zeitschrift für osteuropäisches Recht.
P.M.Z.Bl.	Blatt für Patent- Muster- und Zeichenwesen.
R.	Das Recht.
Rabels Z. (or) Z. f. ausl. int. Priv. R.	Zeitschrift für ausländisches und internationales Privatrecht.
	Das Recht des Kraftfahrers.

Rspr. d. OLG.	Rechtsprechung der Oberlandesgerichte in Zivilsachen. Discontinued.
Sächs. Arch. Rpfl.	Archiv für Rechtspflege in Sachsen, Thüringen und Anhalt.
Seuff. Arch. (or) Seuff. A.	Seufferts Archiv.
St.A.Z.	Zeitschrift für Standesamtswesen.
St.u.W.	Steuer und Wirtschaft.
Ufita.	Archiv für Urheber-, Film- und Theaterrecht.
Warn. Rspr.	Warneyers Jahrbuch der Entscheidungen.
Zschr. d. Akad. f. d. Recht. (or) Z.A.	Zeitschrift der Akademie für deutsches Recht.
Z. f. ausl. intern. Priv. R. (or) Rabels Z.	Zeitschrift für ausländisches und internationales Privatrecht.
Z.f.a.ö.u.V. (Z. für a.ö. und V.) (or) Bruns Z.	Zeitschrift für ausländisches öffentliches Recht und Völkerrecht.
Z.H.R. (or) Z. gesamte Handelsrecht.	Zeitschrift für das gesamte Handelsrecht und Konkursrecht (formerly Goldschmidts Z.).
Z.R.H.	Zentralblatt für Handelsrecht.
Z. Ostr.	Zeitschrift für osteuropäisches Recht.
Z. St.W.	Zeitschrift für die gesamte Strafrechtswissenschaft.
Z. Vergl. R.W.	Zeitschrift für vergleichende Rechtswissenschaft.
Z. Vers.W.	Zeitschrift für die gesamte Versicherungswissenschaft.
Z.V.R.	Zeitschrift für Völkerrecht.
Z.Z.P.	Zeitschrift für (deutschen) Zivilprozess.
Zentral Bl. f. Jug. R. (or) J.J.ZBl.	Zentralblatt für Jugendrecht und Jugendwohlfahrt.

GREECE

See Zeitschrift für ausländisches und internationales Privatrecht, vol. x (1936), p. 636; vol. vII (1933), p. 294; Annuario di diritto comparato, vol. IV/v, 1 (1930), p. 527.

Periodicals, Law Reviews

Archeion Idiotikon Dikaion.
Dikastike.
Ephemeris t. Hellen. Nomikon.
Themis.
Dikaiosyne.

HUNGARY

See Annuario di diritto comparato, vol. IV/v, 1 (1930), p. 695; vol. IV/v, 3 (1930), p. 649; Journal of C.L. (3rd Ser.), vol. XIX (1937), pp. 165 ff. (p. 174).

I. Official Law Reports

Polgári Jogi Határozatok Tára (The Archive of Decisions in matters of private law), containing

(a) Teljes ülési döntvények. (Decisions of the full Court in plenary session.)

(*b*) Jogegységi határozatok. (Decisions affecting the uniformity of the law, decided by one of the three sections (on private, commercial law or the civil procedure.)

(*c*) Elvi jelentöségü határozatok. (Decisions of importance, without being decisions of binding force.) See (*a*) and (*b*).

II.   Other collections of decisions and Law Reviews

M.D.

Magánjogi Döntvénytár. (Collection of decisions in matters of private law.) Published by the Jogtudományi Közlöny döntvénytára. (Journal of Jurisprudence.)

A Jog. (The Law.)

Jogállam. (The State governed by Law.)

Jogi Hirlap. (The Law Journal.)

Jogi Szemle döntvénytára. (Collection of decisions published by the 'Law Review'.)

Kereskedelmi Jog. (Journal of Commercial Law.)

Polgári Jog. (Private Law.)

Ugyvédek Lapja. (Journal of the Advocates.)

ITALY

See Bibliografia Giuridica Internazionale, vol. I, 1 (1932), p. 1; vol. IV, 1 (1935), p. 3; vol. VI (1936), p. 315; Foro Italiano, Repertorio, intr.

I.   Official or general collections of decisions

Foro It.	Il Foro italiano.
Foro It. Rep.	Repertorio del Foro italiano.
Giur. It.	Giurisprudenza italiana.
Giur. It. Rep.	Repertorio della Giurisprudenza italiana.
Mass. Foro it.	Massimario del Foro italiano.
Mass. Giur. it.	Massimario della Giurisprudenza italiana.

II.   Other collections of decisions and Law Reviews

Ann. D. Pr. P.	Annali di diritto e procedura penale.
Annuario.	Annuario di diritto comparato e di Studi Legislativi.
Ar. Giur.	Archivio giuridico 'F. Serafini'.
Assic.	Assicurazioni.
Calabria Giud.	La Calabria Giudiziaria (Catanzaro).
Corte d' Appello.	La Corte d' appello (Naples).
Cor. Ass.	La corte d' assise (Foggia).
Cor. Bari.	La Corte di Bari e del Salento (Bari).
Dir. Aer.	Diritto aeronautico.
Dir. Aut.	Il diritto di autore.

Dir. Autom.	Il diritto automobilistico.
Dir. Co. (or comm.).	Il diritto commerciale (Genoa).
Dir. eccl.	Il diritto ecclesiastico italiano.
Dir. e Giur.	Diritto e Giurisprudenza (Naples).
Dir. Lav.	Il diritto del lavoro.
Dir. Mar.	Il diritto maritimo (Genoa).
Dir. e Pratica Comm.	Diritto e pratica commerciale (Padova).
Foro Amm.	Il Foro amministrativo.
Foro Lomb.	Il Foro della Lombardia (Padova).
Foro Pug.	Il Foro delle Puglie.
Foro Sal.	Il Foro salentino (Lecce).
Foro Sic.	Il Foro siciliano (Palermo).
Foro Tosc.	Il Foro toscano (Florence).
Foro Umb.	Il Foro umbro (Perugia).
Foro Ven.	Il Foro delle Venezie (Padova).
	Il Foro veneto (Venice).
Giur. Cor. reg.	La Giurisprudenza delle Corti regionali (Florence).
Giur. Lav.	La Giurisprudenza del lavoro.
Giur. L. Banc.	La Giurisprudenza e Legislazione bancaria.
Giur. Sard.	La Giurisprudenza sarda (Cagliari).
Giur. Tor.	La Giurisprudenza. Il Foro subalpino (Torino).
Giust. Aut.	La Giustizia automobilistica (Torino).
Giust. Lav.	La Giustizia del lavoro (Bari).
Giust. Pen.	La Giustizia penale.
Mag. Lav.	La Magistratura del lavoro (Milan).
Mag. Lav. Venezie.	La Magistratura del lavoro delle Venezie (Verona).
Mass. Giur. Lav.	Massimario di giurisprudenza del lavoro.
Mon. Trib.	Monitore dei tribunali (Milan).
Il Nuovo Diritto (or) Nuovo Dir.	Il nuovo diritto 'La Pretura' (Tivoli).
Rass. Giud.	Rassegna giudiziaria (Catania).
Rass. Lav.	La rassegna del lavoro (Torino).
Rass. Nissena.	Rassegna giuridica nissena (Caltanisetta).
Riv. Amm.	Rivista amministrativa del Regno (Torino).
Riv. Dir. Aer.	Rivista di diritto aeronautico.
Riv. Dir. Agr.	Rivista di diritto agrario (Florence).
Riv. Dir. Civ. (or) R.D.C.	Rivista di diritto civile (Milan).
Riv. Dir. Col.	Rivista di diritto coloniale.
Riv. Dir. Comm. (or) R.D.Co.	Rivista del diritto commerciale (Milan).
Riv. Dir. Internaz.	Rivista di diritto internazionale.
Riv. Dir. Lav.	Rivista di diritto del lavoro.
Riv. Dir. Matr.	Rivista di diritto matrimoniale (Milan).
Riv. Dir. Navigaz.	Rivista del diritto della navigazione (Naples).
Riv. Dir. Priv.	Rivista di diritto privato (Padova)
Riv. Dir. Pubbl.	Rivista di diritto pubblico.
Riv. Giur. Abbr.	Rivista giuridica abbruzese (Aquila).

Riv. Giur. Giust. Colon. (or) R.G.ME.Dr.	Rivista giuridica del Medio ed Estremo Oriente e giustizia coloniale.
Riv. Giur. Mezz. (or) Riv. Mezzogiorno.	Rivista giuridica del Mezzogiorno (Bari).
Riv. It. Dir. Pen.	Rivista italiana di diritto penale (Padova).
Riv. It. Dir. Internaz. priv. proc.	Rivista italiana di diritto internazionale privato e processuale.
Riv. It. Scienze comm.	Rivista italiana di scienze commerciale (Milan).
Riv. It. Scienze giur.	Rivista italiana per le scienze giuridiche.
Riv. Lav.	Rivista del lavoro (Bologna).
Riv. Pen.	Rivista penale.
Riv. Proprietà intell. ed ind.	Rivista della proprietà intellettuale ed industriale.
Scuola Pos.	La scuola positiva, rivista di diritto e procedura penale (Milan).
Sett. Cass.	Settimana della Cassazione.
Stato Civ.	Lo stato civile italiano (Forli).
Temi Emil.	Temi emiliana (Padova).
Temi Gen.	Temi genovese (Genoa).
Temi Lomb.	Temi lombarda (Milan).
Temi Rom.	Temi romana.
Trib.	Il Tribunale (Rome-Naples).

NETHERLANDS

See Bibliografia Giuridica Internazionale, vol. IV, 4 (1935), p. 405; Zeitschrift für ausländisches und internationales Privatrecht, vol. III (1929), p. 522; vol. XI (1937), p. 194.

A.B.	Advocaten Blad.
A.R.	Arbitrale Rechtspraak. (Suppl. to Weekblad van het Recht.)
I.T.R.	Indisch Tijdschrift van het Recht.
	Magzijn voor Handelsrecht.
N.J.	Nederlandsche Jurisprudentie.
N.Jbl.	Nederlandsch Juristenblad.
R.M.	Rechtsgeleerd Magazijn.
T.v.Str.	Tijdschrift voor Strafrecht.
Th.	Themis.
W.	Weekblad van het Recht.
W.P.N.R.	Weekblad voor het privaatrecht, notarisambt en registratie.

POLAND

See Bibliografia Giuridica Internazionale, vol. 1, 3 (1932), p. 327; Annuario di diritto comparato, vol. IV/V, 1, p. 570.

I. Official or general collections of decisions

O.S.N. (or) Zb.O.S.N.	Orzecznictwo Sądu Najwyższego. (Decisions of the Supreme Court.) Zbiór Orzeczeń Sądu Najwyższego. (Collection of the Decisions of the Supreme Court.)
Zb.W.N.T.A.	Zbiór Wyroków Najwyższego Trybunału Administracyjnego. (Collection of the Decisions of the Polish Supreme Administrative Court.) Orzecznictwo Sądów Najwyższych w sprawach podatkowych i administracyjnych. (The Decisions of the Supreme Courts in matters of Tax Law and of Administrative Law.)
O.S.P.	Orzecznictwo Sądów Polskich. (The Decisions of the Polish Courts.)

II. Other collections of decisions and Law Reviews

Cz.A.	Czasopismo Adwokatów Polskich. (Journal of the Polish Advocates.) Poznań.
Cz.A.P.	Czasopismo Adwokatów Polskich. Organ Związku Adwokatów Polskich. (Journal of the Polish Advocates, Journal of the Society of Polish Advocates.) Lwów. Czasopismo prawnicze i ekonomiczne. (Journal of Law and Economics.) Cracow.
Cz.S.	Czasopismo sędziowskie. (Journal of the Magistrates.)
G.S.W.	Gazeta Sądowa Warszawska. (Judicial Gazette of Warsaw.)
Gl.A.	Glos Adwokatów. (The Voice of the Advocates.)
Gl.P.	Glos Prawa. (The Voice of the Law.) Glos Sądownictwa. (The Voice of the Magistrates.) Miesięcznik Prawa Handlowego i wekslowego. (Monthly Review of Commercial Law and of the Law of Bills of Exchange.) Notarjat i Hipoteka. (Notariate and Mortgages.) Nowe Paústwo. (The New State.)
Pal.	Palestra. (The Advocate, Journal of the Council of the Advocates of Warsaw.) Praca i Opieka Spoleczna. (Labour and Social Assistance.) Przegląd Bankowy i Finansowy. (Review of Banking and Finance.) Przegląd Handlowy. (The Commercial Review.)

P.N.	Przegląd Notarjalny. (Review of the Notariate.)
	Przegląd Polski Ustawodawstwa Cywilnego i Kry- minalego. (Polish Review of Civil and Criminal Legislation.)
P.H.	Przegląd Prawa Handlowego. (Review of Commercial Law.)
P.P.i.A.	Przegląd Prawa i Administracji. (Review for Law and Administration.)
P.S.	Przegląd Sądowy. (Review of the Tribunals.) Cracow.
	Przegląd Ubezpieczeniowy. (Review of Insurance.)
T.P.	Themis Polska. (Publ. by the Faculty of Law of the University of Warsaw.)
	Wileński Przegląd Prawniczy. (The Law Review of Wilna.)

RUMANIA

See Annuario di diritto comparato, vol. IV/F (1930), p. 375; vol. VI, 1 (1930), p. 519; vol. VII, 1 (1933), p. 29; Zeitschrift für ausländisches und internationales Privatrecht, vol. III (1929), p. 967.

Ard. jur.	Ardealul juridic. (The Law in Transylvania.)
Buletinul Curții Casatie. (Bulletin of the Court of Cassation of Bucarest.)	
Buletinul Curților de Apel. (Bulletin of the Courts of Appeal.)	
Buletinul Uniunii Avocaților. (Bulletin of the Union of Advocates.)	
Curierul Judiciar. (The Law Gazette.)	
Cuvântul Dreptății. (The Word of Justice.)	
Dreptatea. (Justice.)	
Dreptul. (The Law.)	
Gazeta juridică. (The Law Gazette.)	
Jur. C. Ap.	Jurisprudența Curților de Apel din Ardeal. (Decisions of the Transylvanian Courts of Appeal.)
Jur. Gen.	Jurisprudența Generală.
Jurisprudența Română. (Rumanian Law.)	
Justiția. (Justice.)	
Pand. Rom.	Pandectele Române. (Rumanian Pandects.)
Pand. sept.	Pandectele săptămânale. (Weekly Pandects.)
Revista de Drept public. (Journal of Public Law.)	
Rev. jur.	Revista juridica. (Lawyer's Journal, published in Cluj as the Official Gazette of the Transylvanian Chambers of Advocates.)
Rev. pen.	Revista penală.
Revista societaților și a Dreptului comercial. (Review of Companies and Partner- ships and of Commercial Law.)	

SCANDINAVIAN COUNTRIES

DENMARK

See Zeitschrift für ausländisches und internationales Privatrecht, vol. 2 (1928), pp. 865, 875.

I. Official or general collections of decisions

U.f.R.	Ugeskrift for Retsvaesen. (Contains all important decisions of the Höjesteret (H.R.E.) and of the Sö-og Handelsret (S.H.E.=Court in maritime and commercial matters.)
H.R.T.	Höjesterets Tidende. (Journal of the Höjesteret.)

II. Other collections of decisions and Law Reviews

J.T.	Juridisk Tidsskrift.
N.F.T.	Nordisk Forsikringstidsskrift.
S.H.T.	Sö-og Handelsretstidende. (Contains a collection of the decisions of the Sö-og Handelsret.)
T.f.R.	Tidsskrift for Retsvidenskab.

NORWAY

See Bibliografia Giuridica Internazionale, vol. IV, 2 (1935), p. 193; Zeitschrift für ausländisches und internationales Privatrecht, vol. VII (1933), p. 941.

Norsk Retstidende. (A collection of the decisions of the Supreme Court (Höiesteret=H.R.).)

Tidsskrift for Retsvidenskap.

SWEDEN

See Zeitschrift für ausländisches und internationales Privatrecht, vol. VII (1933), p. 931; vol. II (1928), p. 871.

N.J.A.	Nytt Juridiskt Arkiv, Part I. (Contains a collection of the decisions of the Supreme Court (Högsta Domstol=H.D.).)
	Svensk Juristtidning. (Swedish Law Journal.)
N.T.I.R.	Nordisk Tidskrift for International Ret.

FINLAND

See Bibliografia Giuridica Internazionale, vol. IV, 2 (1935), p. 159; Zeitschrift für ausländisches und internationales Privatrecht, vol. IV (1930), p. 164.

I. Official or general collections of decisions

H.D.U.	Högsta domstolens utslag. (Decisions of the Supreme Court.)

H.D.D.   Högsta domstolens domar. (Judgments of the Su-
                          preme Court.)

Selostuksia ja tiedonanto ja Korkeimman oikenden ratkaisuista vuonna = (Swedish):
    Redogörelser och meddelanden angående av Högsta domstolen träffade av-
    göranden. (Survey of and annotations to the decisions of the Supreme Court.)
Korkeimman Hallinto-oikeuden päätökset. (Decisions of the Supreme Administra-
    tive Court.)

        II.   Other collections of decisions and Law Reviews

J.F.T.   Tidskrift utgifven av Juridiska Föreningen i Finland.
                          (Journal of the Juridical Society in Finland.)
Lkm.   Lakimies. (Journal of the Association of Finnish
                          Lawyers.)
Df.L.   Defensor Legis. (Journal of the Society of Advocates
                          in Finland.)

SPAIN

See Annuario di diritto comparato, vol. IV/V, 1 (1930), p. 587; vol. VII, 4 (1932),
Part II, p. 71.

        I.   *Law Reviews*

Rev. Der. Priv.   Revista de Derecho privado.
Rev. gen. Legisl. Jurispr. Revista general de Legislación y Jurisprudencia.
Rev. crit. Der. Immob.   Revista critica de Derecho immobiliario.
                         Revista de Ciencias Juridicas y Sociales

        II.   *Collections of decisions*

Gaceta de los Tribunales.
Pleitos y Causas.

PORTUGAL

Boletín da Facultade de Direito. Coimbra.

SWITZERLAND

See Bibliografia Giuridica Internazionale, vol. IV, 4 (1935), p. 421; Annuario di
diritto comparato, vol. IV/V, 1 (1930), p. 602; Zeitschrift für ausländisches und
internationales Privatrecht, vol. II (1928), p. 525.

        I.   Official or general collections of decisions

BGE (or) ATF (or) RO.   Entscheidungen des Schweizerischen Bundesgerichtes
                         (or) Arrêts du Tribunal Fédéral Suisse, Recueil
                         Officiel.
J.d.T.   Journal des Tribunaux et Revue judiciaire (Lausanne).
Praxis.   Die Praxis des Bundesgerichts.

Rep. Giur. Pat.	Repertorio di giurisprudenza patria.
Sem. Jud.	La semaine judiciaire. Journal des Tribunaux. Geneva.

II. Other collections of decisions and Law Reviews

	Blätter f. zürcherische Rechtsprechung. (Neue Folge der Schweizer Blätter für handelsrechtliche Entscheidungen.)
Dr. d'Aut.	Le droit d'auteur.
G.E.	Geistiges Eigentum. (La propriété intellectuelle.)
Pr. Ind.	La propriété industrielle.
S.J.Z.	Schweizerische Juristenzeitung.
S.Z. Beurk. Grundb. R. (or) Z.B.G.R.	Schweizerische Zeitschrift für Beurkundungs- und Grundbuchrecht.
S.Z.Str.	Schweizerische Zeitschrift für Strafrecht.
Z.B.J.V.	Zeitschrift des bernischen Juristenvereins.
Z.B.Z.	Zeitschrift für Betreibungs- und Konkursrecht, sowie Zivilprozess.
Z.S.R.	Zeitschrift für schweizerisches Recht.

TURKEY

See Bibliografia Giuridica Internazionale, vol. IV, 2 (1935), p. 169.

I. Official or general collections of decisions

Paçalioğlu.	Tahşiyeli temyiz mahkemesi mukarrerati hulâsalari. (Extracts from the decisions of the Court of Cassation.)
Paçalioğlu.	Temyiz mahkemesi heyeti tevhid içtihat kararlari. (Decisions of the Court of Cassation in full session.)

II. Other collections of decisions and Law Reviews

Adliye C.	Adliye Ceridesi. (Law Journal.)
İst. Baro M.	İstanbul Baro Mecmuasi. (Journal of the Bar of Istanbul.)
İst.H.F.M.	İstanbul Üniversitesi Hukuk Fakültesi Mecmuasi. (Review of the Faculty of Law of the University of Istanbul.)
	İzmir Barosu Dergesi. (Journal of the Bar of Smyrna.)
Mülkiye.	Mülkiye. Aylik içtimai ilimler mecmuasi. (The Civil Servant.)
Continued as:	
Siyasal Bilgiler.	Siyasal Bilgiler 'Mülkiye'. (Political Science 'Mülkiye'.)

YUGOSLAVIA

See Annuario di diritto comparato, vol. VII, 1 (1932), Part II, p. 5; vol. IV/V, 1 (1930), p. 549.

I. Official or general collections of decisions

Ignjatović-Povoyny.	Zbirka odluka viših sudova. (Collections of decisions of the Higher Courts.)
Kovačević.	Sudska praksa. (Judicial Practice.)
Milanović-Strasser.	Rješenja Kasacijonoga suda u gradjanskim pravnim stvarima. (Decisions of the Court of Cassation in civil matters.)
Milanović-Strasser.	Rješenja Kasacijonoga suda u kaznemin i disciplinskim stvarima. (Decisions of the Court of Cassation in criminal and disciplinary matters.)
Niketić.	Odluke opšte sednice Kasacionog Suda. (Judgments of the Court of Cassation.)

II. Other collections of decisions and Law Reviews

Arhiv.	Arhiv za pravne i društvene nauke. (Archive of law and social sciences, ed. by the Faculty of Law of the University of Belgrade.)
Bran.	Branić. (The Client, Journal of the Advocates of Belgrade.)
Mjes.	Mjeseććik, Glasilo pravničkoga društva u Zagrebu. (Monthly Review, Journal of the Society of Lawyers of Zagreb.)
Odvjetnik. (or) Odvjet.	Odvjetnik, Organ advokatske komore u Zagrebu. (The Advocate, Journal of the Chamber of Advocates of Zagreb.)
Polic.	Policija. (The Police.)
Slov. Prav.	Slovenski Pravnik Glasilo društva 'Pravnika' v Ljubljani. (The Slovene Lawyer, Journal of the Society 'Pravnik' in Ljubljana.)
Zbornik.	Zbornik znanstvenih razprav. (Collection of monographs edited by the Professors of the Faculty of Law of Ljubljana.)

SOUTH AMERICA

Periodicals and Law Reviews (list is incomplete)

ARGENTINE.　Fallos.
　　　　　Gaceta del Foro.
　　　　　Revista del Colegio de Abogados de Buenos Aires.
　　　　　Revista del Colegio de Abogados de los Bancos de la Capital Federal.

Revista de la Facultad de Derecho y Ciencias Sociales, organo de la Universidad de la Plata, Sa. Fe.
Revista de Jurisprudencia Argentina.
'La Ley', Revista Jurídica Argentina.
Revista Argentina de Derecho Internacional.
Buletin de Commercio....

BOLIVIA. Revista de Derecho y Jurisprudencia. Suore.
Revista Jurídica.

BRAZIL. Revista de dereito civil.
Revista de dereito comercial.
Revista da Faculdade de Dereito, Universidad de São Paulo.
Revista forense.
Revista Judiciaria. São Paulo.
Revista Juridica. Rio.

COLOMBIA. Derecho. Medelín.
Ecos del Foro. Ibagué.
Gaceta Judicial. Bogota.
Revista Jurídica.

COSTA RICA. Revista de Ciencias Jurídicas y Sociales. San José.

CUBA. Boletín Judicial.
La Jurisprudencia al Dia. (Organo Official del Colegio de Abogados de la Habana.)
Repertorio Judicial.
Revista de Derecho Internacional.

ECUADOR. Gaceta Judicial. Quito.

GUATEMALA. Gaceta de los Tribunales.

HONDURAS. Foro Hondureño.

MEXICO. Jus.
Los Tribunales.
Noticiero Semanal.
Revista Jurídica.
Semanario Judicial.

PANAMA. Registro Judicial.

PARAGUAY. Revista de Derecho y Ciencias Sociales. Assunción.

PERU. El Foro. Lima.
La Revista del Foro. Lima.
Revista de Derecho y Ciencias Politicas, Lima.

PUERTO RICO. Panfleto del Tribunal Supremo.
Revista de Derecho, Legislación y Jurisprudencia.
Revista Jurídica de la Universidad de Puerto Rico.

URUGUAY. El Derecho. Montevideo.
Revista de Derecho, Jurisprudencia y Administración.
Revista de Jurisprudencia de la Alta Corte, Montevideo.

VENEZUELA. Revista del Colegio de Abogados del Distrito Federal, Caracas.
Revista del Colegio de Abogados del Estado de Merida.
Revista del Colegio de Abogados del Estado Zulia. Maracaito.

Index

For EU product safety concerns, contact us at Calle de José Abascal, 56–1°,
28003 Madrid, Spain or eugpsr@cambridge.org.

www.ingramcontent.com/pod-product-compliance
Ingram Content Group UK Ltd.
Pitfield, Milton Keynes, MK11 3LW, UK
UKHW010335140625
459647UK00010B/622